Contemporary French cinema

Contemporary French cinema is an essential introduction to popular French film of the last twenty-five years. It charts recent developments in all genres of French cinema, with analyses of over 100 movies from *Les Valseuses* to *Les Visiteurs*.

Reflecting the diversity of French film production since the New Wave, this clear and illuminating study includes chapters on the heritage film, the thriller and the war movie alongside the 'cinéma du look', representations of sexuality, and the work of women film-makers. Each chapter introduces the public reception and critical debates surrounding a given genre, interwoven with detailed accounts of relevant films. For the first time, readers will have the opportunity to read at length about the internationally famous work of the 'cinéma du look' directors Luc Besson, Jean-Jacques Beineix and Leos Carax, as well as the blockbusters of the heritage genre, from *Manon des sources* and *Jean de Florette* to *Germinal* and *La Reine Margot*.

A major contribution to both Film studies and French studies, this book is a must for students and fans of French film alike.

Guy Austin is lecturer in French at the University of Sheffield.

For Joanne and Joseph

Contemporary French cinema

An introduction

GUY AUSTIN

MANCHESTER UNIVERSITY PRESS Manchester and New York

distributed exclusively in the USA and Canada by St. Martin's Press

Copyright © Guy Austin 1996

Published by Manchester University Press
Oxford Road, Manchester M13 9NR, UK
and Room 400, 175 Fifth Avenue, New York, NY 10010, USA

Distributed exclusively in the USA and Canada
by St. Martin's Press, Inc., 175 Fifth Avenue, New York, NY 10010, USA

British Library Cataloguing-in-Publication Data
A catalogue record is available from the British Library

Library of Congress Cataloging-in-Publication Data
Austin, Guy.
    Contemporary French cinema : an introduction / Guy Austin.
        p.   cm.
    Filmography: p.
    Includes index.
    ISBN 0–7190–4610–6.—isbn 0–7190–4611–4
    1. Motion pictures—France—History.   I. Title.
PN1993.5.F7A95   1996
791.43′0944′09—dc20   95–43366

ISBN 0 7190 4610 6 *hardback*
ISBN 0 7190 4611 4 *paperback*

First published 1996

00   99   98   97   96   10   9   8   7   6   5   4   3   2   1

Typeset in Photina with Frutiger
by Northern Phototypesetting Co Ltd, Bolton
Printed in Great Britain
by Redwood Books, Trowbridge

Contents

List of illustrations   vii
Preface   ix
Acknowledgements   x

1 French cinema from 1895 to 1968, a brief survey

The birth of cinema   1
The first and second avant-gardes   4
Sound cinema and poetic realism   7
Wartime cinema and *la tradition de qualité*   9
Cahiers du cinéma and *la nouvelle vague*   13

2 Holocaust documentary, the war film, and national identity

May 1968 and political cinema   18
Holocaust documentary   20
La mode rétro   28
The Occupation in fiction films of the 1980s and 1990s   32
The Indochinese and Algerian Wars in fiction film   39
Beur cinema   42

3 Representations of sexuality

Porno and after   46
Woman as object   51
The *récit*: misogyny, desire, spectatorship   54
Woman as subject   64
Masculinities   70
Representing Aids   76

4 Women film-makers in France

Feminism and film in France	81
Avante-garde *auteurs*: Marguerite Duras and Agnès Varda	82
Popular cinema: Diane Kurys and Coline Serreau	87
Late 1980s and early 1990s *auteurs*: Claire Devers, Claire Denis, Martine Dugowson	91

5 The *polar*

The popularity of the *polar*	99
Voyeurism and the Hitchcockian thriller	100
American archetypes and the stylised thriller	106
The naturalistic *polar*	112

6 The *cinéma du look* and fantasy film

Popularity and critical reception	119
Jean-Jacques Beineix	120
Luc Besson	126
Léos Carax	132
Fantasy outside the *look*	135

7 The heritage film

Filming and funding the heritage genre	142
Revolution and empire	144
Filming the arts	152
The Pagnol phenomenon	158
Literary legitimacy	163

Conclusion	171
Filmography	173
Index	183

Illustrations

All illustrations courtesy of BFI Stills, Posters and Designs

1 Pierre Blaise in *Lacombe, Lucien* (courtesy of Nouvelles éditions de films)   31

2 Michel Serrault as *Docteur Petiot* (courtesy of Electric Pictures)   35

3 Michel Blanc, Anouk Grinberg, Charlotte Gainsbourg and Gérard Depardieu in *Merci la Vie* (courtesy of Artificial Eye)   38

4 Myriam Roussell in *Je vous salue Marie* (courtesy of Metro Pictures)   49

5 Miou-Miou in *Les Valseuses* (courtesy of Gala Film Distributors)   53

6 Carole Bouquet and Fernando Rey in *Cet Obscur Object du désir* (courtesy of Artificial Eye)   58

7 Fernando Rey and Angela Molina in *Cet Obscur Object du désir* (courtesy of Artificial Eye)   59

8 Patrick Dewaere and Gérard Depardieu in *Les Valseuses* (courtesy of Gala Film Distributors)   71

9 Delphine Seyrig in *India Song*   83

10 Michel Boujenah and Roland Giraud in *Trois Hommes et un couffin*   91

11 Francis Frappat and Jacques Martial in *Noir et blanc* (courtesy of Electric)   93

12 Michel Blanc in *Monsieur Hire* (courtesy of Artificial Eye)   103

13 Sandrine Bonnaire in *Monsieur Hire* (courtesy of Artificial Eye)   105

14 Bernard Giraudeau in *Poussière d'ange* (courtesy of President Films)   110

15 Fanny Bastien and Bernard Giraudeau in *Poussière d'ange* (courtesy of President Films)   111

16 Marie Trintingant and Patrick Dewaere in *Série noire*   113

17 Marie Trintingant and Patrick Dewaere in *Série noire*   113

18 Frédéric Andrei and Thuy Ann Lu in *Diva* (courtesy of Electric)   121

19 Nastassia Kinski in *La Lune dans le caniveau* (courtesy of
Artificial Eye)   123

20 Christophe Lambert in *Subway* (courtesy of Artificial Eye)   127

21 Denis Lavant in *Les Amants du Pont-Neuf* (courtesy of
Artificial Eye)   135

22 Jean Reno and Christian Clavier in *Les Visiteurs* (courtesy of
Arrow Film Distributors)   139

23 Sabine Azéma and Louis Ducreux in *Un Dimanche à la campagne*
(courtesy of Artificial Eye)   155

24 Jacques Dutronc in *Van Gogh* (courtesy of Artificial Eye)   157

25 Jean-Pierre Marielle and Gérard Depardieu in *Tous les Matins
du monde* (courtesy of Electric)   159

26 Gérard Depardieu in *Tous les Matins du monde* (courtesy of
Electric)   159

27 Daniel Auteuil and Gérard Depardieu in *Jean de Florette*
(courtesy of Electric)   161

Preface

This book is written for students and fans of French cinema of the last twenty-five years or so, and is intended to provide an introduction to French film studies. I have concentrated mainly, though not exclusively, on films which have had either a theatrical or video release in Britain, or which are available on video from France. It seems important to me that the films analysed here be fairly readily available to the readers of this book, and there are other books which bring the attention of an Anglophone audience to more obscure or neglected French films.

For ease of understanding I have provided my own translations of the French comments cited in the text, although all film titles remain in the original.

Acknowledgements

Thanks to my wife Joanne and my brother Thomas, for everything.

To my friends Dave Platten, Nigel Laird, Lee Grieveson and David Wood, for their advice and support.

To the staff and students at Sheffield University French Department, especially to Jean Duffy, Sébastien Grisvard, Val Gritten, Ruth Grundy, Renate Günther, Valérie Larbau, Andy Shoben, Geraldine Walsh-Harrington and Jan Windebank for their valuable suggestions.

Also to Ros Brown-Grant, Rachel Killick, Susan Dolamore and Susan Oldfield at Leeds University French Department, to the staff at the British Film Institute Stills Department and Library, and to my editor Katharine Reeve.

Finally to Arrow, Artificial Eye, Electric, Gala, Metro, Nouvelles éditions de films and President Films for granting permission to publish stills.

French cinema from 1895 to 1968, a brief survey

1

The birth of cinema

The year 1995 saw France celebrating the centenary of cinema as a national achievement, a celebration enhanced by the recent victory over the United States regarding the exemption of films from the GATT free-trade agreement. Numerous film exhibitions and retrospectives were organised, including a showing of the entire catalogue of 1,400 short films made by the pioneering Lumière brothers. A hundred years after the Lumières' break-through in 1895, the film industry remains the barometer by which the French measure the cultural state of their nation.

The pioneers of moving pictures

The development of moving pictures was a piece-meal process, dependent on experimentation and advancement in the recording, reproduction and projection of photographic images. The first steps in this process were the invention of the magic lantern in the seventeenth century, and of photography and various moving-image toys – such as Jacob Plateau's *phénakistiscope* – in the 1830s. By 1895, developments were coming to a head on both sides of the Atlantic. In the States, Eadweard Muybridge had made his photographic studies of people and animals in motion, and Thomas Edison had patented and exported his kinetoscope, whereby a single spectator could watch a tiny image on film. The first kinetoscope parlour in France opened in late 1893, and Parisians could also watch the animated cartoons of Émile Reynaud's *Théâtre optique*. But the first truly collective film show, and hence the birth of cinema, took place on 28 December 1895, when the Lumière brothers' *cinématographe* was watched by an audience paying one franc each at the Grand Café, boulevard des Capucines in Paris. The *cinématographe*, a combined motion-picture camera, projector and printer, had first been patented by the photographers and inventors

Auguste and Louis Lumière in February 1895. Whereas Edison's early films had to be shot in the studio, the *cinématographe* was light enough to be used for filming in the street, and the Lumières captured such unstaged events as a baby playing or workers leaving a factory. Their famous short film of 1895, *L'Arrivée d'un train en gare de La Ciotat*, 'is said to have made the unprepared audiences scatter in alarm as the locomotive seemed to approach them' (Robinson 1994: 9), while *L'Arroseur arrosé* of the same year, the world's first (albeit brief) fiction film, established the visual gag as the basis for film comedy. Besides initiating what later became the documentary and comedy genres, the Lumières also developed film techniques which were to prove fundamental to the grammar of cinema. Their series *Les Pompiers de Lyon* (1895) linked together various shots taken from different angles in a pioneering example of editing; a year later one of their agents developed the tracking shot while shooting from a gondola in Venice (Sadoul 1962: 7).

If the Lumières pioneered the recording of action on film, and the techniques of open-air filming and montage (editing), their contemporary Georges Méliès used *mise en scène* (staging) to create artful and fantastical tableaux. The two strands of cinema that they inaugurated can be traced throughout film history, the Lumières influencing documentary, neo-realist and *nouvelle vague* film, Méliès the fantasy film, literary adaptation, historical reconstruction and *la tradition de qualité* (see below). A professional magician, Méliès built the precursor of the film studio in 1897, a glasshouse with a central stage, which was filmed from a point of view identical to that of the spectator watching a play. This concern with filmed theatre even led Méliès to move the titles of his films up the screen in imitation of the curtain going up on a stage play. Spurning camera movement for static tableaux and close-ups for a wide composition showing all the stage, Méliès had to exaggerate the size of important objects, hence the enormous key in *Barbe-Bleue* (1901). As already noted, the genres established by Méliès were numerous, but he was most famous for his fantasy films, either fairy-tales and legends like *Cendrillon* (1899) or science-fiction films adapted from the novels of Jules Vernes, like *20 000 Lieues sous les mers* (1907). He prefigured the heritage film's obsession with authenticity (see chapter 7) in his careful researching of recent events for films like *L'Affaire Dreyfus* (1899). His tight control over all aspects of staging and filming – including the introduction of innovative effects like the double exposure and the dissolve – and his idiosyncratic style also make Méliès the first *auteur* in French cinema (see below). He seems to have recognised this himself when declaring that the success of film as a medium was due not to its inventors the Lumières, but to those who used it to record their own personal productions (Sadoul 1962: 8).

Early French cinema as a global force

Following Méliès' lead, the cinema entrepreneurs Charles Pathé and

Léon Gaumont built studios in Paris in the early years of the twentieth century. Both men also headed powerful French companies,
Pathé Frères originally specialising in the phonograph, L. Gaumont
et Compagnie in photography. Between them, they established the
French film industry as a commercial force of such global influence
that in the years 1908 to 1910 the majority of films distributed in
the world were French (Billard 1994: 56). Commercialising the new
medium far more rapidly than their American counterparts, Pathé
and Gaumont were responsible not only for developing technical
hardware, but also for producing and distributing films, and for setting up chains of cinemas in France and in England.

While Méliès, having failed to adapt his rigid film style, ceased
independent production in 1909, the directors employed by Pathé
and Gaumont ensured that innovation continued, particularly by
launching new and extremely popular genres. At Pathé, for example, Ferdinand Zecca introduced the crime film and the use of seedy,
realistic settings with *L'Histoire d'un crime* (1901) and *Les Victimes
de l'alcoolisme* (1902). In the ensuing years, the melodramas, crime
stories and comedies of Zecca and his colleagues at Pathé were distributed with great success through a series of agencies in Europe,
Japan and America, and in 1908 Pathé sold twice as many films to
the United States than all the American production companies combined (Sadoul 1962: 12). Meanwhile Léon Gaumont, who had
given up directing in 1900, turned to his secretary Alice Guy, who
thus became the first woman film-maker. Guy directed numerous
films before setting up a branch of Gaumont in New York in 1907.
After Guy's departure, her co-director on *La Vie du Christ* (1906),
Victorien Jasset, launched the detective film with the *Nick Carter*
series, filmed between 1908 and 1910 for the third major production company, Éclair. The immediate popularity of the genre led
Louis Feuillade, Guy's replacement at Gaumont, to emulate and
indeed surpass Jasset's success, by filming the *Fantômas* novels written by Pierre Souvestre and Marcel Alain. If Nick Carter was the
world's first film detective, Feuillade's Fantômas, star of a cycle of
adventures shot in 1913 and 1914, was its first arch-villain, known
as 'the emperor of crime'. Set in realistic urban surroundings, and
combining a documentary attention to the streets of pre-war Paris
with an evocation of mystery and lyricism, the *Fantômas* series was
to prove a major influence on surrealism (see below). It also
ensured, along with Jasset's *Nick Carter* films, French dominance in
popular cinema before World War One. The formula employed by
Jasset and Feuillade was imitated across the world, by the *Homuncu-
lus* series in Germany, *Ultus* in Britain, *Tigris* in Italy and *The Perils
of Pauline* (filmed for Pathé by a French director) in the United
States.

France was pre-eminent in the field of the art film. Founded in
1908 and reliant first on Pathé and later on Éclair for production
and distribution, the *Film d'Art* company brought the 'high' culture
of the theatre into the realm of cinema. Using stage actors from the

Comédie Française and prestigious writers from the Académie, the company achieved its greatest success with Charles Le Bargy's film *L'Assassinat du Duc de Guise* (1908), followed by literary adaptations from Victor Hugo, Eugène Sue, and others. Like the work of Méliès, the *film d'art* is a major precursor of *la tradition de qualité* and the heritage film. But in pre-war cinema, it was overshadowed by popular genres, notably the crime story and also the Pathé comedies starring the first international film star, Max Linder.

French dominance of world cinema was curtailed by the outbreak of the First World War in 1914. The Russian and eastern European markets were lost immediately, while the threat to Paris from the German army halted film production for a year, and subsequent French production included nationalistic propaganda films which were far less successful than the pre-war offerings. Moreover, as was to happen in 1940, a number of French technicians and directors left the country to work elsewhere. Coincidentally, American cinema was beginning to compete successfully both in the United States and in Europe. In return for exporting French productions, Pathé, Éclair and Gaumont imported American films into France, notably the popular comedies starring Mack Sennett and Charlie Chaplin. Aware that France was on the point of losing its Anglophone markets in Britain and the United States, Charles Pathé decided in 1918 to pull out of film financing and production, and to concentrate on distribution. Emerging from the war victorious but damaged, France found that in terms of cinema, the United States was now the dominant force. By 1919, only 10 per cent of films on French screens were home-produced, and an unprecedented 50 per cent were American (Billard 1994: 57).

The first and second avant-gardes

In the aftermath of World War One, not only was French cinema commercially in decline, it was also aesthetically stagnant. While Germany, the United States, Britain and Sweden all boasted emergent national film movements of considerable artistic importance – the most influential being German expressionism – French productions were still in the pre-war vein. Yet within ten years, France had provided cinema with its first avant-garde movement – impressionism – and with surrealist film, known as 'the second avant-garde'.

Impressionism

The prime mover behind impressionism was Louis Delluc, a journalist and director who is often credited with inventing film criticism. Having established the first *ciné-club* in 1920 to promote alternative films, the following year Delluc launched the review *Cinéa*, in which he declared: 'Que le Cinéma français soit du cinéma, que le Cinéma français soit français' [Let French Cinema be true cinema, let French Cinema be truly French] (Sadoul 1962: 24). Reacting against the literary adaptations of the *film d'art* -although far from commending the popular genres of comedy and crime story – Delluc asserted that cinema was an artistic medium in its own right, distinct from theatre or literature. Influenced by D. W. Griffith's *Broken Blossoms* (1919), Delluc sought in his own films to convey, through editing, the motions of human psychology, and to this end developed the flashback technique in *La Femme de nulle part* (1922). Similar aims were held by the film-makers associated with Delluc and forming the impressionist avant-garde. Germaine Dulac, who had directed *La Fête espangole* from Delluc's scenario in 1919, summarised impressionist practice in assessing her film *La Mort du soleil* (1920): 'I used, in addition to facial expressions, [...] objects, lights and shadows, and I gave these elements a visual value equivalent in intensity and cadence to the physical and mental condition of the character' (Williams 1992: 101). The innovations in film technique which resulted from the impressionists' desire to evoke human subjectivity included close-ups, camera movements, rapid editing, flashbacks and subjective point-of-view shots. Marcel L'Herbier's *El Dorado* (1921) featured 'semi-subjective' sequences to express a character's psychological state: 'The most famous of these is set in a cabaret where a dancer [...] distractedly sits with other women, thinking about her sick young son. She is out of focus, the other characters perfectly in focus' (Williams 1992: 105). Rhythmic cutting to express a drunken or unstable state of mind, first evident in Abel Gance's *La Roue* (1922) and subsequently in Jean Epstein's *Cœur fidèle* (1923), was perhaps the technique most closely linked with the movement. In *Napoléon vu par Abel Gance* (1927), the most famous and idiosyncratic member of the group combined a commercial, conventional subject—the historical epic—with radical new forms. His use of three screens for the projection of the film predated Hollywood's Cinerama by over twenty years, while the subjective camera was employed in a number of startling new ways, all facilitated by the portable movie cameras available in France at the time. For chase scenes, Gance attached a camera to a horse; when Napoléon dived into the sea, a camera was thrown off a cliff to record his point of view; at the staging of the siege of Toulon, a tiny camera in a football evoked the experience of a soldier blown into the air.

With the exception of Gance's *Napoléon* and L'Herbier's *L'Argent* (1928) – neither of which was purely impressionist – no major productions came out of the movement after 1923. Out of favour with the large production companies and the public, impressionism had nevertheless established film in France as a complex artistic medium supported by a critical discourse and an alternative screening and debating network, the *ciné-clubs*. It was this network, and in particular the avant-garde Parisian cinemas, Studio des Ursulines and Studio 28, which provided the second avant-garde – surrealism – with an audience.

Surrealism

Born out of the pacifist and absurdist Dada group, surrealism developed as a major artistic movement in Paris during the 1920s, under the authoritarian leadership of André Breton. The year 1924 saw the publication of Breton's first surrealist manifesto, and the group proceeded to demand a revolution in the arts and indeed in lifestyle, subverting received norms of expression in many fields including literature, painting, photography and cinema, and aiming to liberate the unconscious from codes of civilised behaviour. The first surrealist film was the ironically titled *Le Retour à la raison* (1923), a short collection of animated photos by the American photographer Man Ray. The film's première, a Dadaist evening, in fact degenerated into a riot. The riot produced a schism out of which the surrealist group was formed. The following year René Clair, a young film-maker not directly associated with either group, was asked by the Dadaist painter Francis Picabia to direct his short scenario. The result, *Entr'acte* (1924), was an absurdist 'rewriting of a pre-war chase movie' (Williams 1992: 144), in which a coffin chased by mourners zoomed about the streets of Paris. Clair's subsequent success as a director of comedies such as *Un Chapeau de paille d'Italie* (1927) was however dependent on the very narrative structures subverted in *Entr'acte*. In a 1924 review of Jean Epstein's *Cœur fidèle*, Clair compared impressionism's gratuitous optical effects unfavourably with 'American film technique, which is completely at the service of the progression of the story' (Williams 1992: 134), and in the 1940s he was to work in Hollywood as part of that classical narrative tradition.

Another director from outside the group who nonetheless created a seminal surrealist work was the former impressionist Germaine Dulac. Her adaptation of a scenario by Antonin Artaud, *La Coquille et le clergyman* (1928), used optical effects and clever editing to convey the repression of unconscious desires. Premièred at the Studio des Ursulines, the film was not well received by the generally misogynistic surrealists who accused Dulac of 'feminising' Artuad's scenario (Williams 1992: 148). In contrast, Salvador Dali and Luis Buñuel's *Un Chien andalou* of the same year was immediately hailed by Breton as a surrealist masterpiece. Although only twenty minutes long, the film managed to disrupt the codes of cinematic representation (time, space, character definition, narrative structure – even silent titles are all subverted), and to create disturbing dream-like episodes dynamised by violent desires. The infamous opening scene, showing a woman's eyeball sliced in half with a razor, was both a deliberate shock tactic and a warning that, in the words of the surrealist-inspired young director, Jean Vigo, 'dans ce film, il s'agira de voir d'un autre œil que de coutume' [in this film, one will have to see things with a different eye than usual] (Prédal 1972: 194). Contrary to Dali and Buñuel's intentions, *Un Chien andalou* was a success with middle-class audiences, running for nine months at the Studio des Ursulines. Two years later,

Buñuel's feature-length sound film *L'Age d'or* (1930) attempted to put this right by launching a violent attack on the bourgeoisie, parodying the Church, the police, and all manner of Establishment conventions, presented as so many obstacles to the consummation of a couple's sexual desire. Again, the Dali-inspired images were startling – a cow in a luxury bedroom, a burning giraffe being thrown out of a window – but were also more determinedly sacrilegeous, as in the concluding sequence which portrayed Christ as a libertine from the Marquis de Sade's *Cent vingt journées de Sodome*. Unsurprisingly, the right wing took offence, and the film was prohibited by the *préfet de police* after a fascist mob destroyed the Studio 28 cinema during a screening in December 1930. Buñuel went on to have a long and brilliant career, making numerous films in France, Spain and Mexico, and carrying his own brand of surrealism into the 1970s (see chapter 3). But most avant-garde film-makers, including Germaine Dulac, were unable to continue in the 1930s, faced with the technical demands and high production costs of the sound film.

Sound cinema and poetic realism

The late 1920s and early 1930s saw French cinema in crisis. Production became increasingly dependent on foreign input, either in the form of technology or finance, usually of American origin. In 1924 Gaumont in France merged with MGM, and in 1927 Pathé joined George Eastman's production company to form Kodak-Pathé. In terms of overall production, 1929 marked a nadir, with only fifty-two feature-length films made in France, as compared with hundreds annually before World War One (Prédal 1972: 114). The crisis was compounded in 1927 when *The Jazz Singer*, made in Hollywood for Warner, inaugurated the era of the 'talkie'.

The coming of sound and the crisis of the early 1930s

The Jazz Singer was premièred in France in February 1929. By that time, French film studios and cinemas alike had begun to re-equip for the new medium of sound cinema, an expensive process requiring American technology. For the studios in particular, the coming of sound was ill timed. Dating mostly from the early 1920s or the pre-war period, French film studios had only just finished modification to accommodate electricity. The first French sound studio at Épinay was ready in February 1929, but the earliest French 'talkies' were actually shot in Britain or Germany, while other films, like L'Herbier's *L'Argent* (1929) were partly sonorised half way through production (Crisp 1993: 104). Many French cinemas, meanwhile, were not equipped to screen sound films until 1934, and when they did so, relied on the American Vitaphone system rather than Gaumont's own underdeveloped Cinéphone (Crisp 1993: 100).

The technical problems associated with the advent of sound were compounded by the purist attitude of many leading French film-makers – including Abel Gance and initially René Clair – who deemed it fit only for musicals and vaudeville. To turn 'silent' films into 'talkies' would be to 'produce talking films that were restricted to a specific-language community' and to lose the 'universality' of the original medium (Crisp 1993: 97). Such a stance only weakened French cinema further in the face of Anglophone dominance. Ironically, it was René Clair, one of the vociferous opponents of sound, who directed the first great French sound film, *Sous les Toits de Paris*, at the Épinay studio in 1930. Although the film did manifest an adventurous use of sound – privileging songs while reducing dialogue to a minimum, and including some counterpoint experiments, in which sound and image were not synchronised – it was most notable for Lazare Meerson's set design, which evoked a realistic yet lyrical picture of working-class Paris. At first ignored by the French public, *Sous les Toits de Paris* became an enormous world-wide success, fêted in Berlin, London, New York and Tokyo (Sadoul 1990: 317). By late 1934, however, Clair had left France for England and subsequently Hollywood, after the commercial failure of *Le Dernier Milliardaire* (1934). The same year saw the death of Jean Vigo, whose *Zéro de conduite* (1933) and *L'Atalante* (1934) had suggested a fruitful integration of surrealist imagery into realistic narrative cinema. French film production also entered a crisis in 1934 to rival that of 1929. Exacerbated by the Depression, which struck France later than it did Britain or the United States, and above all by the financial collapse of both Gaumont and Pathé, film production fell from 158 features the previous year to only 126 in 1934, and 115 in 1935 (Prédal 1972:114). But although production remained at this level for the rest of the decade, the industry was to be revitalised in aesthetic terms by poetic realism, the key genre of classic French cinema.

Poetic realism

In general terms, the evolution of sound cinema shifted film-making from location shooting to studio production and from modernism to realism (Crisp 1993: 104). The coming of sound was a particular catalyst in the development of poetic realism: for technical and economic reasons, sound film was best shot in the studio, hence the increased importance of set design. Poetic realism, a naturalistic but lyrical genre shot almost exclusively on carefully designed studio sets, was given its characteristic atmosphere by art directors like Lazare Meerson and Alexandre Trauner. As Colin Crisp has noted, 'The set decorators' contribution to this style was crucial, and [...] helps to clarify a "movement" which is notoriously difficult to define' (Crisp 1993: 367). Like poetic realism as a genre, the set design which served it was a stylisation of reality, in which the guiding principle was realism, simplified, exaggerated and rendered symbolic. Whether in historical farce (Meerson's reconstruction of seventeenth-century Flanders for Jacques Feyder's *La Kermesse héroique* (1935)) or contemporary tragedy (Trauner's urban sets for

Marcel Carné's *Quai des brumes* (1938) and *Le Jour se lève* (1939)) set design established the tone of the film. As Trauner said, it was essential to isolate and emphasise the principal details of the setting (Crisp 1993: 372). In a similar way, characterisation was based in reality but was also larger than life, with certain types representative of social class or position, the most prevalent and famous example of which is Jean Gabin's iconic status as the working-class hero. Gabin's roles in particular tended to be tragic heroes trapped by fate. Fatalism – which was also found in the slightly later American genre of the film noir (see chapter 5) – was manifest, indeed often personified, in a number of films written by Jacques Prévert and directed by Marcel Carné. Their first great film of the period, *Quai des brumes*, featured Gabin in a fog-bound Le Havre as a deserter driven by love to murder, while in *Le Jour se lève*, a year later, Gabin was again the doomed working-class hero, this time trapped in a house by the police and recalling his past love and his motives for murder. With Gabin's tragic hero, Trauner's realistic yet symbolic sets, and the theme of fate – here personified by a blind man – *Le Jour se lève* epitomises the poetic realism of the 1930s. But the reception of Carné and Prévert's *Les Portes de la nuit* (1946) proved that the genre was out of place after the harsh realities of World War Two and the German occupation of France.

While poetic realism was at its height, Jean Renoir – the most important film-maker of the era, a talismanic figure in post-war film and arguably the greatest ever French director – was faced with a generally lukewarm reception from critics and audiences. Renoir had met popular success with his version of Émile Zola's *Nana* in 1926, but in the ensuing decade his work was not well received despite encompassing a variety of genres from the comedy of *Boudu sauvé des eaux* (1932) to the political propaganda of *La Vie est à nous* (1936). In 1937 the pacifist *La Grande Illusion* was a success, but the cool reception of *La Règle du jeu* two years later, combined with the outbreak of war, led Renoir to leave France for Hollywood. It was only in the 1950s, thanks largely to *la politique des auteurs* (see below), that his importance was recognised. Often cited as an exemplary director of actors, Renoir also displayed a technical mastery of the medium. Throughout the diversity of setting and tone, his films are characterised by fluid camera movements (particularly tracking shots), by deep focus photography, and by a careful *mise en scène* which contrasts foreground and background. These techniques allowed him to develop a humanist concern for the place of the individual in society, filmed with a realism far less stylised than that of his contemporaries. He has proved a major influence not only on the *nouvelle vague* cinema of the 1950s and 1960s (see below), but also on the heritage genre of the 1980s (see chapter 7).

Wartime cinema and *la tradition de qualité*

In 1940, France suffered a humiliating defeat at the hands of the

German army. The resultant period of occupation – in which the country was initially divided into a northern zone administered by the invaders and a 'free' southern zone governed by Marshal Pétain's neo-fascist Vichy regime – was to prove one of the most traumatic eras of French history. While responses varied from active collaboration with the Germans to flight or underground resistance, most of the population struggled to continue living as before. Cinema-going increased, and, ironically, the German occupation actually saw a flowering of classical French cinema.

Film during the Occupation

Naturally enough, 1940 saw French film production reduced to an unprecedented low of thirty-nine films (Prédal 1972: 115). Many film personnel were lost to the industry. A few (such as composer Maurice Jaubert) were killed in action, but most simply fled the country. Directors Jean Renoir, René Clair and Max Ophüls began new careers in Hollywood, while Alexandre Trauner and a number of other Jewish technicians sought the temporary safety of the south (the 'free' zone was later invaded by Germany). Although many personnel resettled in Nice or Marseilles, production facilities and capital remained in Paris. As a result, 'Almost the only producer in a position to work on a film was Marcel Pagnol, who had his studio, actors, technicians, and bank accounts all in the Marseilles region' (Williams 1992: 248). Pagnol was thus able to follow his popular comedies and melodramas of the thirties with *La Fille du puisatier* in 1940.

Thanks largely to German finance and also to an influx of film-makers replacing those who had departed, after 1940 French film production began to increase, more than doubling in quantity by 1943 (Prédal 1972: 115). During the 1930s the German companies Tobis and U.F.A. had produced many French films, and they were now joined by Continental. With imports from America and Britain banned, the French film industry, censored and to some extent controlled by the Germans, could monopolise its captive audience. Many German and some Italian films were also screened, but French-produced cinema claimed 85 per cent of box-office receipts during the Occupation (Sadoul 1962: 89). Moreover, despite the desire of Joseph Goebbels, the German Propaganda Minister, that the French public should be fed a diet of empty and stupid films (Prédal: 91), a vibrant French film industry was a useful tool to placate the population and thus to deter resistance. The result was indeed a highly successful era for French cinema, albeit one characterised by escapism and fantasy, and shot almost entirely in a closed studio environment (Crisp 1993: 375). Constrained by censorship but also reflecting a national desire for an escape from the present, Occupation cinema has been characterised as a cinema of isolation and immobility, dominated by historical subjects, lyrical fantasies and remote settings (Williams 1993). Thus Christian-Jacques' *L'Assassinat du Père Noël* (1941) took place in a snowed-in mountain village and Jacques Becker's *Goupi Mains-Rouges* (1943) in a remote inn, while the major successes at Parisian cinemas – Marcel L'Herbier's *La Nuit fantastique* (1942), Marcel Carné's *Les Visiteurs du soir* (1942) and *Les Enfants du paradis* (1945), and Jean Delannoy's *L'Éternel Retour* (1943) – were either fantastical or historical subjects or both at once. Even Henri-Georges Clouzot's controversial thriller *Le Corbeau* (1943) was set in a small provincial town isolated from the outside world. None the less, the contemporary setting and bleak plot of *Le Corbeau* – in which poison-pen letters ultimately provoke murder – did spark a critical debate about the film's relation to the realities of the Occupation. Although the film could be interpreted as a comment on the neuroses and betrayals of life in occupied France, as resistance intensified and the Occupation was lifted, Clouzot was subjected to attacks from the Comité de Libération du Cinéma, which contrasted the defeatist pessimism of *Le Corbeau* with the spirited optimism of Jean Grémillon's aviation story *Le Ciel est à vous* (1944). With the Liberation of Paris in 1944, Clouzot was driven out of the film industry. But after three years he returned, just as the themes and styles of Occupation cinema were to return in the immediate post-war period.

Postwar 'quality' production

In the decade following the Liberation, the French film industry exploited to commercial success the trends established by the cinema of the Occupation. Literary screenplays, historical or nationalistic subjects, and an increasing attention to production values were predominant in the postwar era, resulting in what came to be known as *la tradition de qualité*. This was a period of consolidation and of competition with the Hollywood films which, banned under the Occupation, flooded post-war France. The Blum–Byrnes agreement of 1946 had reduced the industry's protectionism against American imports and this decision, combined with the appeal of high-quality Hollywood studio productions fronted by famous stars, appeared to jeopardise the commercial viability of French cinema. But the domestic industry was aided in its efforts by two institutions originally set up by the Vichy regime during the war. The Comité d'Organisation de l'Industrie or COIC, established in 1940 to revitalise French production and distribution, was continued in a modified form as the Centre National de la Cinématographie (CNC) after 1946. In addition, the national film school IDHEC (Institut des hautes études cinématographiques), which dated from 1943, was given government support (as was the prewar film archive, the Cinémathèque française). In a policy which was to be echoed by government aid for the prestigious heritage genre in the 1980s (see chapter 7), from 1949 a CNC committee 'began to select projects deemed worthy of *primes de la qualité* or "bonuses for quality"', including literary adaptations of classics by Zola, Stendhal and Maupassant (Williams 1993: 278). European co-productions, especially with Italy, were also encouraged, and the average film budget rose from 50 million old francs in 1950 to 100 million five years later (Sadoul 1962: 103). Such tactics proved invaluable in the competition with Hollywood: whereas in 1948 American films accounted for 51 per cent of French box-office receipts and home product only 32 per cent, by 1957 the situation had been reversed (Sadoul 1962: 145).

Among the literary adaptations central to the success of the *tradition de qualité* were Christian-Jacques' *La Chartreuse de Parme* (1948) and Claude Autant-Lara's *Le Rouge et le Noir* (1954), both taken from nineteenth-century novels by Stendhal. Both films also featured the actor Gérard Philipe who, along with Martine Carol, played in numerous films of the period and epitomised the new French star system. The acting style of the 1930s, in which characters embodied a given social class and gave an 'extrovert expressiveness' to poetic realist film, was now superseded by the 'anguished interiority' of literary adaptations in which the psychology of the individual characters was paramount (Crisp 1993: 365). The decline of poetic realism was most clearly marked in the hostile reception of Marcel Carné and Jacques Prévert's *Les Portes de la nuit* (1946). Although the film was set in post-war Paris, the fantastical plot and Alexandre Trauner's stylised sets 'already seemed dated, belonging to a past era' (Crisp 1993: 375). After the commercial and critical failure of *Les Portes de la nuit*, Carné's fantasy film *Juliette ou la clé des songes* (1951) met a similar fate, as did Jean Cocteau's cryptic fantasy *Orphée* (1950). If the historical drama flourished in the 1950s, the fantasy genre entered an almost terminal decline, not arrested until the coming of the *cinéma du look* in the 1980s (see chapter 6).

For all the popularity of the costume drama – and in particular of films set at the turn of the century, such as Jacques Becker's *Casque d'or* (1952) or Jean Renoir's *French Cancan* (1954) – French post-war cinema included a number of more contemporary dramas. As under the Occupation, the thriller genre allowed a cynical and pessimistic portrayal of society, witness Yves Allegret's *Une Si Jolie Petite Plage* (1948) and Henri-Georges Clouzot's *Les Diaboliques* (1954). A more documentary-style realism was provided by René Clément's depiction of the war, *La Bataille du rail* (1945). Although Clément went on to film typical 'quality' projects, such as the Zola adaptation *Gervaise* (1955), *La Bataille du rail* belonged to the realist style of post-war European cinema, as did Robert Bresson's *Le Journal d'un curé de campagne* (1950), *Un Condamné à mort s'est échappé* (1956) and *Pickpocket* (1959). Bresson's films, although stylised to an extent, used real locations and amateur actors, as did the most important realist movement of the period, Italian neo-realism. And although such examples were relatively rare in French cinema during the 1940s and 1950s, they prefigured the emergence of *la nouvelle vague*, a style of film-making which sought to destroy the high production values and orthodox format of *la tradition de qualité*.

Cahiers du cinéma and la nouvelle vague

In the decade after the Liberation, a fresh conception of cinema evolved in parallel with the development of *la tradition de qualité*, but in strident opposition to the values embodied by 'quality' productions. First formulated by young critics in the magazine *Cahiers du cinéma*, the new film theories were put into practice in the late 1950s and early 1960s by many of those same critics who, as directors, became known as *la nouvelle vague*.

La politique des auteurs

Cahiers du cinéma was launched in April 1951 by Jacques Doniol-Valcroze, Lo Duca and André Bazin. As editor, Bazin became the mentor to the young critics who contributed to the magazine, including François Truffaut, Jean-Luc Godard, Claude Chabrol and Eric Rohmer. These critics tended to praise the work of idiosyncratic French directors such as the comic actor and director Jacques Tati, along with many Hollywood productions, especially the film noir and the B-movie thriller (see chapter 5), but they reserved contempt for the French offerings of *la tradition de qualité*. This position was most strongly stated in François Truffaut's polemical article 'Une certaine tendance du cinéma français', published in *Cahiers* on New Year's Day, 1954. Targeting the scriptwriters Jean Aurenche and Pierre Bost, who had worked on numerous 'quality' films for various directors since the war, Truffaut contrasted the 'abject characters' they created with the more personalised creations of Jean Renoir, Robert Bresson, Jean Cocteau and Jacques Tati, all of them *'authors ["des auteurs"]* who often write their own dialogue and in some cases themselves invent their own stories, which they then go on to direct', (Crisp 1993: 234). Truffaut went on to write: 'I cannot see any possibility of peaceful coexistence between the *Quality Tradition* and an *auteur cinema*' (Crisp 1993: 234–5).

La politique des auteurs, or in other words, the conception of 'an *auteur cinema*' in which the film-maker, like an author or an artist, uses the medium (including not just the direction but the screenplay and even the production) to express a personal view of the world, was not invented by Truffaut in 1954. The idea of cinema as art had been first propounded in 1908 by the *film d'art* group (see above). More recently, an article by Alexandre Astruc for *L'Écran français* in 1948, had suggested the concept of 'la caméra-stylo' – the movie-camera used like a pen – by declaring: 'After having been successively a fairground attraction, an amusement analogous to boulevard theatre, or a means of preserving the images of an era, [cinema] is gradually becoming a language [...] by which an artist can express his thoughts' (Williams 1993: 306). Nevertheless, it was the *Cahiers* group who popularised the concept during the 1950s. Most significantly, they applied the term to almost all of their favourite film-makers, irrespective of nationality or cultural status. Among French directors, Jean Renoir was considered the classic *auteur*, writing, directing and even starring in his own films. The first special issue of *Cahiers* was devoted to him in January 1952. The reappraisal of Renoir was facilitated by the re-release of *La Grande Illusion* (1937) in 1946, and the first showing of the unfinished *Une Partie de campagne* (1936) the same year. These films, along with post-war Hollywood productions, were watched by the *Cahiers* critics at the Cinémathèque française. But the subsequent veneration of popular Hollywood directors like Alfred Hitchcock, Howard Hawks and Sam Fuller proved controversial: 'Part of the scandal created by the *politique* was caused by its application to popular American cinema, generally thought of as mass entertainment reproducing dominant ideology and incompatible with the interests of art' (Cook 1985: 126). Ironically, whereas in the 1950s *la politique des auteurs* attacked *la tradition de qualité* while granting Hollywood directors like Hitchcock serious critical attention for the first time (see chapter 5), since the 1970s auteurist criticism in France has been used to defend 'quality' French art cinema against the very notion of anonymous Hollywood product which the *politique* originally challenged.

La nouvelle vague

In 1957 François Truffaut acted on his auteurist convictions and founded his own production company, Les Films du Carrosse, which was to produce nearly all his work from his second short, *Les Mistons* (1957) to his final feature *Vivement dimanche!* (1983). One year later, in June 1958, a new wave of French cinema – *la nouvelle vague* – was launched, with the preview at the Cinémathèque française of Claude Chabrol's first feature, *Le Beau Serge*. Set in a small rural community and shot with a rigorous realist style in bleak locations, the film was not a popular success. But it was followed in 1959 by three films which gave *la nouvelle vague* a commercial as well as an aesthetic impact: Chabrol's *Les Cousins*, Truffaut's *Les 400 coups* and Godard's *A bout de souffle*. While the latter was a fine example of collaboration within *la nouvelle vague* - conceived by Truffaut, it was scripted and directed by Godard, with Chabrol as artistic supervisor – *Les 400 Coups* was a personal triumph for its director. Banned from the 1958 Cannes film festival for his outspoken views as a critic, Truffaut won the best director award at Cannes a year later for *Les 400 Coups*, his first feature film. This 'instant critical and commercial success not only afforded Truffaut considerable artistic independence [...], but also made it much easier for other *Cahiers* critics turned film-makers to finance their own projects' (Monaco 1976: 13).While *Les Cousins* and *A bout de souffle* owed a particular debt to the Hollywood thriller, *la nouvelle vague* as a whole brought a fresh sensibility and a radical style of filming to French cinema, indeed arguably to world cinema. Godard's *A bout de souffle* startled audiences with the systematic use of jump-cuts, and Truffaut's *Les 400 Coups* ended in stunning fashion with a freeze-frame. In contrast with *la tradition de qualité*, 'the aesthetic of New Wave cinema was improvisational (unscripted), and its photography and editing were far less mannered than its predecessors' (Cook 1985: 40). Working with low budgets, using the new cheaper and lighter equipment, able to film in real locations and at night if required, influenced by television practices like hand-held shooting and the interview straight to camera, the *nouvelle vague* film-makers paradoxically achieved a vibrant and graphic realism while at the same time experimenting self-consciously with the medium of film.

La nouvelle vague is usually taken to encompass five principal directors: François Truffaut, Jean-Luc Godard, Claude Chabrol, Eric Rohmer and Jacques Rivette, all of whom wrote for *Cahiers du cinéma* in the 1950s (Monaco 1976). However, this canonical list, and indeed the dating of the movement as beginning in 1958/9, should be qualified. Agnès Varda, a major omission from some accounts of the movement, predated Chabrol, Truffaut and Godard by shooting her first feature, *La Pointe courte*, in 1954. Shot independently on a very small budget, the film alternated between realism and symbolism, as does much of Varda's subsequent work (see chapter 4). Everyday life in a fishing village provided a graphic background to a young couple's rather literary discussions about their struggling relationship. *La Pointe courte* was given a limited release in 1956, the year which saw another important precursor of *la nouvelle vague*, Roger Vadim's *Et Dieu créa la femme*, prove a great commercial success. Despite its low budget, Vadim's film benefited from the presence of Brigitte Bardot in her first screen role, and its performance at the box office encouraged production companies to finance projects by unknown directors, a policy which was instrumental in the evolution of *la nouvelle vague*. Contrary to the rhetoric of cinematic revolution which surrounds *la nouvelle vague*, the emergence of the movement was thus prepared not only by technical factors, allowing more flexible filming techniques, but also by the commercial significance of *Et Dieu créa la femme*, and even by the post-war system of state subsidy, which saw Chabrol's *Le Beau Serge* gain a *prime de la qualité* alongside the 'quality' productions more readily associated with this prestige bonus (see above). One might conclude that, for all its stylistic innovations, 'the New Wave does not represent a sharp break with past practices, but the culmination of a development which had been apparent [...] ever since the war' (Crisp 1993: 376).

Among the forms explored by *la nouvelle vague* and related film-makers were fantasy genres hitherto neglected in France: science fiction in Chris. Marker's *La Jetée* (1963), Godard's *Alphaville* (1964) and Truffaut's *Fahrenheit 451* (1966); the musical in Godard's *Une Femme est une femme* (1961) and Jacques Demy's *Les Parapluies de Cherbourg* (1964) and *Les Demoiselles de Rochefort* (1966). The New Wave also tended to mix previously distinct genres, thus making use of generic structures while submitting them to a personal, auteurist vision. Truffaut's *Tirez sur le Pianiste* (1960), for example, although an adaptation of an American crime novel by David Goodis, added comic and fairy-tale elements to the basic thriller narrative. By the middle of the decade, however, Truffaut had become much more conservative in terms of both narrative structure and genre, a development which resulted in his becoming the most commercially successful film-maker to come out of *la nouvelle vague*. Meanwhile, Chabrol had started to work consistently within the thriller genre (see chapter 5), but both Eric Rohmer and Jacques Rivette did not break through commercially until the late 1960s and early 1970s (see chapter 3). If the mid-sixties marked the dissipation of the movement, it did not see any diminution in the formal innovations carried out by the most radical of the group, Jean-Luc Godard. While Truffaut and Chabrol had become auteurs in a fairly conventional mould, Godard remained at the cutting edge of both cinema and politics. Experimenting with colour in *Le Mépris* (1963) and *Pierrot le fou* (1965), he also challenged the traditional identification between audience and characters through his use of interview techniques in *Masculin-Féminin* (1966) and *Week-End* (1967). The latter, with its violent attack on the bourgeoisie and depiction of counter-culture terrorists, has been interpreted in retrospect as heralding the social unrest which shook France in May 1968 (see chapter 2). Godard's political activism was also evident in his collaboration with a group of film-makers including Agnès Varda, Alain Resnais and Chris. Marker, on the protest film *Loin du Vietnam* (1967).

For all its artistic influence – manifest not just in Europe but in the work of American directors such as Arthur Penn and Martin Scorsese – *la nouvelle vague* was not a major commercial form. The French box office of the 1960s was dominated by the popular genres of the thriller and the comedy. Although cinema-going in France declined over the decade, from 355 million spectators in 1958 to 185 million in 1970 (Prédal 1991: 212), there were notable hits, including Yves Robert's childhood comedy *La Guerre des boutons* (1962) with 9.6 million spectators, and Gérard Oury's Resistance comedy *La Grande Vadrouille* (1966) with over 17 million (Prédal 1991: 404). The late 1960s also saw increasing numbers of pornographic films being made in France, a trend which was to culminate in the mid-seventies with the temporary acceptance of pornography into mainstream French cinema (see chapter 3).

References

Billard, P. (1994), France–États-Unis: Une guerre de cents ans, Paris, *Le Point*, 1163, 56–8.

Cook, P. (1985), (ed.), *The Cinema Book*, London, BFI.

Crisp, C. (1993), *The Classical French Cinema 1930–1960*, Bloomington and Indianapolis, Indiana University Press.

Monaco, J. (1976), *The New Wave*, New York, Oxford University Press.

Prédal, R. (1972), *La Société française (1914–1945) à travers le cinéma*, Paris, Armand Colin.

Prédal, R. (1991), *Le Cinéma français depuis 1945*, Paris, Nathan.

Robinson, D. (1994), *The Chronicle of Cinema, 1: The Beginnings*, London, Sight and Sound/BFI.

Sadoul, G. (1962), *Le Cinéma français (1890–1962)*, Paris, Flammarion.

Williams, A. (1993), *Republic of Images: A History of French Filmmaking*, Cambridge, Massachusetts and London, Harvard University Press.

2 Holocaust documentary, the war film and national identity

May 1968 and political cinema

In May 1968 French students, workers and professionals united briefly in a wave of demonstrations, strikes and sit-ins – known as 'the events of May '68' – which challenged the institutions of President Charles de Gaulle's Fifth Republic and the ideals of the consumer society. The official reporting of the violent clashes between protestors and police throughout May 1968 revealed the extent to which the complicit French television system functioned as an apparatus of the State. The response of independent film-makers and collectives was to report the struggle from a viewpoint outside state control. Already in February of 1968 film-makers had been mobilised against government control of the media by the sacking of Henri Langlois as secretary of the national film archive, the Cinémathèque française. In May came the establishment of the States-General of the Cinema, with the declaration that 'free speech does not exist in either cinemas or television in this country, as a very small minority of writers and technicians control both production and the means of expression'. As the States-General reported later, eyewitness films were made during 'the events' and distributed from mid-June onwards (Fisera 1978: 303, 304). Despite the continuation of de Gaulle's presidency until 1969, and a general return to the political *status quo*, in terms of film culture the 'events' had a profound effect, facilitating the development of politicised and collective film-making, and contributing to the rise of gay film and women's cinema in the decade that followed. Above all, and naturally enough, it was documentary film-making which was most directly influenced by what happened in May 1968.

Documentary film-making in France in the 1960s had been dominated by *cinéma-vérité* – the recording of everyday life and events – as in Jean Rouch's *Chronique d'un été* (1961) and Chris. Marker's *Le Joli Mai* (1963). This style was gradually supplanted by more formally experimental and politically-motivated forms of documentary from the late sixties onwards; the anti-war film *Loin du Vietnam* (1967), a group venture including Marker, Jean-Luc Godard, Agnès Varda and Alain Resnais, prefigured 'the collective production' and 'interventionist role [...] which was characteristic of political and documentary film making after 1968' (Forbes 1992: 15). Moreover, after May 1968 the very distinction between documentary and fiction was questioned, nowhere more so than in Jean-Luc Godard and Jean-Pierre Gorin's *Tout va bien* (1972).

Tout va bien: new subjects, new forms

Godard's attacks on the consumer society in *Week-End* and *La Chinoise* (both 1967) seem in retrospect to have heralded the upheavals of May 1968. In the years that followed he worked with the Maoist Jean-Pierre Gorin on a number of political projects outside mainstream cinema, usually financed by foreign television companies. In an explicit break with his career as a key *auteur* in *la nouvelle vague* (see chapter 1), Godard no longer worked under his own name but in collaboration with Gorin as the Dziga-Vertov Group, named after a revolutionary Soviet film-maker. The primary aim of the group was to 'faire politiquement des films politiques' [make political films politically], and more precisely to situate themselves 'historically' in regard to May 1968 and contemporary political struggles (Godard 1991: 116–17). *Tout va bien*, filmed in 1972 with Yves Montand and Jane Fonda, was an attempt to consider the legacy of 1968 from within mainstream cinema, a strategy facilitated by the box-office power of the two stars. The film that resulted is 'perhaps the single best cinematic description of France in the aftermath of '68' (MacCabe 1992: 20).

Interviewed about *Tout va bien* in April 1972, Godard and Gorin rejected the *cinéma-vérité* style of documentary associated with Rouch as unable to answer the questions raised by May 1968 (Godard 1991: 127). The only response was to marry new subjects to new forms, breaking down what Gorin called the 'bourgeois' distinction between fiction and documentary in order to create 'materialist fictions' (Godard 1991: 131, 133). In other words, both form and content were to be politicised, in what Godard had already termed in 1967, with regard to *La Chinoise*, a 'struggle on two fronts' (Godard 1991: 10–58). The political, yet not documentary, nature of *Tout va bien*, its status as a 'materialist fiction', is best illustrated by the images in the film of demonstrations and clashes with the police. Although alluding explicitly to situations from 1968, and particularly to the death of student Gilles Tautin while fleeing from police dispersing a demonstration at the Flins Renault factory in June 1968, these sequences are clearly not documentary footage but staged versions of what took place. The fictionalising of events characteristic of May 1968 also provides the film with its central narrative, the story of a factory occupation set in May 1972, during which the characters played by Montand and Fonda are locked in with the boss by striking workers. Accusing the strikers of being 'contaminated by May '68', the boss renders explicit the political symbolism of the factory occupation, after which the protagonists, like France itself after 1968, appear to return to the *status quo*. The strike is not filmed, however, as documentary nor even as realism. The non-realistic use of colour, the cross-sectional staging interpreted by tracking shots, and the playing of several scenes as farce all distance the factory sequences from the ostensibly truthful forms of documentary and naturalism, and place the fictional nature of cinema in the foreground. (The use of a 'low' cinematic form, such as farce, supposedly inappropriate to serious referential content is raised again by Godard in the context of Holocaust representation (see below).) If *Tout va bien* does propose any final truth, it is in the male and female voice-overs which conclude the film, stating of the protagonists that 'ils ont commencé à se penser hi-stor-ique-ment' [they have begun to think of themselves hi-stor-ic-ally], and proposing that 'chacun sera son propre historien, [...] moi ... toi ... lui ... elle ... nous ... vous!' [everyone will be their own historian, [...] me ... you ... him ... her ... us ... you!]. This proposed fragmenting of history into personalised narratives perhaps predicts Godard's retreat into non-commercial video projects in the mid-seventies. It also subverts the dominant historical discourse of the period, the Gaullist myth that France had been united (in resistance) during the Second World War and ever since. This view of history was to be readdressed in the representations of the Occupation and the Holocaust which began to proliferate in the aftermath of 1968.

Holocaust documentary

The extent of French collaboration with the Germans during the Second World War, and most crucially the role of the Vichy government in the deportation of French Jews, were taboo subjects in the 1950s and 1960s. But they were addressed with increasing urgency during the 1970s and 1980s. This concern was ultimately manifested in the trials of the collaborator Paul Touvier and 'the Butcher of Lyons', Klaus Barbie, in the investigation surrounding Vichy police chief René Bousquet, and the debate over the wartime actions of the Catholic Church and of François Mitterand. It was also manifested in French cinema, both in documentary and fiction form. Documentary images of the Holocaust were first seen in French cinemas during 1945, with footage of the concentration camps shown in the Actualités Françaises newsreel, *Les Camps de la mort* (Colombat 1993: 14). The major Holocaust documentaries are Alain Resnais's *Nuit et brouillard* (1955), Marcel Ophüls's *Le Chagrin et la pitié* (1971) and Claude Lanzmann's *Shoah* (1985). Each of these seminal films marks a new stage in Holocaust representation, and raises distinct questions: '"What exactly happened?" "How could we allow the Holocaust to take place?" and "What memory of these horrifying events should be kept alive for future generations?"' (Colombat 1993: xiv).

Nuit et brouillard and the myth of le résistancialisme

The Gaullist myth of a united France was based on *le résistancialisme*, the theory that, during the Occupation, the French nation had supported Charles de Gaulle and the Resistance rather than collaborating. Established during the post-war Fourth Republic, the myth was perpetuated with the founding of the Fifth Republic by de Gaulle in 1958. In the determinedly forward-looking context of the 1950s, Resnais's *Nuit et brouillard* was a warning not to forget the atrocities of the past. Following a commission by the Comité d'Histoire de la Deuxième Guerre Mondiale, Resnais worked with the writer and Holocaust survivor Jean Cayrol to produce a short, stylised film of great poetic resonance. (They were to work together again on the fiction film *Muriel* (1963) which, like much of Resnais's work, presents a world akin to the enclosed, traumatic world of the concentration camp (see below).) *Nuit et brouillard* establishes the classic photographic dichotomy of the Holocaust film, according to which the past is seen in black and white and the present in colour. The aesthetic quality of the film stems from the inter-relation of Cayrol's text and Eisler's music with Resnais's editing, which juxtaposes colour images of the ruins of the death camps with black and white archive footage of the camps and their victims during the war. Resnais thus excavates the horrors lying beneath the deceptively banal landscapes of the present day, landscapes which like those in Lanzmann's *Shaoh* are at times startlingly beautiful with blue or pink skies and orange trees. It has even been remarked that these colours are too bright, like open wounds or 'draining blood' (Ward Jouve 1994). The disembodied and anonymous narration in *Nuit et brouillard*, the film's universal concerns, and the absence of any reference to the extermination of the Jews might be taken as conforming to the myth of *le résistancialisme*. Although a specifically French context is given by brief allusions to the camps at Pithiviers and Compiègne, and to the deportation of Jews from the Vélodrome d'Hiver in Paris, the image which most explicitly challenged the Gaullist myth – a French policeman surveying the camp at Pithiviers – was censored (Colombat 1993: 27). Cinema was not to demythologise the official version of French history during the Occupation until after 1968. Nevertheless, *Nuit et brouillard* remains a powerful call to awareness, particularly via the archive images of the dead and dying, and in the concluding voice-over which warns of 'the coming of new executioners' whose faces are not 'really different from ours'. It is notable that in May 1990, after anti-Semitic attacks on Carpentras and other Jewish cemeteries, all five French state television channels simultaneously broke their programming to broadcast Resnais's film.

History on trial: from *Le Chagrin et la pitié* to *Hotel Terminus*

Faced with Hitler's rise to power, the young Marcel Ophüls and his family fled from Germany to France in 1933, only to leave for the United States eight years later to escape the Occupation. After the war, Marcel worked as assistant on his father Max's last film, *Lola Montès* (1955), before embarking on a career as a director of fiction films and ultimately documentaries. In 1967, working with André Harris and Alain Sedouy for French state television – the ORTF (Office de radio et télévision française) – he made *Munich*, the first third of a projected documentary series on the Second World War. In the aftermath of May 1968, and following the resignation of the three film-makers from the ORTF, the series ended. In 1969 Ophüls began filming *Le Chagrin et la pitié* (1971) for German and Swiss television, with Harris and Sedouy as executive producers. The ORTF subjected the completed film to what Ophüls called 'censorship by inertia' (Insdorf 1983: 242), and it was not broadcast on French television until after the Socialists came to power in 1981. Its cinema presentation in 1971 was however a success, attracting a large, predominantly young audience. Subtitled 'Chronicle of a French town under the Occupation', the film focuses on the choice between collaboration and resistance for the people of Clermont-Ferrand. Black and white throughout, it combines interviews with French, German and British witnesses with newsreel footage and propaganda films of the period. It has been noted that throughout *Le Chagrin et la pitié*, and especially in the interview with Madame Solange, resistance is portrayed as masculine and collaboration as feminine (Reynolds 1990). A more complex portrayal of women's experience under the Occupation is given in Claude Chabrol's 1988 fiction film *Une Affaire de femmes* (see below).

In contrast with the impersonal quality of Resnais's *Nuit et brouillard*, Ophüls favours a personalised filmic style. Although not as strong an authorial presence as in his later work, Ophüls does exercise his political commitment and strong sense of irony throughout *Le Chagrin et la pitié*, most notably through the editing and a frequent disjuncture between sound and image, as in the parodic 'tourist guide' introduction to the town of Clermont-Ferrand, which is undermined by solemn images of a war memorial. As in Lanzmann's *Shoah*, the staging functions to symbolise the role of each witness: hence the SS volunteer Christian de la Mazière is interviewed in the German castle of Sigmaringen, and a British pilot in the cockpit of a Lancaster bomber. In a sequence which prefigures Abraham Bomba's testimony in *Shoah*, the right-wing hairdresser Madame Solange is filmed in a hairdresser's, her interview ironically preceded by images of *l'épuration* – the post-war purges – showing women suspected of collaboration having their heads shaved. The politician and war veteran Pierre-Mendès-France is privileged as a surrogate narrator, complementing the unidentified narrative voice-over which punctuates the film, adding a political discourse and raising in particular the spectres of anti-Semitism,

Anglophobia and anti-Communism as factors in the collaboration with Germany. The testimony of Mendès-France is addressed from the beginning at younger generations, that is, directly at the film's audience.

The reception of *Le Chagrin et la pitié* was determined by the debate over Gaullism initiated in 1968. Although de Gaulle himself had died in 1970, President Pompidou continued the Gaullist regime. From such a perspective, Ophüls's portrayal of de Gaulle was startlingly negative. Not only was he rarely mentioned in his mythical role as leader of the Free French, when he was referred to it was as much in relation to his loss of power after the 1969 referendum defeat as to his wartime activity. The film also drew an unmistakable visual parallel between de Gaulle and Marshall Pétain, the head of the collaborationist Vichy government. Part one ended with an image of Pétain and part two with a shot of de Gaulle. This parallel was to be drawn even more strongly in Harris and Sedouy's *Français si vous saviez* (1973), the poster for which shows statues of de Gaulle and Pétain side by side, the one being constructed out of the other. *Le Chagrin et la pitié* also caused controversy over the glaring rift it presented between German and French interpretations of events 'at a time when the Franco-German Collaboration was the key-stone' of Gaullist European policy (Colombat 1993: 182). Ironically, the film was also unpopular with militant film-makers like Godard and Gorin, who judged the film to be empty of political analysis and hence 'revolting' (Godard 1991: 139). Critics have subsequently attacked *Le Chagrin et la pitié* as being 'politically vacuous', specifically for ignoring the role of the Catholic Church within Vichy (Avisar 1988: 19). Nevertheless, the film does engage with the internal conflicts of the Resistance, illustrating the rupture between Catholic and Communist elements in the juxtaposed testimonies of Du Jonchay and Duclos. It was this even-handed portrayal of the 'popular struggle', and the revelation that collaborators were mostly ordinary people rather than ideologues, which saw the film condemned by some on the left – along with Louis Malle's controversial fiction film *Lacombe, Lucien* (1974) – for epitomising *rétro* cinema (see below). Ophüls followed *Le Chagrin et la pitié* with a film on Northern Ireland, *A Sense of Loss* (1972), and *The Memory of Justice* (1976), a documentary on the Nuremberg trials which also considers the wars in Algeria and Vietnam. *Hôtel Terminus* (1987) was filmed in tandem with the development of the trial of the Nazi war criminal Klaus Barbie, 'the Butcher of Lyons', who was eventually sentenced to life imprisonment for crimes against humanity. Barbie is in fact an absence rather than a presence in the film – he was not present at the trial until the verdict – while Ophüls establishes a running contradiction between the testimonies of Barbie's colleagues, both in Germany and the Americas, and of his victims. Partly because it concerned war crimes committed by a German Nazi rather than French collaborators, *Hôtel Terminus* proved less controversial than *Le Chagrin et la pitié*. It was also overshadowed by the release two years earlier of the mammoth Holocaust documentary *Shoah*, whose director Claude Lanzmann may have been right when he said of the Barbie trial: 'All of this will be forgotten while *Shoah* will not be forgotten' (Colombat 1993: 108).

Shoah: reliving the Holocaust

Ophüls has described Claude Lanzmann's *Shoah* (1985) as 'the greatest documentary about contemporary history ever made, bar none, and by far the greatest film I've ever seen about the Holocaust' (Insdorf 1983: 254). Lanzmann had fought with the French Resistance as a youth before travelling to Israel after the war and making the film *Pourquoi Israël*. But his major achievement is undeniably *Shoah*, a project which took eleven years to make – from 1974 to 1985 – the first six years recording testimony in fourteen different countries, the next five years editing the film from 350 hours of footage into the $9^{1}/_{2}$ hour result. 'Shoah' is Hebrew for 'annihilation', and Lanzmann's film challenges the conscious and unconscious annihilation of the Holocaust as a lived experience. The film is therefore about the so-called Final Solution in its terrible specificity, evoking the very logistics of a genocide that exterminated six million European Jews. In this regard, the historian Raul Hilberg is a key influence on Lanzmann, both via his book *The Destruction of the European Jews*, and via his presence in the film as a commentator, much like Pierre Mendès-France in Ophüls's *Le Chagrin et la pitié*. It is Hilberg who stresses the importance of asking small questions about the details of 'the bureaucratic destruction process', rather than attempting to address the Holocaust as an abstract concept. Following this line of enquiry, Lanzmann elicits testimony from his interviewees about the actual process of extermination in camps which functioned as what the SS guard, Franz Suchomel, calls 'a primitive but effective production line of death'. The Final Solution demanded of its perpetrators, as Hilberg notes in the film, 'Do these things, do not describe them'. In *Shoah*, Lanzmann records at length a testimony which, shot in long takes, expressed in a diversity of languages, delayed while it is translated into French and punctuated with silences, presents an agonised description of the indescribable.

Shoah was made and released during an extended period of debate and controversy surrounding the Holocaust. In France the late seventies and early eighties saw a rise in anti-Semitic terrorism, the arrest of Klaus Barbie, the beginnings of proceedings against Touvier and other collaborators, and also the emergence and eventual trial, in 1983, of the revisionist historian Robert Faurisson (Colombat 1993: 99). Faurisson's stance is epitomised by his claim in 1979 that: 'I have tried in vain to find a single former deportee capable of proving to me that he had really seen, with his own eyes, a gas chamber' (Felman 1992: 215). In such a context, Lanzmann's filming of the gas chambers and the sites of the death camps, and above all his recording of testimony from numerous Jewish survivors, Polish onlookers and Nazi perpetrators, assumes an even more urgent relevance. The essential difference between *Shoah* and other Holocaust documentaries, in particular *Nuit et brouillard* and *Le Chagrin et la pitié*, is that Lanzmann avoids using archive footage, and that consequently no photographic distinction is set up between the past and the present. All of the material in *Shoah* is shot in the present and practically all of it in colour, partly because Lanzmann felt that archive film of the death camps was losing its impact upon audiences, and also to establish the continuity between past and present which is fundamental to the film. If there is a structural dichotomy in *Shoah* it is between sound and image, establishing 'an absolute contrast between the beauty of the landscape and the horror of what is said' (Lanzmann 1993). Thus the first images in the film are of a beautiful green Polish landscape, through which Simon Srebnik, one of only two survivors from the Chelmno death camp, travels slowly by boat. Srebnik comments that 'It was always this peaceful here', even when the Germans were burning two thousand Jews a day. Srebnik's return to Chelmno forms the introduction to the film, which is structured in two halves. *The First Era* and *The Second Era* correspond to the development of the extermination process in the death camps of Treblinka, Auschwitz, Belzec, Chelmno and Sobibor. Although *Shoah* is characterised by repetition in terms of both testimony and image, it presents a loose narrative development, whereby the eyewitness accounts, like Lanzmann's camera, slowly approach and ultimately enter the camps. Certain images recur throughout the film: green Polish forests, trains and railtracks, the stones commemorating the dead, and a long, slow dolly shot of Auschwitz for which he himself pushed the dolly.The two halves are both introduced by a witness singing: in the first case, Srebnik sings precisely as he used to while under SS guard on the river at Chelmno; in the second, the former SS man Suchomel sings the song the worker Jews at Treblinka were forced to learn, a song which he alone knows, since the Jews were all killed. In a further irony, it is the blurred, monochrome images of Suchomel (and of the other Nazis filmed secretly with hidden cameras) which are closest to the images of death captured in the black-and-white archive footage of traditional Holocaust documentary.

Shoah has often been described as not so much a historical documentary as the director's personal obsession. Lanzmann himself has called the film a crime film and a Western, in which he (and survivors like Srebnik) 'come back to the scene of the crime' (Felman 1992: 256, n.34). As he told *Cahiers du cinéma*, the film is a 'fiction of reality', with the witnesses turned into 'actors' in order to 'relive' and 'transmit' their experiences (Colombat 1993: 312–13). Hence the importance in *Shoah* not just of montage – as in the cross-cutting between Hilberg citing Czerniakow's diary and Grassler denying the atrocities in the Warsaw ghetto – but of the traditionally fictional strategies of *mise en scène*. Most notably in the case of Abraham Bomba, a survivor who had to cut the hair of those about to be gassed, it is the staging of the interview – in a Tel Aviv barbershop – as much as Lanzmann's relentless questioning, which results in a 'transmission' of intense personal suffering from the interviewee to the film spectator, as Bomba breaks down on what Lanzmann terms 'the border of the unspeakable' (Colombat 1993: 343). Like the barbershop, the locomotive driven towards Treblinka by Henrik Gakowski was rented by the director in order to bring the past more graphically to life for witness and spectator. Such 'reactivation' turns the film into what Lanzmann calls 'an incarnation, a resurrection' (Felman 1992: 214). This is evident not only in the celebrated sequence wherein Srebnik, returning to the church at Chelmno, is confronted with the rekindled anti-Semitism of the villagers, but also in the clandestine filming of Suchomel which presents the secrecy of the Holocaust even as the SS guard testifies to the camouflaging and invisibility of the death camps.

The concluding hour or more of *Shoah* – the interviews with Karski, Grassler and Rottem, and Hilberg's readings from Czerniakow's diary – concerns the acknowledgement of the Holocaust as an event which, however secret, must be told. The precise focus is the Warsaw ghetto, the site of a physical struggle and also the subject of a struggle over the reality of the Holocaust. The testimony of Jan Karski in particular, edited by Lanzmann from eight hours of footage into forty minutes, enacts the movement from ignorance to awareness and then to 'reactivation' of the past which is crucial to the film and to the spectator's response. As the former courier to the Polish government in exile, a man whose mission was to report what he saw in Warsaw and elsewhere to the Allies and to plead for action, Karski stands on the threshold between the 'inside' of the Holocaust and the outside world. His position thus parallels that of the spectator of Holocaust film, and of *Shoah* especially: 'I never saw such things, I never ... nobody wrote about this kind of reality. I never saw any theatre, I never saw any movie ... this was not the world.' Karski's struggle to comprehend what he saw, to be believed, and also to speak to Lanzmann of something he has not mentioned for twenty-six years, is followed in the film by the Nazi administrator, Grassler's, revisionist account of the ghetto against which Lanzmann himself fights, telling Grassler 'I'll help you to remember'. The interview with Karski is also subject to Lanzmann's most dramatic and unexpected use of imagery: while in voice-over Karski recounts his own anguished visits to the ghetto and the urgent pleas he was to give the Allied leaders, we see serene blue skies over American skyscrapers and German factories. The impassive symbols of American wealth and democracy – the New York skyline, the White House – and of German industrial strength – the Ruhr – implicitly give the response to Karski's messages, and also suggest a collective guilt shared by the Allies and the Germans. Lanzmann's editing and camerawork then link the present to the past explicitly, as an image of a German factory flame gives way to a slow pan down a bare tree to the debris of Auschwitz and close-ups of the piles of shoes and brushes taken from the dead. The last interviewee in *Shoah*, the ghetto fighter Rottem, describes himself alone in the Warsaw ghetto as 'the last Jew'. This has been compared to Srebnik's comment early in the film that if he survived the camps, he would become 'the only one left in the world'. Asked about this apparently cyclical conclusion, Lanzmann has responded that the Holocaust 'still goes on' and that therefore 'I decided that the last image of the film would be a rolling train, an endlessly rolling ... train' (Felman 1992: 242). As with the shot of the Saurer lorry – the same make as the gas vans – in motion at the end of *The First Era*, the 'continuous, incomplete motion' of the train 'reminds us that there is no end to *Shoah*' or to the Holocaust (Colombat 1993: 338).

La Guerre sans nom: breaking the silence on the Algerian War

The films of Ophüls and Lanzmann established documentary film as a means of breaking taboos on political or historical subjects. The influence of Ophüls, in particular, is manifest in the work of Bertrand Tavernier, who appeared in *Hôtel Terminus* before in turn producing Ophüls's film on the war in Bosnia, *Veillées d'armes* (1994). Ophüls's *The Memory of Justice* had included testimony about the torture practised by the French army during the Algerian War. *La Guerre sans nom* (1992), Tavernier and Patrick Rotman's four-hour documentary, considers in much greater depth this forgotten period of French history which, as Tavernier's narration makes clear, has never been officially acknowledged as a war, but euphemistically termed an operation to keep law and order. Tavernier had already explored the wounds left by the First World War in his 1989 fiction film *La Vie et rien d'autre* (see chapter 7). He felt *La Guerre sans nom* to be, in a sense, a continuation of this work (Tavernier 1993: 267). The documentary also makes a brief allusion to Tavernier's jazz movie *Autour de Minuit* (1986), in the closing interview with a traumatised veteran. Indeed, music is used very effectively throughout, whether it be live – the final scene in which the jazz-loving veteran plays 'The Girl from Ipanema' on the piano – or added to the sound-track, in the form of the sixties pop songs which punctuate the film. Recordings of gunfire and of the radio messages sent by troops to their families are also employed to revivify the events described in the interviews. *La Guerre sans nom*, like Ophüls' *Le Chagrin et la pitié*, has a specific geographical focus; the film begins in Grenoble, with evocations of a protest against conscription to fight in Algeria. When the film was due to be shown on French television (it also received a cinema release), Tavernier was asked by the station concerned, Canal Plus, to cut the demonstration sequence. He refused, 'because it anchors the film within a precise French context, one that has never been shown before' (Tavernier 1993: 257). In Tavernier's words, the aim of the film was 'to give a voice to people who had been silent, who had been excluded from history; to bring back to life a forgotten memory'. To this end, the film-makers interviewed former conscripts and 'recalled' soldiers, none of them ranked higher than lieutenant, from the Grenoble area: 'No volunteers, no professional soldiers or senior officers [...]. And we've left out any archive or newsreel footage, anything "official". We have only used amateur photographs taken by our witnesses' (Tavernier 1993: 267). The decision to rely solely on present testimony recalls Lanzmann's strategy in *Shoah*, while the numerous witnesses are in many cases breaking thirty years of silence to talk about their experiences in Algeria. The tension of their hesitation on what Lanzmann calls 'the border of the unspeakable', a tension ultimately released by the cathartic power of music in the final scene, conveys not only the horrors of the Algerian War but also the suffering involved in breaking the taboo which has surrounded it.

La mode rétro

As already noted, although Charles de Gaulle died in 1970, Gaullist policy was continued by his chosen successor as President, Georges Pompidou. It is thus 1974, the year of Pompidou's death in office and the election of Valéry Giscard d'Estaing, that marks the end of the Gaullist dominance of post-war France. Hence François Nourrisier's comment in an article of the time: 'Le Père est mort, on fait l'inventaire de l'héritage' [The Father is dead, time to take stock of the inheritance] (Morris 1992: 105). The death of Gaullism coincided with a wave of re-interpretations of the Occupation on the part of writers and film-makers who had been children during the war. In literature, this trend began with Patrick Modiano's 1968 novel *La Place de l'étoile*, while in cinema it was Ophüls's *Le Chagrin et la pitié* (1971) which set the tone. Despite the positive reception of such works by the public, the critical response – from both Gaullists and the Left – was often to denigrate them as stylised and apolitical revisions of French history, in short, as inaugurating *la mode rétro*. This critique was fundamentally a response to the revision of Gaullist history taking place across French culture and society, exemplified by Giscard d'Estaing's decision in 1975 to replace the 8 May celebrations of Germany's defeat with a festival of Europe.

Those who attacked *la mode rétro* saw themselves as guardians of a historical truth under threat; hence *Le Chagrin et la pitié*, intended according to Ophüls and Harris to 'eliminate mythology' and challenge *le résistancialisme* by addressing French collaboration, was rejected by the director-general of the ORTF because it destroyed myths which the French people still needed (Morris 1992: 43-4). Subsequent critiques of *la mode rétro* were launched in Ganier-Raymond's 1975 history of anti-Semitism during the war, *Une Certaine France*, and by *Cahiers du cinéma* in the summer of

1974 under the heading 'Anti-rétro'. Apart from *Le Chagrin et la pitié*, two fiction films bore the brunt of these attacks: Louis Malle's *Lacombe, Lucien* (1974, co-written by Modiano) and an Italian film of the same year, Lilianna Cavanni's *The Night Porter*. All three films generated controversy by representing collaborators or Nazis rather than Resistance fighters, a choice of subject compounded in *Lacombe, Lucien* and *The Night Porter* by an attractive *mise en scène* and elements of eroticism. Since the visual style of *la mode rétro* did not extend to any disruption of form, contesting the myth of Gaullism via content and ironic tone instead, it elicited criticism from avant-garde film-makers like Godard and Gorin (Godard 1991: 139). *Cahiers du cinéma* succinctly defined *rétro* cinema as a snobbish fetishising of old costumes and décors combined with a contempt for history, while in an interview for the magazine, Michel Foucault epitomised the anger of the Left faced with the demythologising of the struggle against Occupation, observing with dismay that if a 'positive' film were made in 1974 about the Resistance, it would be either ignored or laughed at by the audience (Bonitzer and Toubiana 1974: 5, 8). Foucault was right to say that if the Gaullist myth of *le résistancialisme* (all of the French were Resistance fighters) was not accurate, then neither was the new myth of *la mode rétro* (all of the French were collaborators), and that the historical truth lay in a gradual movement during the war years from collaboration to resistance. In French cinema after *la mode rétro*, however, this movement was not always perceived as purely 'positive' or ideological, but also – in response to the ongoing scandals about the wartime past of François Mitterand and René Bousquet, among others, – as contaminated by a cynical opportunism and leading to the horrors of *l'épuration*, the post-war purges against anyone suspected of collaboration (see below).

Lacombe, Lucien: the collaborator not as monster but as 'youth of today'

Although belonging to the same generation as the film-makers of the *nouvelle vague* (see chapter 1), Louis Malle is a classical rather than an experimental director. His career has comprised fiction and documentary films, the latter including *Calcutta* (1969) and *Place de la République* (1974). Despite his liberal sympathies, even before the making of *Lacombe, Lucien* in 1974 Malle had been faced with suggestions of right-wing allegiance for working with Roger Nimier on *Ascenseur pour l'échafaud* (1957) and for basing *Le Feu follet* (1963) on a novel by Drieu La Rochelle (Colombat 1993: 77). The project that was to become *Lacombe, Lucien* was always intended as a portrayal of collaboration: it was first to be about Algerian *harkis* (Algerians who fought with the French and against the FLN – the Algerian independence movement) helping the French maintain control of their country, before Malle settled on the subject of France during the Occupation. This subject would have proved taboo in the 1960s by Malle's own admission, but by the early seventies he felt that *Le Chagrin et la pitié* had 'prepared the ground by forcing Frenchmen to question themselves on this matter' (Morris 1992: 105). Consequently shocked at the furore surrounding his film, Malle stressed in interviews that the characters in *Lacombe, Lucien* – including the incongruous figure of the black Gestapo foot-soldier – were in fact based closely on historical research, while comparing the 'objective' stance of the film to his documentary work, an assertion supported by the use of non-professional leads and by the (false) authentication of the narrative as historical fact in the final caption. He later declared that 'What they teach French school-children about the Occupation period is a bunch of lies' (Insdorf 1983: 123), and that to conform to the prevalent mythology a collaborator should have been presented as a club-footed monster to be exterminated rather than understood (Morris 1992: 58). Far from demonising Lucien in this way, the film portrayed him – according to the press release – as 'un jeune d'aujourd'hui' [a youth of today] (Bonitzer 1974: 44).

The film is set in 1944 as the Allied advance begins. Lucien (Pierre Blaise) is a peasant youth living in the rural south-west. Having been rejected by the Resistance as too young, he stumbles into the local Gestapo headquarters by accident after his bike gets a puncture. While drunk he betrays the Resistance contact who refused him, before being given a machine gun and kitted out in fashionable clothes as the newest member of the Gestapo. Meeting a Jewish tailor and his family, Lucien begins an affair with the daughter, France (Aurore Clément). After the tailor has given himself up, and when he sees France and her grandmother being deported, Lucien rescues them and the trio flee to the backwoods. A caption at the film's close asserts that Lucien was tried and shot for collaboration. Significantly, the narrative is generated by chance – and by Lucien's apolitical and often petty motivations – rather than by ideology. The same is true of Cavanni's *The Night Porter*, where 'by chance' the former Nazi Max comes across Lucia, his 'favourite victim' from the camps, in post-war Vienna (Daney 1974: 30). It was this absence of ideology – in the representation of the most crucial period of ideological choice in recent French history – which proved so controversial. As an uneducated peasant who ignores the radio broadcasts of both sides, who loves a Jewish woman and who uses Pétain's image for target practice, Lucien is as apolitical as an active collaborator can be. His responsibility for the fates of the *résistant* schoolteacher and France's father is carefully qualified. Even during his apparently 'good' act of rescuing France and her grandmother from deportation, Lucien kills the guard merely in order to reclaim a watch he considers his. The closing sequence in the woods places Lucien and France as young lovers outside the realm of history and politics in a pastoral idyll into which the war makes only a perfunctory return in the final freeze-frame and caption.

The erotic and pastoral aspects of the film, strongest in the clos-

1   Pierre Blaise (left) in *Lacombe, Lucien*

ing reel, were particularly confusing to the extreme Left, as noted in *Cahiers* (Bonitzer and Toubiana 1974: 15). Foucault claimed that the eroticism functioned to rehabilitate the anti-hero Lucien (Bonitzer and Toubiana 1974: 10), while Jean Delmas writing in *Jeune Cinéma* in 1974 described the film as 'la récupération senti-mentale d'un salaud' [the sentimental rehabilitation of a swine] (Prédal 1989: 116). It is in fact typical of Malle to be more inter-ested in sex, psychology and adolescence than in history or politics – witness *Au Revoir les Enfants* (1987) and *Le Souffle au cœur* (1971) (see below) – and thus Foucault and Delmas misread *Lacombe, Lucien* as a film on history with sexuality added, instead of the reverse. Of course, war films are traditionally concerned with male psychology and sexuality – a rare exception is Claude Chabrol's *Une Affaire de femmes* (see below) – and *Lacombe, Lucien* conforms to this trend. In Malle's portrayal of masculinity, Lucien is defined as a man through the power he exercises as a member of the Gestapo; this power is symbolised in his machine gun (which replaces the rifle of his absent father) and is exercised over women, principally France but also those queuing in the street for food. When Lucien confronts other men he seeks to emasculate them, remarking to France's tailor father that only women sew, humiliating a *résistant* prisoner by gagging him with a piece of tape on which he draws a mouth in lipstick. Reviewing the film for *Cahiers*, Pascal Bonitzer observed that in the latter sequence the prisoner, like the audience, expects Lucien to enter history either as a *résistant* or as a *collabo*. In fact Lucien neither frees the prisoner nor tortures him, side-step-ping these ideological choices first by asking why the prisoner addresses him as *tu*, and second by gagging him. As Bonitzer observes, the act of gagging, thus emptied of any ideological mean-

Holocaust documentary and the war film

ing, epitomises Lucien's function throughout the film as a political cipher (Bonitzer 1974: 44). It is however in terms of sound rather than image that *Lacombe, Lucien* most clearly exhibits the *rétro* sensibility of privileging style over history. While historical discourse, contained in the radio broadcasts which punctuate the film, remains a barely audible background presence, the sound-track is dominated by jazz tunes of the 1940s carefully chosen by the director to evoke the style of the period.

In the wake of *la mode rétro*, the Occupation became the premise for comedies and sex films, two tendencies combined in Francis Girod's *René la canne* (1977). With *Emmanuelle* star Sylvia Kristel the female lead, and Gérard Depardieu and Michel Piccoli as a pair of rogues, the film relies on comic stereotypes. Depardieu's thief and Piccoli's policeman team up to fight the Germans and both survive the war unscathed: the challenging of *le résistancialisme* inherent to *la mode rétro* is thus absent while only a stylised *mise en scène* remains; the Citroën cars, berets and ragtime music all derived directly from *Lacombe, Lucien*. In playing the Occupation for farce, however, the film prefigures Bertrand Blier's much more thoughtful parodying of the war movie in *Merci la Vie* (1991) (see below).

The Occupation in fiction films of the 1980s and 1990s

By the 1980s, Foucault's judgement that a 'positive' portrayal of the Resistance was impossible no longer held true. *Le Dernier Métro* (1980), François Truffaut's rather facile representation of Resistance – effortlessly embodied by the two leading stars of the day, Catherine Deneuve and Gérard Depardieu – attracted over three million spectators and proved Truffaut's most popular film ever in France (Prédal 1991: 402). And after a decade in the United States following the reception of *Lacombe, Lucien*, Louis Malle made a triumphant return to French cinema and to the war period with *Au revoir les enfants* (1987), a world-wide success which gained an Oscar nomination and seven Césars, and was watched by two million spectators in France (Prédal 1991: 403). More melancholic and less controversial than *Lacombe, Lucien*, the film has an understated narrative, a subdued *mise en scène* and a bleak music track. With the exception of the secondary character, Joseph, who is a reprise of Lucien, this is a positive portrayal of the French during the Occupation, especially of the priests who – in contrast with the complicity of the Catholic Church in the Vichy regime – shelter Jewish boys in their school. The narrative functions as a mystery story about the true identity of new boy Jean Bonnet/Kippelstein, and is viewed through the eyes of the young schoolboy Julien. The historical reality of the Holocaust is thus present for the spectator and for Jean, but not for Julien: it lies hidden behind the enigma of Jean's identity. *Au revoir les enfants* is also an evocation of boyhood, with constant echoes of Jean Vigo's *Zéro de conduite* (1933). The lengthy forest scene is exemplary in combining Julien's innocent exhilaration with the historical apprehension shared by Jean and the audience. Ultimately, Julien inadvertently betrays Jean to the Germans, and here as throughout, the narrative is authorised by Jean's point of view, the final image switching from Jean's exit to a reaction shot of Julien. As at the end of *Lacombe, Lucien*, history intrudes upon innocence, here in the form of a voice-over declaring that Jean, the other Jewish boys and the priest who sheltered them, all died in the camps. Yet despite this conclusion, the film remains essentially a childhood buddy movie rendered poignant by its historical resonance, just as *Lacombe, Lucien* is a love story complicated by the Occupation and *Le Souffle au cœur* (1971) an incest narrative set against the war in Indo-China (see below).

Gender in the war film: *Une Affaire de femmes*

With rare exceptions – such as Diane Kurys' *Coup de foudre* (1983) (see chapter 4) – French representations of the Occupation and the Holocaust concentrate on male experience, as do war films in general (Selig 1993). This masculine discourse, epitomised by Pétain's speeches in Claude Chabrol's compilation of Vichy newsreels, *L'Œil de Vichy* (1993), is challenged by Chabrol's fiction film on female experience, *Une Affaire de femmes* (1988). Co-written by Colo Tavernier O'Hagan, and based on a true story, the film follows the efforts of Marie Latour (Isabelle Huppert) to bring up her two children in Cherbourg during the Occupation. As a favour to a friend, Marie carries out an abortion, and gradually begins to make money through this illegal activity. Her husband, Paul (François Cluzet), a prisoner of war, is released and returns to Cherbourg. It is he who finally betrays Marie to the police; tried in Paris for crimes against the state, she is found guilty and guillotined in July 1943.

Chabrol films this story in a bleakly realist style, using music sparingly and shooting in brown tones which evoke deprivation and poverty. Marie's activity as an abortionist is a double threat to the official policy of collaboration, first by depriving the Germans of potential French workers, and second by contradicting the Vichy dogma of family and motherhood, inscribed in the motto *travail, famille, patrie* and in the celebration of *la fête des mères*. Chabrol portrays the process of abortion with the neutral, unspectacular realism which characterises the film, but ultimately turns to the structures of melodrama to realise Marie's personal tragedy. Hence she rises highest in her creative ambition – to be a singer – at the moment of her impending downfall and arrest. A plot-line typical of the 'woman's film' thus dramatises the female war experience. In *Une Affaire de femmes* the Occupation is an experience that women have come to terms with and one which in a sense, does not concern men, who are largely absent. Marie rents out a room to her prostitute friend Lulu as a deal 'between women'; she cryptically tells Paul that she does 'women's favours' for her friends and neighbours; her tarot reading makes no mention of men, but suggests she will have many women in her life; throughout the film she enjoys female companionship with her Jewish friend Rachel, with Lulu and with the prisoners who share her cell in Paris. This iterative stress on the common concerns and responses of women in wartime sidelines the 'masculine' arena of combat, as it sidelines Paul within the narrative. He eventually takes his revenge for this – and for Marie's affair with a young spiv – by denouncing his wife to the (male) authorities. Marie's response to her sentence is emblematic of the film as a whole and subverts the claims of the conventional war movie: 'Qu'est-ce que tu veux qu'ils comprennent, les hommes?' [What do you expect men to know about it?]. Enduring and ameliorating the conditions of war is here a woman's business, condemned and punished by the patriarchal Vichy state.

Docteur Petiot: the Holocaust as horror film

The question of cinematic form is a particularly fraught one for films on the Holocaust and the Occupation; these subjects are conventionally considered susceptible either to a documentary approach or to classical realism. Culturally 'low' genres like horror, fantasy and farce seem inappropriate and are therefore rare. The enormity of the Holocaust as a historical event may determine not only the choice of genre, but also of monochrome rather than colour, as in *Schindler's List* (1993) by Spielberg. Such delineations of what is considered appropriate have been challenged in the nineties by films which run counter to the classical realist tradition of French cinema and of the war movie: Christian de Chalonge's *Docteur Petiot* (1990), Bertrand Blier's *Merci la Vie* (1991) (see below), and Jeunet and Caro's *Delicatessen* (1990) (see chapter 6).

Despite being based on the actual case of a serial killer operating in Paris during the Occupation, *Docteur Petiot* rejects historical realism for something altogether more unexpected, the horror genre. The plot concerns Petiot's double life. Ostensibly a respectable doctor and family man, he takes on a vampiric persona at night, secretly promising Jews fleeing from the Nazis safe passage out of France before murdering them and stealing their possessions. Thus there is a truly horrific referent behind the generic horror style. Petiot's efficient and systematic murder of Jews – whose bodies are subsequently burned in his enormous basement stove – is clearly analogous to the horrors of the Holocaust. The stereotypical portrayal of some of the Jewish characters notwithstanding, the film thus engages effectively not just with the Occupation but with the Holocaust. By representing the casual and banal logistics of Petiot's murders, albeit distanced by the fantastical and at times farcical style, Christian de Chalonge comes close to making what Godard has defined as the intolerable but necessary film which has yet to be made about the camps: 'The only real film to be made about them [...] would be if a camp were filmed from the point of view of the torturers and their daily routine. [...] The really horrible thing about such scenes would be not their horror but their very ordinary everydayness' (Godard 1986: 198). In this regard, de Chalonge's

2   Michel Serrault as *Docteur Petiot*

choice of genre has two consequences. By choosing a fantasy genre
which has a monster as its usual protagonist, he is able to show
what Godard calls 'the torturer's daily routine' without departing
from a popular and accessible generic format. (In other words, the
horror film naturally allows the representation of horrors which
would be unrepresentable in a realistic mode.) Second, by juxta-
posing Petiot's grotesque appearance as an archetypal vampire with
the 'everydayness' of his efficient, murderous routine, the director
asks where the real horror lies: in the style of Petiot's behaviour or
the specific (anti-Semitic) content of his actions.

The opening sequence of the film suggest what is to come by submitting historical images to a sense of theatrical spectacle, with
black-and-white newsreel footage of Paris in 1942 framed by the
red curtain of a movie theatre. The newsreel (history) is then suc-
ceeded by 'Hangman's Castle', a German monochrome horror film
in the style of Murnau's expressionist masterpiece *Nosferatu* (1922).
The sequence which follows is an exemplary piece of self-conscious
cinema: finding the vampire movie ridiculous and clumsy, Docteur
Petiot himself emerges from the audience to remonstrate at the film,
at which point his shadow appears on the screen opposite the figure
of the vampire. While Petiot's words thus cast him as more realistic and less ridiculous than the generic vampire on the screen, the
image – which is then frozen for the opening credits – equates the
two as similarly horrific and fantastical. After the credits, the stilled
image moves again and Petiot tears through the screen to enter the
horror film, stirring cauldrons as a black-and-white version of his
'historical' self. This invasion of the horror space situates *Docteur
Petiot* within the genre both explicitly – via the monochrome photography, shadowy expressionist *mise en scène* and eerie music – and

implicitly, since the self-referential motif of crossing the screen that separates cinematic fantasy from the 'real world' is a staple of the horror film from *King Kong* (1933) onwards (Clover 1992: 195). As Petiot goes on his rounds, the black-and-white photography fades to situate the action once more in Paris, 1942, shot in colour and with some realism. Generic horror elements remain throughout the film, however, in the suspenseful music and moaning sound effects which accompany Petiot's nocturnal movements, in the gloomy expressionism of the *mise en scène*, and above all in the person of Petiot himself (Michel Serrault), whose theatrical gestures, black cape and pale make-up continue to characterise him as a vampire. There are realistic glimpses of poverty and deprivation under the Occupation, such as the shot of Parisians catching pigeons to eat. Until the final reel, however, horror overrides history, with Petiot laughing maniacally as he cycles through the dusk, hiding under the bedclothes when dawn light comes through the shutters, or described as 'le vampire' in newsreels after his crimes come to light.

After the police discover the scene of Petiot's crimes, the doctor goes into hiding, before reappearing during the Liberation of Paris with a false identity as Captain Valéry, a Resistance war hero. As the film nears its close, Petiot's new disguise and eager involvement in anti-collaboration purges – *l'épuration* – render him no longer a personification of war crimes against the Jews, but of French post-war manoeouvrings and myth-making. The myth of *le résistancial-isme* and the controversial conduct of public figures such as René Bousquet and François Mitterand is addressed through Petiot's seemingly effortless metamorphosis from murderer to hero. In 1990, the year *Docteur Petiot* was released, the role of former Vichy police chief, René Bousquet, in the deportation of Jews – a question subsequently broached in Jean Marbœuf's biopic *Pétain* (1992) – and the friendship between Bousquet and Mitterand were under great scrutiny. Bousquet's trial was being delayed by the French judiciary; in April 1991 he was indicted for crimes against human-ity, only to be assassinated in 1993. Moreover, in May 1990, the desecration of a Jewish cemetery at Carpentras, and the revisionist theories of Bernard Notin, contributed to a picture of 'une France sur la défensive, inquiète dans son identité' [France on the defen-sive, unsure of its identity] (Jeambar 1990). This is the very situa-tion personified by Petiot's change of identity at the close of the film, a change complemented by a transformation of genre, from the horror film to the thriller. In a reprise of the opening sequence, and an ironic allusion to the escapist function of cinema during the war period (see chapter 1), Petiot again crosses the screen, this time in order to evade capture by the police. His attempt to enter the thriller he is watching fails, however, and he is arrested behind the screen. Nevertheless, this scene clearly signals the shift in genre which has taken place: no longer coded as horror, the narrative concludes both as a thriller – the pursuit and capture of the suspect – and also as historical realism. The return of history is realised in the form of a voice-over which explains that Petiot was found guilty of twenty-seven murders, and guillotined on 24 May 1946. The image track meanwhile shows a lingering slow pan on the fifty-three suitcases full of possessions recovered after Petiot's trial, an image which recalls the discovery of personal belongings horded in the death camps, and more precisely, Lanzmann's filming of the piles of brushes and shoes in the documentary *Shoah* (1985). The closing images of *Docteur Petiot* thus confirm this horror film's urgent relation to the historical enormity of the Holocaust.

Merci la Vie: parodying the French war movie

Bertrand Blier's *Merci la vie* (1991) is a mix of genres, part buddy movie, part sex comedy and part war film. Blier had already worked consistently within the first two genres, but this interest in history was novel. The narrative of the film shifts throughout between the present and the past, allowing Blier to explore two crises: the trauma of the Occupation and the threat of Aids. The two are equated metaphorically, rather as disease and occupying powers were conflated in the wartime epithet 'la peste brune' [the brown plague] and in Albert Camus's post-war novel *La Peste*. Blier's protagonists, Joëlle (Anouk Grinberg) and Camille (Charlotte Gainsbourg), pursue sexual adventures in much the same fashion as their male counterparts in his first film, *Les Valseuses* (1974). They find themselves caught up, however, in the fantasies of two male film directors, the second of whom is shooting a movie set during the Occupation. This allows Blier to parody not only the conventional representation of women in film (see chapter 3), but also conventional modes of filming the Occupation.

While Blier's films are often characterised by farce and black comedy, a wartime subject might appear to preclude such a treatment. Jean-Luc Godard was attacked in 1963 for combining newsreel footage with what he called 'improvised farce' in his war film *Les Carabiniers* (Godard 1986: 198). In *The Holocaust and the Literary Imagination*, however, Langer asserts that rather than verisimilitude (so often the recourse of films on the Occupation and the Holocaust), the farcical, the fantastic and the grotesque are best suited to the representation of 'the unimaginable' (Avisar 1988: 1–2). These elements are of course used to great effect in Christian de Chalonge's *Docteur Petiot* and Jeunet and Caro's *Delicatessen* (both 1990). For his part, Blier combines the comic and the grotesque, reducing the torture of Raymond (Jean Carmet) to a farce, and revealing the artifice of the war film when the Blier-lookalike film director asks if he is being shot by fake or real bullets. The functioning of monochrome and colour in the Holocaust documentary, epitomised by Resnais's *Nuit et brouillard* (1955), is also kept in the foreground throughout *Merci la Vie*. Michel Drach had reversed the conventional dichotomy – black and white for the past, colour for the present – in *Les Violons du bal* (1973), but Blier's alternation of colour and monochrome is completely random, divorced

Michel Blanc, Anouk Grinberg, Charlotte Gainsbourg
and Gérard Depardieu in *Merci la Vie*

from the chronology of the narrative. The director has compared *Merci la Vie* to channel-zapping between six different movies, including a black-and-white film by Jean Renoir and a colour fantasy film by Joe Dante (Mény 1991). The list might also include the recent French war films parodied through Blier's *mise en scène*, such as Malle's *Lacombe, Lucien* (1974), Girod's *René la canne* (1977), Truffaut's *Le Dernier Métro* (1980) and Jean-Marie Poiré's *Papy fait de la Résistance* (1983). The latter – a comedy in which the policy of Franco-German collaboration degenerates into a farcical cohabitation – is a clear precursor for *Merci la Vie*, parodying as it does previous war films, including Jean-Pierre Melville's *Le Silence de la mer* (1949) and *L'Armée des ombres* (1969) (Nevers and Strauss 1993: 85). Blier and Poiré also share a close relation to the *café-théâtre* of the 1970s. This style of comic drama, based at the Café de la Gare and le Splendid in Paris, produced such actors as Michel Blanc, Miou-Miou, Thierry Lhermitte and Christian Clavier, and first made an impact on French cinema in 1974 with Blier's own *Les Valseuses* (see chapter 3). Blier worked frequently in the next two decades with actors from the Café de la Gare – Miou-Miou, Depardieu, Patrick Dewaere – and also with Josiane Balasko and Michel Blanc from le Splendid. Poiré's films remain more genuinely popular – and populist – than Blier's: *Papy fait de la Résistance*, a product of le Splendid starring Clavier, Blanc, Balasko and Lhermitte, attracted nearly four million spectators in 1983 (Prédal 1991: 402), while a decade later, Poiré and Clavier were responsible for the hugely popular comic fantasy *Les Visiteurs* (see chapter 6).

The Indochinese and Algerian Wars in fiction film

On 7 May 1954, the French army in Indochina was heavily defeated by the Vietminh at Dien Bien Phu. The fall of Dien Bien Phu was a turning point not just in Indochina but in French colonial power, heralding the futile conflict in Algeria (1954–62), decolonisation, and the decline of the French empire. Moreover, 'Psychologiquement, Dien Bien Phu devient le symbole du désastre' [Psychologically, Dien Bien Phu symbolises disaster] (Accoce and Stavridès 1991: 23). Precisely because the colonial wars fought in Algeria and Indochina proved so traumatic, they remained taboo, practically absent from the French cinema of the period. When films were made which referred to the conflicts they ran the risk of censorship, as with Godard's Le Petit Soldat (1960), which was banned until 1963, a year after Algerian independence. The impossibility of representing on screen the Algerian War – and particularly the war crimes associated with it – is addressed in Alain Resnais's Muriel (1963). Set in Boulogne in November 1962, the film concerns memories of both the Second World War and the Algerian'War. The mysterious Muriel is the personification of the latter conflict. Apparently the fiancée of the male protagonist Bernard, she in fact remains invisible, unrepresentable except via sound in Bernard's recollections and in a tape recording which seems to capture her torture and death at the hands of French soldiers in Algeria. As one of the soldiers later declares, 'Muriel, ça ne se raconte pas' [Muriel's story cannot be told].

The Algerian War was first subjected to a direct, naturalistic portrayal in Gillo Pontecorvo's Italian-Algerian co-production, The Battle of Algiers (1966). In France, however, the colonial wars were still approachable only at a tangent. In Le Souffle au cœur (1971) Louis Malle characteristically uses the fall of Dien Bien Phu as historical background for an evocation of adolescent sexuality. Here the conflict in Indochina assumes a function analogous to its place in the work of Malle's collaborator on Lacombe, Lucien, Patrick Modiano, for whom wars are merely a chronological index: 'les meilleurs repères, ce sont les guerres' [wars are the best landmarks] (Modiano 1975: 19). Claude Chabrol explores the legacy of the two wars in Le Boucher (1969), a thriller about a serial killer at large in a small French town. From the outset, Chabrol makes it plain that the butcher Popaul (Jean Yanne), is an army veteran who has been marked by his experiences in Algeria and Indochina. An uneasy tension is established between the ostensible normality and continuity of provincial life – evoked by the dancing and folk songs during the long wedding sequence – and the hidden traumas arising from the past, realised in iterative shots of the war memorial accompanied by haunting and suspenseful music. The anguish and violence implicit in the symbol of the war memorial is rendered explicit when Popaul, aggressively chopping slabs of meat in his shop, almost involuntarily tells his customers about the mutilated bodies he saw as a soldier. When the local headmistress Hélène (Stéphane Audran) finds the victim of the first murder, she tells Popaul that the body resembles the atrocities he has described. Although from this point on Chabrol moves from psychological concerns to a more generic suspense narrative in the style of Alfred Hitchcock, through the character of Popaul a connection between present violence and past traumas has clearly been made. As with Hollywood representations of the Vietnam war in the 1970s, it is obliquely through the figure of the returning veteran that the conflict itself is addressed. And as with the films on Vietnam, in *Le Boucher* 'the authenticity of [the veteran's] experience and the reconstitution of a masculine identity require the ultimate exclusion of women and female sexuality' (Selig 1993: 10). Popaul's victims are all women, while he makes friends only with the overtly desexualised Hélène, who has been celibate for ten years. At the film's close, he tells Hélène that it was only in her company that he was free from the visions of blood which have haunted him since his war experiences.

Stimulated both by the reappraisal of history following 1968 and by their increasing distance from the colonial wars, film-makers began to engage directly with Algeria and Indochina during the 1970s. In 1972, René Vautier, who had worked with the independence-seeking FLN (Front de libération nationale) during the conflict, directed *Avoir 20 ans dans les Aurès*, credited as 'the first fictional film about the Algerian War' (Tavernier 1993: 289). This was followed swiftly by Yves Boisset's less well-received *R.A.S.* (1973). But the director most consistently concerned with the two wars in question is the veteran Pierre Schoendoerffer.

Hearts of darkness: *Le Crabe-Tambour* and *Dien Bien Phu*

Having volunteered to go to Indochina, Schoendoerffer served as a cameraman with the French army until his capture at Dien Bien Phu. In 1963 he published *La 317e Section*, a novel based on his experiences in Indochina which he himself filmed the following year. The same pattern over a decade later produced first the novel, then in 1977 the film version, of *Le Crabe-Tambour*. Like Resnais's *Muriel*, the film explores memories of war through an enigmatic central figure – who may or may not be imaginary – and through the juxtaposition of different conflicts.

Willsdorff, nicknamed 'Le Crabe-Tambour' (Jacques Perrin), is a mysterious officer who has served in both Indochina and Algeria. Crucially, he is identified with the traumatic disasters which concluded those conflicts, having been captured at Dien Bien Phu and implicated in the *putsch* of 1961 which sought to prevent de Gaulle granting Algerian independence. Evoked throughout the film by the recollections of Pierre, a naval doctor (Claude Rich), and his skipper (Jean Rochefort), Willsdorff becomes a partly historical, partly mythologised figure, a mixture of Moby Dick, Lawrence of Arabia and Kurtz from Joseph Conrad's *Heart of Darkness*. Schoendoerffer's

narrative is, besides, explicitly Conradian. It follows a French naval
vessel, the *Jaureguiberry*, heading towards the Arctic in the hope of
finding Willsdorff, who is apparently in charge of a boat crewed by
veterans of Algeria and Indochina. As the *Jaureguiberry* nears its
quarry, the sailors and fishermen encountered tell of Willsdorff's
growing isolation and madness. Two years before *Apocalypse Now*
(1979), Coppola's celebrated representation of the Vietnam War
through the journey towards 'Colonel' Kurtz, Schoendoerffer
realises a hellish quest, not through the jungle but through the ice,
for a symbol of colonial warfare and defeat. During this quest the
red décor and lighting on the ship suggest the bloodshed of the past,
while the grey emptiness of the ocean functions as a screen upon
which both doctor and skipper project memories of Willsdorff as a
soldier, an adventurer, an opium junkie and a traitor (he is given
twenty years for his part in the *putsch*). The constant cross-cutting
between sequences in the Arctic (the present) and in Indochina and
Algeria (the past) is complemented by the use of radio and television broadcasts about the Vietnam War. By setting *Le Crabe-Tambour* in 1975 during the fall of Saigon, and by insistent
juxtapositions, Schoendoerffer establishes a grim continuity
between the conflicts of four decades, as when one character's story
about U-boats in the Second World War is interrupted by television
images from Vietnam. Ultimately, radio contact is made with Willsdorff, but he remains unseen, present only as the protagonists'
obsessive memory/fantasy. In an attempt to exorcise the traumas
that Willsdorff represents, the skipper who has relentlessly pursued
him simply says 'Adieu' over the radio before turning back for
France. It is precisely this evocation and hence exorcism of the past
which Schoendoerffer attempts in *Dien Bien Phu* (1992), which he
called his farewell to Indochina (Stavridès 1991: 26).

After years of struggling to finance his films, Schoendoerffer was
able to spend $25 million on an epic account of the defeat in
Indochina (Stavridès 1991: 25). Despite the high production values
and the hundreds of extras, however, *Dien Bien Phu* is not quite the
sumptuous mythologising of the past suggested by both the press
and the producers. Schoendoerffer's prime means of distancing himself from this stance, so typical of the heritage film (see chapter 7),
is the ironic use of a theatrical frame for the narrative. The opening sequence shows an orchestra warming up, then the lights going
up on a stage set for a concert in Hanoi by French violinist Béatrice
Vergnes (Ludmila Mikael) against a backdrop of the tricolour and of
Marianne, personification of France. The frame is closed at the end
of the film as the concert finishes and the lights dim, implying that
the empire, and indeed its filmic representation, is mere spectacle.
Framed within this ironic device, however, is Schoendoerffer's personal account of Dien Bien Phu, an autobiographical and realistic
portrayal of the confusion and monotony of two months of fighting.
The film is shot largely from the point of view of the French soldiers
who took part, including an army cameraman who evokes the

director himself. But both the images and the sound-track present a tension between the autobiographical and the theatrical: the general realism of the combat scenes is modified by a spectacular *mise en scène* during the nocturnal bombardments, while the battle is at once introduced by an unidentified first-person plural voice-over, and mediated by the melancholic and wordless chorus of Béatrice's violin. The theatrical gives way to the personal in the film's conclusion as, after the narrative frame is closed with Béatrice playing the swan song of the French empire, the screen fades to black and the commentary passes into the present, speaking of the shattering experience of returning to Dien Bien Phu after forty years in order to shoot the film. In its final statement the voice, saying 'I' for the first time, is identifiable as the director's, as the credits immediately confirm. Thus although framing the film as a spectacle about the fall of empire, Schoendoerffer in the final analysis charts a personal journey analogous to the quest undertaken in *Le Crabe-Tambour*.

Beur cinema

Beur, derived from the word 'Arabe' backwards, 'denotes a second-generation child of North African immigrants who was born in France, or else came to France at an early age', and is usually applied to 'the Algerian, rather than the Moroccan or Tunisian, immigrant community' (Bosséno 1992: 47). Consequently, *Beur* cinema has been defined as 'any film directed by a young person of North African origin who was born or who grew up in France, usually featuring *Beur* characters' (Bosséno 1992: 49). Already in the 1960s and early 1970s first generation North-African immigrants in France were making films, mostly documentaries or realistic narratives on social themes such as racism, a choice of subject later termed 'miserabilism'. *Beur* cinema developed in the 1980s, when second generation Algerians started making commercial feature films with professional actors, linear narratives and themes concerning suburban youth. The realism of the urban settings was at odds with the heritage-film trend which developed at about the same period in white French cinema (see chapter 7), but may have influenced directors such as Beineix and Carax to set films in the Parisian suburbs (Bosséno 1992: 51).

Bosséno claims that *Beur* cinema 'displays enough characteristics to be classified as a genre on its own,' and that its 'influence on the French cinema is quite out of proportion with the number of films' it comprises (Bosséno 1992: 56) Essentially, the major *Beur* films are Abdelkrim Bahloul's *Le Thé à la menthe* (1984), Mehdi Charef's *Le Thé au harem d'Archimède* (1985), *Camomille* (1987) and *Miss Mona* (1987), Cheikh Djamai's *La Nuit du doute*, Rachid Bouchareb's *Bâton rouge* (1986) and *Cheb* (1991), and most recently Malik Chibane's *Hexagone* (1993). Several enjoyed success at the box office, in particular *Le Thé au harem d'Archimède*, which attracted 100,000 spectators in Paris, played at Cannes and won the Prix Jean Vigo for best first feature (Bosséno 1992: 56). There are also 'alternative' *Beur* films, usually fictionalised documentaries, financed and distributed within the *Beur* community, which 'form part of a cinema of social intervention' (Bosséno 1992: 49). The young characters in commercial *Beur* cinema are not solely Beurs but also white French, witness the cross-racial friendships in *Le Thé au harem d'Archimède* (1985) and *Bâton rouge* (1986). Since social integration is the main aspiration for these characters, racism tends not be a central issue here, while comedy and the buddy movie are the principal genres used. Bosséno argues that *Beur* cinema is essentially transitional, an 'exorcism' of North-African concerns and identity which precedes and facilitates integration into French society. Hence Charef's first film concentrates on questions of ethnic identity, while his subsequent work considers other marginalised groups, but not in racial terms (Bosséno 1992:55-6). This tendency has resulted in some critics terming these films an unrealistic and submissive 'harki' cinema (Bosséno 1992: 50). One could respond to this accusation by pointing out the metaphorical representation of *Beurs* through outsider figures such as the transvestite in *Miss Mona*. In 1993 Carrie Tarr reported that 'As yet no *Beur* women have achieved funding to make a feature film' (Tarr 1993: 325), although they have directed alternative, low-budget films (Bosséno 1992: 54).

Rites of passage in *Hexagone*

Shot in only twenty-four days, *Hexagone* is Malik Chibane's début film, financed by a local association which he established in the Parisian suburb of Goussainville. Set and filmed in this deprived urban environment, the film was intended to increase the 'cultural visibility' of Chibane's generation of *Beurs* (Bouquet 1994: 11). In this regard, Chibane claimed that Hexagone was the first French film to have five *Beurs* in lead roles (Bouquet 1994), playing a group of friends: Ali the student (Karim Chakir), Nacera who seeks independence as a *beurette* (Faiza Kaddour), Staf the dandy (Hakim Sarahoui), Samy the drug addict and petty criminal (Farid Abdedou), and his unemployed brother Slimane (Jalil Naciri). It is Slimane who, sparingly, narrates the film: he introduces the setting and characters; later he explains the significance of the Islamic holiday celebrating Abraham's sacrifice of his son; and his voice-over concludes the film.

Particularly in the establishing shots, Hexagone is documentary in style, Chibane's handheld camera exploring urban locations in a style reminiscent of Maurice Pialat. The director also makes a sparing and effective use of pictorial compositions, such as the shot of Goussainville station, the icon showing Abraham's sacrifice, or the symbolic image of the dead sheep lying on the grass which immediately follows Samy's death, and which evokes the Abraham myth. The absence of sound-track music – apart from during the end credits – and the preponderance of street patois in the dialogue, commingling *verlan* (backwards slang), Parisian slang and Arabic, maintains a realism which is complemented by the naturalistic acting of the non-professional actors. Unemployment, integration and questions of cultural identity are addressed for the most part directly in the film, while racism is evoked more obliquely in a comic episode wherein Staf pretends to be an Italian called Xavier in order to sleep with a racist white French woman, only revealing to her afterwards in a cryptic message that he is a *Beur*. The buddy-movie genre and the at least partially comic observation of every-day life are staples of *Beur* cinema, but Chibane adds a more tragic, symbolic strand to his narrative via the religious story of Abraham sacrificing his son to God. This mythical paradigm is applied to Samy's death on the feast of Aid El Kebir. Arrested for shoplifting, Samy is rescued by Slimane, but, having escaped from the police, collapses and dies from an overdose. Slimane's concluding voice-over attempts to find some sense of continuity after his brother's death. The rite of passage characteristic of the buddy movie is here given a mythical dimension, as well as being emblematic of the *Beur* situation, where a passage to integration is advocated both by Ali in the film, and by Chibane in interview (Bouquet 1994).

References

Accoce, P. and Stavridès, Y. (1991), Retour à Dien Phu, Paris, *L'Express*, 9 May 1991, 24–5.

Avisar, I. (1988), *Screening the Holocaust: Cinema's Images of the Unimaginable*, Indianapolis and Bloomington, Indiana University Press.

Bonitzer, P. (1974), Histoire de sparadrap (Lacombe Lucien), Paris, *Cahiers du cinéma*, 250, 42–7.

Bonitzer, P. and Toubiana, S. (1974), Anti-rétro: Entretien avec Michel Foucault, *Cahiers du cinéma*, 251/2, 5–15.

Bosséno, C. (1992), Immigrant cinema: national cinema – the case of *Beur* film, in R. Dyer and G. Vincendeau (eds), *Popular European Cinema*, London and New York, Routledge, 47–57.

Bouquet, S. (1994), Malik Chibane, Paris, *Cahiers du cinéma*, 476, 11.

Clover, C. J. (1992), *Men, Women, and Chain Saws: Gender in the Modern Horror Film*, London, BFI.

Colombat, P. A. (1993), *The Holocaust in French Film*, London, Filmmakers, No.33, The Scarecrow Press.

Daney, S. (1974), Anti-rétro (suite), Fonction critique (fin), Paris, *Cahiers du cinéma*, 253, 30–36.

Felman, S. (1992), The Return of the voice: Claude Lanzmann's *Shoah*, in S. Felman and D. Laub, *Testimony: Crises of Witnessing in Literature, Psychoanalysis, and History*, London and New York, Routledge, 204–83.

Fisera, V. (1978) (ed.), *Writing on the Wall. May 1968: a documentary anthology*, London, Allison and Busby.

Forbes, J. (1992), *The Cinema in France After the New Wave*, London, BFI/Macmillan.

Godard, J.-L. (1986), *Godard on Godard*, ed. by T. Milne, London, Da Capo.

Godard, J.-L. (1991), *Godard par Godard: des années Mao aux années 80*, Paris, Flammarion.

Insdorf, F. (1983), *Indelible Shadows: Film and the Holocaust*, Cambridge and New York, Cambridge University Press.

Jeambar, D. (1990), La Profanation, Paris, *Le Point*, 921, 49.

Lanzmann, C. (1993), Interview for *Moving Pictures*, BBC Television.

MacCabe, C. M. (1992), Jean-Luc Godard: A life in seven episodes (to date), in R. Bellour and L. Bandy (eds), *Jean-Luc Godard: Son + Image 1974–1991*, New York, The Museum of Modern Art, 13-21.

Malle, L. (1993), *Malle on Malle*, ed. by P. French, London, Faber and Faber.

Mény, J. (1991), *Making* Merci la vie, FR3 television.

Modiano, P. (1975), *Villa triste*, Paris, Gallimard.

Morris, A. (1992), *Collaboration and Resistance Reviewed: Writers and the Mode Rétro in Post-Gaullist France*, New York and Oxford, Berg.

Nevers, C. and Strauss, F. (1993), Entretien avec Jean-Marie Poiré et Christian Clavier, Paris, *Cahiers du cinéma*, 465, 84–9.

Prédal, R. (1989), *Louis Malle*, Paris, Edilig.

Prédal, R. (1991), *Le Cinéma français depuis 1945*, Paris, Nathan.

Reynolds, S. (1990), *The Sorrow and the Pity* revisited, or be careful, one train can hide another, Chalfont St Giles, Bucks., *French Cultural Studies*, 1:2:2, 149–59.

Selig, M. (1993), Genre, gender, and the discourse of war: the a/historical and Vietnam War films, Glasgow, *Screen*, 34:1, 10–18.

Stavridès, Y. (1991), 'Notre adieu à l'Indochine ...', Paris, *L'Express*, 9 May 1991, 24–8.

Tarr, C. (1993), Questions of identity in *Beur* cinema: from *Tea in the Harem* to *Cheb*, *Screen*, 34:4, 321-342.

Tavernier, B. (1993), I wake up, dreaming, London, *Projections*, 2, 252–378.

Ward Jouve, N. (1994), A woman in black and white, London, *Sight and Sound*, July 1994, 29.

3

Representations of sexuality

Porno and after

If 1968 marked a watershed in French cinema's engagement with politics and history (see chapter 2), 1974 did the same for representations of sexuality. In that year, pornography entered mainstream French cinema.

Emmanuelle and the legitimising of the porn film

The gradual relaxation of censorship in the late 1960s had seen a steady increase in the number of erotic films made in France, culminating in Jean Rollin's vampire series. But the increase in sexual candour in films like Bertrand Blier's *Les Valseuses* (1974) still met with controversy and complaint. The watershed came with the enormous success of *Emmanuelle* (1974), which achieved a genuine cross-over from porn to mainstream. Based on a novel by Emmanuelle Arsan, the film starred Sylvia Kristel and was directed by a former fashion photographer called Just Jaeckin. The plot – the sexual initiation of a French woman in Bangkok – was merely a premise for glossy soft-porn photography. Playing to packed houses in cinemas usually given over to mainstream hits, *Emmanuelle* eventually became the best-attended French film of the decade, attracting nearly nine million spectators (Prédal 1991: 404). Its phenomenal success legitimised the porn film, and was followed by other hits including the hard-core porn of Jean-François Davy's *Exhibition* (1975). In response, the Government passed a law on 30 December 1975, which greatly increased taxation on the production and exhibition of pornographic films, and subjected them to an X classification. These measures were intended to reduce the porn sector to its previous 10 per cent of the market (Forbes 1992: 8). But because foreign porn was also targeted, France continued to produce and consume large numbers of X-rated films. The porn vogue peaked at the end of the seventies: 1978 saw 167 X-rated films released in France, but by 1987 production had completely dried up (Prédal 1991: 434). Porn films are now almost totally dependent on the video market, and are indeed usually shot straight on to video. But the explosion of the mid-seventies inscribed explicit sexual representation in French film to such an extent that in the work of certain directors, porn has become a metaphor for cinema itself.

Post-porn: from *Sauve qui peut (la vie)* to *Je vous salue Marie*

After playing a major role in the *nouvelle vague* of the 1960s (see chapter 1), Jean-Luc Godard retreated into 'research' on the video image before making his return to the cinema in 1979 with *Sauve qui peut (la vie)*. This work also inaugurated a quartet of films – culminating in the controversial *Je vous salue Marie* (1985) – which explore the role of sexuality in cinema. Godard had already explored prostitution as a metaphor for the consumer society in *Deux ou Trois Choses que je sais d'elle* (1966), and the relation between sex and politics in video material such as *Numéro deux* (1975). But *Sauve qui peut (la vie)* is distinguished by the fact that it comes after the porn boom, and after the law of December 1975 which relocated porn outside the realm of mainstream French film. Godard has said of this watershed: 'I think that one of the great defeats for the French cinema was the moment when they passed the law on pornography and when film-makers let them close up pornography by failing to defend it' (Godard 1980: 12).

In *Sauve qui peut (la vie)* pornography and cinema are brought together again, via a narrative which concerns the inter-relations between Denise (Nathalie Baye), her lover Paul (Jacques Dutronc) and Isabelle, a prostitute (Isabelle Huppert). It is primarily through the stunning use of stop-motion photography that Godard investigates the desires and ordeals of these three characters. Affectionate or erotic embraces in the film are slowed to a point at which the violence underlying them becomes visually apparent: Paul's desire for Denise is translated into an assault; his attempt to kiss his daughter Cécile becomes heavy with an incestuous threat. Although these examples involve Paul, whose death at the close of the film is also filmed in stop-motion, most of the slowed sequences in the film present decompositions of the movements of women. As Godard says of his video experiments, 'when one changes the rhythms, [...] one notices that there are so many different worlds inside the woman's movement. Whereas slowing down the little boy's movements was a lot less interesting' (Penley 1982: 49). In this regard, Godard seems to conform to the voyeurism which has always linked pornography and cinema: 'one intractable direction of cinematic narrative evolution follows the pleasure of seeing previously hidden parts, or hidden motions, of the woman's body' (Williams 1990: 53). Godard nevertheless uses the 'hidden motions' of the women in *Sauve qui peut (la vie)*, and of Isabelle in particular, not to uncritically realise pornography, but rather to interrogate it.

When Isabelle picks up Paul in a cinema queue, the image slows and freezes on her staring eye, framed by the shadow of Paul's face. The voyeuristic, male gaze accommodated by pornography is challenged by this lucid, female eye. The subsequent sex scene between Paul and Isabelle evacuates the pornographic image through its submission to an obdurately non-pleasurable sound-track. Godard shoots Isabelle's face in close-up during sex, so that she becomes 'the inevitable icon of the pornographic love-making scene, the close-up of the moaning woman's face serving as the guarantee of pleasure' (Penley 1982: 47). This pleasure is undermined, however, first by Isabelle's overacting – Paul has to tell her to stop faking it – and then by Isabelle's own thoughts, which are spoken in voice-over. This interior monologue not only contradicts the visual simulation of sexual pleasure central to the porn film, but does so by introducing Isabelle's most banal plans: to tidy her room, clean the windows, send for a plumber. The deconstruction of pornography is however most evident in the orgy sequence, wherein Isabelle, another prostitute, and a male employee are ordered into certain positions by a businessman. Their choreographed sexual activity resembles the act of filming itself, with the boss/director creating first an image track, then a sound-track: 'l'image ça va, maintenant on va faire le son' [the image is OK, now for the sound]. Moreover, the mechanical slowness of the actions involved recalls Godard's own decomposition of movement throughout the film. Thus *Sauve qui peut (la vie)* presents pornography – or more precisely, the laborious creation of faked sexual pleasure – as a metaphor for cinema. A similar process, though one informed by pleasure rather than excluding it, can be observed in Alain Tanner's *Une Flamme dans mon cœur* (1987), where the sex show becomes the encapsulation of both cinema and theatre.

Just as cinema and porn are analogous in *Sauve qui peut (la vie)*, Godard also links sex and filming in certain sequences of *Passion* (1982), for instance, when a film technician has sex with a woman while urging her to say her lines. The dialogue also focuses on penetration, openings and closings, a bodily discourse which is continued in *Prénom Carmen* (1983) and *Je vous salue Marie* (1985). The question of representing the female body is crucial to the latter film, which retells the story of the Virgin Birth and thus has to represent the Mother of God. Setting the narrative in contemporary Switzerland, Godard dramatises his/our relation to the body of Marie (Myriem Roussel) through the terrestrial desires of her husband Joseph (Philippe Lacoste). The early sequences of the film are dominated by close-ups of Marie's almost child-like face, reminiscent of both Catholic iconography and of Godard's framing of his wife, Anna Karina, in his sixties films. There are also occasional images of Marie's body, for example in the bath, which tend to be shot from above, from the perspective of God or Godard, and which are not visible to Joseph, who longs to see his prospective wife naked. But although the angle of vision here, and Marie's own voice-over –

4   Myriam Roussel in *Je vous salue Marie*

which offers her body to 'the gaze of He who had become my master forever' – suggest that Godard is ironically identifying both director and spectator with God, it is in fact Joseph's struggle to look at Marie without desire which dynamises the filming of the female body in *Je vous salue Marie*. The key sequence concerns Joseph's efforts to touch Marie's virgin/pregnant stomach. When this contact is finally achieved, it is framed in the first close-up of Marie's body (her naked stomach), and is immediately followed by luminous images of meadows, trees and skies. From this point on, Joseph disappears, and Godard proceeds to explore visually the contradiction within the narrative, the virginity/sexuality of Marie's body. Bridged by Marie's monologue which declares 'Il n'y aura plus de sexualité en moi' [There will be no more sexuality in me], explicit shots of her naked body give way to images of the sun, plants, animals. Marie's divine and yet human body thus belongs not to pornography but to the 'virgin' imagery of natural history. In a similar gesture, Agnès Varda films Jane Birkin's naked body in extreme close-up as a kind of human landscape in *Jane B. par Agnès V.* (1987) (see chapter 4).

Identifying in French cinema of the 1980s a turning away from porn and towards the sacred, René Prédal has written that *Je vous salue Marie* is characteristic of 'l'après-porno' in its submission of sexuality to an intellectual approach (Prédal 1991: 435). Such a perspective is shared by the novelist and film-maker Marguerite Duras, who contributed to Godard's *Sauve qui peut (la vie)* between working on her own films (see chapter 4). Most recently, however, Duras has seen her novel *L'Amant* turned into a glossy sex film which seems to reverse the post-porn trend.

L'Amant: a return to Emmanuelle?

Jean-Jacques Annaud is associated with cosmopolitan casts, large budgets and high production values. Having begun his career in advertising, he was responsible for eighty television adverts per year from 1970 to 1975. His first two feature films failed to make a great impact in France, but in 1981 *La Guerre du feu*, and five years later *Le Nom de la rose*, brought him international success. *L'Ours* (1988) proved the highest-grossing French film of the year, attracting over nine million spectators (Prédal 1991: 403). *L'Amant* (1992) was originally to be a collaboration between Annaud and Marguerite Duras, the author of the novel. As it turned out, Duras not only pulled out of the project, but responded to the film with her own rewritten version of the story, *L'Amant de la Chine du Nord*. The narrative of both Duras's original novel of 1984 and Annaud's film, concerns the relation between an unnamed French girl at boarding-school in 1930s Saigon and a similarly nameless Chinese landowner. Where the film version diverges from the text is not so much in the substance of the narrative as in the exotic style of representation employed. Serge Daney, the editor of *Cahiers du cinéma* during the seventies, has attacked the film for compiling 'promotional objects, from the virgin car to the designer girl' (Daney 1992: 16). This photogenic approach to a sexual narrative runs the risk of steering towards soft porn, of becoming in Daney's terms 'a kind of *Emmanuelle* with a bit of literary gloss' (Daney 1992: 16).

The photography in the film is minutely realistic and yet stylised and fetishistic. The location is Vietnam, there are numerous extras, and yet as Daney remarks, 'How utterly pointless it was for Annaud to have shot the film in the real Vietnam', since the style of the film already precluded any chance of 'his camera accidentally recording a few seconds of unprocessed reality' (Daney 1992: 16). Spectacle overrides narrative, be it in the sex scenes or the street scenes. Jane Marsh as the young girl is composed from a number of fetishised constituent parts – her shoes, the man's hat she wears, her pigtails – and frequently introduced by such itemisation or by the panning of the camera slowly up her body from the feet and legs. Annaud's tendency to avoid the more complex and brutal qualities present in Duras's text is highlighted by the slippage between Jeanne Moreau's frequent voice-over and these images. The gulf is best exemplified during the scene in which the girl loses her virginity to her Chinese lover. While the voice-over, following the text, speaks of the blood which results, and which the lover washes from her body, the image track shows no such image. Annaud's coyness here contrasts with the frank deflowering scene from Truffaut's *Les Deux Anglaises* (1971). Truffaut's film is also a literary adaptation, of Henri Roché's novel *Les Deux Anglaises et le continent*, but when the text, and hence the voice-over, declares that 'Il y avait du rouge sur son or' [There was red on her gold], Truffaut actually presents a stunning close-up of the sheet slowly turned red by Muriel's blood. It is perhaps significant that *Les Deux Anglaises* was made before the porno vogue of the mid-seventies, while the decorative sex in *L'Amant* seems like a return to soft porn.

Woman as object

The representation of the female body by means of itemisation and close-up is not confined to porn. As critics, including Noël Burch, have demonstrated, voyeuristic objectifications of the female body are central to cinema's representations of women, and date back to the very beginnings of cinema at the turn of the century: in early cinema, 'the frequent presence of a voyeur on screen constituted a veritable inscription in the film of a predominantly male audience's relationship to the stripping woman' (Burch 1979). After the decline of the 'voyeur films' of early cinema, voyeuristic desires were no longer explicitly embodied by a character so much as institutionalised in the classical framing of women's bodies by the close-up, the lascivious pan and the point-of-view shot: 'cinema can and does fragment the body [...] the movement up is the appraising sweep of the male gaze fixing the woman for the film [...], film plays on the passage between fragmented body and the image possession of the body whole' (Stephen Heath, cited in Burch 1979). Perhaps the most consistent example of this in contemporary French film is the work of François Truffaut, a director acutely influenced by both early cinema and classical models such as Hitchcock and *film noir* (see chapter 1).

Fetishising the female body: from *Domicile conjugal* to *La Lectrice*

The women in Truffaut's films are fragmented and fetishised, with a particular emphasis on images of their legs. Indeed, the archetypal Truffaudian shot could be said to show a woman's legs in close-up as she ascends or descends a stairway, from Madame Doinel in *Les 400 coups* (1959) to Marion Steiner in *Le Dernier Métro* (1980). It is above all from the representation of women in American *film noir* that Truffaut takes his cue: 'The *femme fatale* is characterised by her long lovely legs [...]. In *Double Indemnity* Phyllis' legs [...] dominate Walter's and our own memory of her as the camera follows her descent down the stairs, framing only her spike heels and silk-stockinged calves' (Place 1980: 45). In *La Femme d'à côté* (1981) Truffaut introduces the *femme fatale* Mathilde (Fanny Ardant) by identical means: she descends a staircase into view, her legs the focus of the image. Similarly, *Domicile conjugal* (1970) begins with a tracking sequence in which Christine (Claude Jade) walks down the street, her legs framed in close-up. *Domicile conjugal* is the fourth and penultimate film – after *Les 400 Coups*, *Antoine et Colette* (1962) and *Baisers volés* (1968) – in the Antoine Doinel series concluded by *L'Amour en fuite* (1979). In the last two films of the cycle the character of Antoine, played throughout by Jean-Pierre Léaud, is gradually reduced to a series of tics, repeating gestures and lines of dialogue from previous works. Moreover, certain images are duplicated exactly from one film to the next – Antoine and Christine kissing in the cellar in *Baisers volés* and *Domicile conjugal* – and eighteen minutes of footage from the other films of the cycle is uneasily integrated into the narrative of *L'Amour en fuite*. Thus, Truffaut fetishises not just the female body but cinema itself, whether it be his own (the Doinel cycle reprised throughout *L'Amour en fuite*), that of the pioneers (the Lumière brothers' first fiction film pastiched in *Les Mistons* (1957)), or the basic techniques of modern filmmaking depicted in *La Nuit américaine* (1973). A similar doubling of the fetish is presented in Michel Deville's *La Lectrice* (1988), an erotic and self-conscious adaptation of the novel by Raymond Jean. While Marie (Miou-Miou) reads a suggestive text to the wheelchair-bound Eric, close-ups of her thighs as she crosses her legs alternate with shots of Eric looking at her. Throughout the film, point-of-view shots belonging to Marie's predominantly male clients fragment and objectify her body, concentrating on her legs and breasts. These close-ups and lascivious pans up her body coincide regularly with erotic passages from the books she is reading aloud, such as Maupassant's *La Chevelure* and Duras' *L'Amant*. In *La Lectrice* it is at once the female reader's body and the various texts she reads which are fetishised.

Woman/nature/dirt: *Buffet froid, Les Valseuses*

Bertrand Blier, who first came to prominence in 1974 with the controversial hit *Les Valseuses*, has consistently presented absurdist variations on sexual themes. His films conform to many archetypes, and transcend or invert many others, but in his early work women tend to function solely as objects. It is not just through fragmentation and framing that women are objectified in cinema. The representation of women in Western culture has tended to reduce them to certain idealisations or metaphors. Woman has for instance become synonymous with nature. At the end of Blier's *Buffet froid* (1979), a surreal nightmare in which women are either absent, dead, or idealised as Death (Carole Bouquet), the three male protagonists escape from Paris to a country retreat. What might have been a pastoral idyll in another film is here an ordeal, in which nature becomes a feminised threat, embodying the 'female' principles of dampness, fertility and dissolution. The police chief (Bernard Blier, the director's father) complains about the 'hole' they have ended up in, where everything is 'damp.' Blier does not however privilege a 'male' environment over this metaphorical representation of the female body. The 'masculine' urban landscape of *Buffet froid* is sterile, violent and alienating, epitomised by the cold geometry of the Parisian district of La Défense.

Buffet froid became a cult classic in France, without ever making much money. The reception of *Les Valseuses* was the opposite: a success at the box office, it met with a stiff critical response because of its explicit portrayal of sex. Critics described the film as pornography and, incredibly, as a 'nazi' work (Haustrate 1988: 19). This is

5   Miou-Miou in *Les Valseuses*

self-evidently not the case; but the representation of women in the
film, and especially of the hairdresser Marie-Ange (Miou-Miou),
does conform closely to patriarchal codes. These codes include the
association of women with nature, but also with dirt: 'the bodies of
erotic women, especially proletarian ones, become so much wet
dirt' (Theweleit 1987: 421). In *Les Valseuses*, it is not so much
Marie-Ange's social status (nearly everyone in the film is also working-class) as her sexually-active behaviour which qualifies her as
'dirty.' After he himself, Pierrot (Patrick Dewaere), and the scrapyard dealer have all slept with Marie-Ange, Jean-Claude (Gérard
Depardieu) asks her if he can touch her intimately, since 'it's good
luck to touch something dirty, like stepping in shit'. As the incident
in the scrapyard shows, Marie-Ange also functions as a commodity, an object of exchange: she is given to the dealer by Jean-Claude
and Pierrot as 'payment' for his help. Marie-Ange is also replace-
able by other female objects (Jeanne Moreau, Isabelle Huppert). But
unlike the 'dirty' woman, Marie-Ange does not experience sexual
pleasure, only indifference. Ironically, it is neither Jean-Claude nor
Pierrot but the virgin Jacques with whom she first achieves orgasm.
Through this twist, and the characterisation of both Pierrot and
Jean-Claude as slightly effeminate (see below), Blier thus undercuts
the male archetype of the macho stud, while never really challenging the filmic objectification of women.

La Grande Bouffe: the edible woman

Jill Forbes has identified a 'crisis of masculinity' in *Les Valseuses* and
other films of the period, including *La Grande Bouffe* (1973), a
French/Italian co-production by the Italian director Marco Ferreri

(Forbes 1992: 184). But as well as representing the 'social and sexual malaise' of the male protagonists (Forbes 1992: 184), Ferreri's film explores the objectification of women, primarily through a combination of woman-as-nature and as commodity. In *La Grande Bouffe*, woman has become food. The plot concerns a collective suicide by four middle-aged men. Philippe the judge (Philippe Noiret), Marcello the pilot (Marcello Mastroianni), Ugo the cook (Ugo Tognazzi) and Michel the television director (Michel Piccoli) shut themselves in a large house and eat themselves to death over a number of weeks. They are joined briefly by a group of prostitutes and then by a primary-school teacher, Andréa (Andréa Ferréol), who promises to marry Philippe but in fact acts as nurse and lover to all four men. One by one the men die, but Andréa survives.

The central metaphor is first introduced by the cook Ugo, who compares a prostitute's behind to a chocolate meringue. But above all it is Andréa who is equated with food. Ugo inscribes her name in sauce, creates 'la tarte Andréa' by having her sit in the dough, and 'tastes' her body as he does his own cooking. After Ugo's death (which identifies sex and food: masturbated by Andréa, he dies on the kitchen table), Andréa turns cook for the last survivor, Philippe. She serves him two cakes in the shape of breasts, a parody of her own maternal body, to which he clings in death. The last scene of the film places Andréa in the garden of the house as a now redundant delivery of meat is hung on the trees and bushes. In this context, Andréa is just one more piece of meat. Unlike those who consume her, she will not die: she survives as an eternal object, as nature itself. The serene idealisation of Andréa (who eats as much as the men but shows no change) thus only exaggerates the 'crisis of masculinity' in the film, characterised by impotence, repetition and mortality.

The *récit:* misogyny, desire, spectatorship

As we have seen, the framing of the female object of desire is crucial to representations of sexuality, particularly within male-authored heterosexual cinema. Laura Mulvey's celebrated feminist reading of classic narrative cinema explains how women function on the level of spectacle while both narrative drive and spectatorship are construed as 'male' (Mulvey 1975). In some ways this model is analogous to the structure of the French short novel or *récit*. Naomi Segal has defined this literary form as a first-person narrative, 'usually embedded in a frame narrative, in which a male protagonist tells [his] story'. The central object of the narrative is a woman who 'usually ends up dying, while the man lives on to tell "his" tale' (Segal 1988: 9). This pattern is common in French cinema, with male narrator–protagonists recounting the story of their doomed relations with female objects of desire. Patrice Leconte's *Le Mari de la coiffeuse* (1990) and *Tango* (1993), Luis Buñuel's *Cet Obscur Objet du désir* (1977), Jean Becker's *L'Été meur-*

trier (1983) and Jean-Jacques Beineix's *37,2 le Matin* (1986) either conform to or modify the format.

Le Mari de la coiffeuse and *Tango*: the *récit* as misogynistic

Patrice Leconte worked as a cartoonist for the fantasy magazine *Pilote* before turning to film. After directing films derived from the *café-théâtre* (see chapter 2) and concerning the exploits of *les Bronzés*, he moved into a more fully cinematic genre in 1989 with the thriller *Monsieur Hire* (see chapter 5). The plot of *Le Mari de la coiffeuse* (1990) is simple: a young boy, Antoine, develops a fascination for having his hair cut by the maternal hairdresser Madame Schaeffer, to such an extent that he declares it his ambition to marry a hairdresser when he grows up. His youthful fetish is only strengthened when Madame Schaeffer is found dead in her salon. Antoine next appears as a middle-aged man (Jean Rochefort) intent on carrying out his ambition. He encounters a beautiful hairdresser, Mathilde (Anne Galiena), and marries her. They are happy together, and have a lively sex life in the salon, which they rarely leave until one night after making love Mathilde runs off and drowns herself. Antoine is left to sit in the salon and reflect on his story.

The *récit* form is manifest in the framing of this narrative as well as in the plot. Although the opening shot is of the young Antoine dancing to his favoured Arab music, a close-up immediately after the credits of the older self (Jean Rochefort) soon establishes the presence of a narrator, and his thoughts in voice-over cast the film as one long flashback. Moreover, at salient points throughout the film, such as the moment Mathilde accepts his proposal of marriage, the close-up image of Rochefort 'recalling' the events of the narrative (and the melancholy Michael Nyman sound-track which first accompanied it) recurs. 'The connexion with the outside world of the frame narrative, the significance of the story, belong [...] to the hero who speaks, not to the heroine who dies' (Segal 1988: 12). A woman – in this case Mathilde – may form the ostensible focus of the *récit* form, but her story is mediated by the man who tells it: 'If women have pleasure, then men alone have a knowledge of that pleasure which can be spoken' (Segal 1988: 5). The sequence which culminates with Mathilde's suicide equates female sexual pleasure with death in the archetype of the hysterical woman, and leaves the hero alone to muse on the meaning of her actions. This pattern, and the reprise of the opening scene which it entails, is also present in Beineix's *37,2 le Matin* (1986) (see below). Throughout *Le Mari de la coiffeuse* Mathilde is presented by Leconte as generic, just another of her sex/just another hairdresser: first introduced by Antoine's voice-over as 'une coiffeuse,' it is some time before she is named. She is identified with her trade/shop, which she rarely leaves (except to visit her former boss and to commit suicide by drowning), thus proving not so much a discrete individual as a repetition of the first hairdresser of the film, Madame Schaeffer. It is through Mathilde that Antoine restores his youthful obsession with Madame Schaeffer's maternal body: 'the narcissist seeks his own image within the frame of the mother's body' (Segal 1988: 9). Through his marriage to Mathilde, Antoine is freed to return to the pleasures of childhood: not required to work, he sits in the salon where he frequently dances to rai music (Arab music), as did the young Antoine in the opening scene of the film. This is also his response to Mathilde's suicide, in the final scene which repeats the sign of narrative framing (the dancing). But the *récit* model – the male survivor narrates the woman's death – is however attenuated by the final silence as Antoine and the customer wait for Mathilde's return. The narrator has lost his voice (-over), and hence the film has moved beyond the narrative frame of the *récit*. No image of Antoine-as-narrator mediates the final sequence, although the melancholy music returns. There is grief and poignancy in this ending. But it is again a repetition, of the moment earlier in the film when Antoine saw Madame Scheaffer's dead body. And just as Mathilde replaced the first hairdresser, so there is the possibility in Antoine's ambiguous last words, that Mathilde will be replaced by another hairdresser, thus allowing the narrator to continue to define himself in relation to that maternal body: 'La coiffeuse va venir [The hairdresser will be here soon].'

There is no narrative frame or voice-over in Leconte's subsequent film, *Tango* (1993) but it is his most crudely misogynistic work. The film is characterised by cartoon-like action sequences, brightly coloured photography, fragmented compositions of women's bodies (the framing of Madeleine's torso through the car window, frequent close-ups on legs or breasts) and consistently misogynistic dialogue, declaring that women are either nymphomaniacs or prudes. The prologue concerns a pilot, Vincent (Richard Bohringer), who repays his wife's infidelity by causing her death in a loop-the-loop. The pattern is repeated when, cleared of murder by François (Philippe Noiret), a chauvinistic judge, Vincent is then blackmailed into tracking down Marie (Miou-Miou), the unfaithful wife of the judge's womanising nephew Paul (Thierry Lhermitte), in order to kill her. The main body of the film is hence a buddy movie/road movie in which the three men follow Marie to Africa. Although in the rather facile conclusion, Marie is spared and finally reconciled with Paul, women are for the most part absent, dead, or silent in the film. Indeed the film ends with the judge's 'joke' that even when dead, women continue to 'piss off' men.

It is not Leconte, but Bertrand Blier, who explores the implicit desires of the all-male buddy/road genres (see below). Leconte does not challenge the form, he merely inhabits it, rather like the second-rate Blier of *Calmos* (1976). Perhaps most kindly interpreted as an *hommage* to Blier, although one which repeats Blier's chauvinistic stereotypes without any of his attempts to deconstruct them, *Tango* includes a clear allusion to the episode from *Les Valseuses* in which Jacqueline asks to be deflowered by Jean-Claude and Pierrot. In

Leconte's film, a young woman, Madeleine (Judith Godrèche) asks for the buddies to give her a baby, and Vincent obliges. The other major intertext for Leconte is Alfred Hitchcock, long considered the epitome of cinematic voyeurism: the aeroplane sequences in which Vincent terrorises his wife's lover recalls *North by North-West* as strongly as the voyeurism of *Monsieur Hire* (1989) recalls *Rear Window* (see chapter 5). *Le Parfum d'Yvonne* (1994), Leconte's film of Patrick Modiano's novel *Villa Triste*, repeats the *récit* structure, beginning with the male protagonist's voice-over, which narrates the story of his relationship with an enigmatic young woman, and punctuated by voyeurism (the narrator uses a cine-camera to film the object of his desire). The only twist concerns the situation of the narrator, whose remembering of the narrative is signalled by facial close-ups lit by flames which come, as we learn in the final scene, from the crashed car in which a man has died.

Interrogating desire: *Cet Obscur Objet du désir*

Luis Buñuel, although Spanish, directed films in Mexico and France as well as in Spain. The architect of surrealist cinema in the 1920s (see chapter 1), his mature work in the sixties and seventies consisted mainly of French productions, and included explorations of female sexuality – *Belle de jour* (1966), *Tristana* (1970) – and satires of bourgeois society – *Le Charme discret de la bourgeoisie* (1972), *Le Fantôme de la liberté* (1974). His final film, *Cet Obscur Objet du désir* (1977), was based on Pierre Louÿs's novel *La Femme et le pantin*. This text had been filmed several times before, most notably by Duvivier with Brigitte Bardot, and by Sternberg with Marlene Dietrich. Laura Mulvey has taken Sternberg's framing of Dietrich to embody 'the ultimate fetish' where the image of the woman is 'in direct erotic rapport with the spectator' (Mulvey 1975: 203). What is at stake in Buñuel's film is the rapport between male subject (the narrator, the film-maker and ultimately the 'male' spectator) and female object of desire. But, as the title implies, there is no 'direct erotic rapport': for Buñuel, the transparency of possession is replaced by obscurity, constant deferral and slippage.

Most of the film consists of a flashback, introduced by the narrator–protagonist Mathieu (Fernando Rey), and interrupted at several points by his audience, the passengers who share his train carriage on the journey from Seville to Paris. Mathieu is a wealthy and lecherous man who has just terminated, or so he claims, an erotic obsession with a young Spanish woman called Conchita (played alternately by Carole Bouquet and Angela Molina). The flashback reveals the origins and the development of this obsession, which is characterised by Conchita's infuriating deferral of sexual consummation (infuriating both for Mathieu and, via the narrative structure of his tale and of the film, for the passengers and the spectator) and, even more bizarrely, by Mathieu's complete ignorance of the fact that Conchita is, in a sense, two women. (The duality of Conchita's identity, which is alternately coolly composed (Carole

6 Carole Bouquet and Fernando Rey in *Cet Obscur Objet du désir*

Bouquet) and provocatively voluptuous (Angela Molina), operates as a visual comment on the generalised expectations that male desires place on women, and also parodies the virgin/harlot stereotype.) When Mathieu's tale is finally ended, the object of it – Conchita – appears on the train and the couple recommence their relationship in Paris.

As is usual with the *récit* form, the female object of desire is absent from the opening scenes which establish the narrative frame. In the absence of Conchita herself, the first representation of her in the film is through objects and clothes belonging to her which are scattered about Mathieu's villa: a shoe, a bloodstained cushion, a pair of knickers. These objects are presented to Mathieu by his servant, Martin, who maintains a misogynistic discourse throughout the film, describing women as 'sacks of shit'. The realisation of misogyny in Buñuel's work is however far from that manifested by Leconte. In *Cet Obscur Objet*, Martin's chauvinism is ludicrously literalised in the series of sacks carried by various characters in the film, including Mathieu himself. Mathieu's attitudes towards women (and indeed the spectator's own) are submitted to a more complex interrogation. Conchita's appearance in the film (as Mathieu's new maid) does not preclude her representation by synecdoche (parts standing for the whole). Indeed it is only parts of her body, or objects belonging to her, that Conchita will allow Mathieu to possess, always deferring the moment of consummation when he will, he imagines, have 'all' of her. Hence the gradation of objects which Mathieu is permitted to grasp or consume: first the handkerchief she

7   Fernando Rey and Angela Molina in *Cet Obscur Objet du désir*

drops at the hotel in Lausanne, then the sweet she feeds him out of a box held suggestively on her lap, eventually her body itself, but not entire: she remains dressed in a nightgown or, when that obstacle is overcome, protected by a chastity belt or the bars of a gate. Like the film's spectator, Mathieu is restricted to visual pleasures; voyeurism is his only access to Conchita's body as a whole, whether he is watching her as she dances nude for tourists or, in his culminating humiliation, staring despite himself as she puts on a show of sex with her young lover in the very house that he has bought for her as a preliminary to consummation.

Mathieu concludes his tale by declaring 'C'est terminé maintenant' [it's over now']. But unlike the archetypal *récit*, which depends on the woman's absence, Mathieu's story is interrupted by Conchita's very real presence: she appears on the train and pours a bucket of water over his head. In the crucial final scene Mathieu, now reconciled – for the umpteenth time – with Conchita, pauses to look at some objects in a shop window and lets her walk out of shot unnoticed. The objects which grab his attention are a number of nightgowns like those worn by Conchita earlier in the film, and which have just been taken out of a sack. He thus desires a return to the synecdochic objectification of Conchita which characterised his own narrative. The female object of desire can only exist as an object and can never finally be possessed. Furthermore this object ('woman') is itself a cultural construct, epitomised for Buñuel by the bourgeois domestic activity of embroidery, represented in Vermeer's painting *The Lacemaker* which appears in Bunuel's first film, *Un*

Chien andalou (1928) and which informs the closing scenes of *Belle de jour* and of *Cet Obscur Objet du désir*. The final sequence of the latter shows a female window-dresser completing a piece of embroidery (leaning on a bloodstained nightgown, perhaps representative of the forever absent consummation) and Mathieu catching up with Conchita again before a terrorist explosion ends the cycle of desire. The French feminist Luce Irigaray has said of Freud that he 'cracked his head against all that remains irreducibly "obscure" to him in his speculations. Against the non-visible [...] nature of woman's sex and pleasure' (Irigaray 1985: 139). Mathieu, like Freud, has had to rely on the fetishisation of objects to come anywhere near a possession of female sexuality, and to be able to narrate the story of male desire. Buñuel, however, demonstrates in the constant slippage of the film away from the expected moment of possession/closure that female sexuality remains obscure to the male desiring subject.

The gender of genre: 'male' *récit* and 'female' melodrama in *L'Été meurtrier*

Jean Becker, like Jean-Jacques Annaud, found success in the 1980s after making adverts for television. In this case, however, the director had previously made four thrillers in the 1960s, before spending seventeen years in television. His cinematic comeback with *L'Été meurtrier* (1983) was spectacular: the fourth most-viewed French film of 1982/3, attracting four and a half million spectators (Prédal 1991: 402), it owed a great deal of this success to its female lead, Isabelle Adjani. The pulling power of Adjani, at its peak in the mid-eighties, was again evident in 1988 with the marketing of *Camille Claudel* (see chapter 7).

It is principally through the fluctuating power/impotence of Éliane, the female protagonist played by Isabelle Adjani, that *L'Été meurtrier* achieves its tension, and in particular its startling oscillation between the male-narrated *récit* form and melodrama, traditionally gendered as feminine (the 'women's movie' or 'weepie'). The film has not been fully credited, however, for its exploration of genre and gender. René Prédal's comments are emblematic of the critical response, enjoying the film's opening, in which the 'male' *récit* is toned as sexual comedy, but dismissing the rest of the film as ridiculous and over the top (Prédal 1991: 501). This dismissal of the melodrama which constitutes much of the film is not however surprising. As Linda Williams has noted, melodrama and other 'body genres' are considered culturally inferior because they mobilise coincidence, repetition and non-naturalistic plot strategies, and because they present the spectacle of bodily excess – orgasm in the porn film, terror in the horror/slasher film, and weeping in the melodrama (Williams 1991). (The strategies which characterise the sexual comedy and the *récit*, and which are present in the first reel of *L'Été meurtrier*, are also components in the porn film: a presumed male (active) audience, and a fantasy of seducing/being seduced.)

Becker's film initiates a complex interference between gendered genres. The film begins (after a cryptic credit sequence which will only be decodable halfway through the film) with a male voice-over in which Pin-Pon (Alain Souchon) introduces himself, his village, and his first glimpse of Éliane. At this stage, sexuality is comic and unproblematic, exemplified by the scene in which Pin-Pon and the projectionist's wife make love in the aisle of the cinema immediately after a showing. The implication in this choice of location, and in the reaction of Pin-Pon's friends and his brother, who are practically an audience to his actions – they wait outside in a lorry for him to finish – is that the film will reassure spectators about how uncomplicated heterosexuality can be. In this context, the arrival of Éliane in the village is not perceived as a threat, but as an object for conquest/seduction. In the world of the sex comedy and of the *récit*, Woman (Éliane's nickname is 'Elle') is expected to function as a sexual object. This is an impression which Éliane deliberately cultivates with her flirtatious behaviour and revealing outfits, and in which the camera implicates the spectator, as Adjani's body is shot in close-up from Pin-Pon's point of view, interpreted by his voice-over.

After Éliane and Pin-Pon have gone out on their first date, the narration switches from his voice to hers, and there are the first hints at an ulterior motive for her behaviour. From this point onwards, the film oscillates from one genre, and one voice-over, to the other. Scenes of Éliane's seduction of Pin-Pon, her introduction to his family, and her frequent provocative nakedness alternate with glimpses of Éliane's parents, her crippled father and anguished mother. The crucial relation within the *récit* form, the heterosexual couple, is replaced by the staple of melodrama, the mother–daughter dyad. The bodily excess of the genre is evident not only in Éliane and her mother's tears when they talk to each other, but in the disturbing scene in which Éliane is suckled by her mother. Éliane's narration while she looks at a photograph of Pin-Pon's father and later at the barrel organ stored in the barn mobilises brief flashback sequences relating to her secret, but it is a third switch of narration, to Éliane's mother, which entails a full flashback. While she tells her daughter 'for the hundredth time' what happened, we see how the mother was raped by three men twenty years previously, while her husband was away visiting his sister. The scene is directed as almost unbearably grotesque, with screams, blood, swaying lights, and finally the nightmarish jollity of the barrel organ as the men force Éliane's mother to dance with them in the snow. This is the primal scene which governs Éliane's actions in the film, and which has already been repeated in fragmented flashbacks before it is shown entire. One body spectacle, the daughter as sex object, has been deciphered as a screen for an earlier and excessive body spectacle, the rape of the mother. As Williams suggests, 'melodramatic weepie is the genre that seems to endlessly repeat [...] the loss of origins impossibly hoping to return to an earlier state which is perhaps most fundamentally represented by the body of the mother' (Williams 1991: 10–11).

The central section of *L'Été meurtrier* develops a sense of female solidarity reminiscent of the 'weepie,' with Éliane and Pin-Pon's grandmother becoming friends and allies. The grandmother's narration introduces another version of the flashback scene, and allows Éliane to identify the men she believes responsible. Éliane also makes use of her lesbian former schoolteacher's desire in order to further her plan, which requires the appropriation of the conventionally male/patriarchal role of avenger which her father was apparently too weak to carry out. It is through killing the men who raped her mother that she hopes to restore 'normal' family relations. Yet the twist in the film's conclusion not only reappropriates revenge as a male action but negates both Éliane's mission and therefore her identity. Discovering that her father has in fact already murdered the real perpetrators, Éliane suffers a breakdown in which she regresses to the age of nine (before she realised that she was 'de père inconnu'). The belatedness characteristic of melodrama (Williams 1991: 11) is thus doubled: it is too late now to prevent the rape or to accomplish the revenge. And yet this is also the moment at which the film spectacularly reaffirms itself not as melodrama but as *récit*. Having visited Éliane in an asylum (like Zorg visiting Betty in Jean-Jacques Beineix's *37,2 le Matin*), Pin-Pon, the original narrator of the film, is left to finish her misconceived revenge. By a stroke of excessive and coincidental plotting, Éliane has left the names of her two suspects (the third, Pin-Pon's father, is long dead) with the schoolteacher. Pin-Pon retrieves the names and retrieves the film as a male-motivated genre by shooting both men. The voice-over of the opening scenes and its cryptic references to terrible decisions and doomed destinies is now identifiable as Pin-Pon's narration from prison awaiting judgement. The final image of the film is of Pin-Pon firing, in slow-motion, at the camera (from the point of view of his second victim), reinscribing the film as his story, not Éliane's. The *récit* again, but placed in a dynamic relation to genre (melodrama) and hence to gender.

37,2 le Matin and the female spectator

During the seventies and eighties various shifts have taken place in theories of film spectatorship, as summarised for instance in Klinger (1988). The dominant theories in film studies tend to remain apparatus theory, epitomised by Mulvey (1975) – wherein an essentially passive spectator is positioned ideologically by the film they watch (for instance, the male spectator posited as desiring a female object) – and the closely-related field of psychoanalytical theory. Recently, however, studies such as Jackie Stacey's *Star Gazing* have challenged the canonical views of spectatorship by exploring the patterns of identification and consumption that exist between female spectators and female stars, asking 'What pleasures can [women] gain from the feminine images produced for the male gaze?', and suggesting that 'female spectatorship might be seen as a process of negotiating the dominant meanings of [...] cinema, rather than one of being passively positioned by it' (Stacey 1994: 11–12). This is particularly relevant to those films within the *récit* sub-genre whose 'dominant meanings' might be negotiable by the spectator to produce something other than a misogynistic objectification of hysterical women. Two key examples are Becker's *L'Été meurtrier* and Beineix's *37,2 le Matin*, both popular films featuring female stars, and which owe a great deal of their success at the box office (attracting audiences of four and a half million and two million respectively) to female viewers. The success of *L'Été meurtrier* and *37,2* with female as well as male spectators suggests that the *récit* form, and cinema in general, may draw on a more flexible model of viewer identification than previously assumed, a model which has been identified in the horror genre by Carol Clover (Clover 1992).

37,2 le Matin, the third film by Jean-Jacques Beineix (see chapter 6), is closely based on a novel by Philippe Djian. (The version originally released was shorter by an hour than the 'version intégrale', and thus necessarily less faithful to the text.) The opening scene of the film, an extended slow zoom on Betty (Béatrice Dalle) and Zorg (Jean-Hugues Anglade) naked on a couch having sex, is a microcosm or 'a metaphor for the whole film' (Norienko 1991: 194), which concerns the torrid and doomed love affair of this young couple. The first scene also lies 'outside the hero's trajectory' (Norienko 1991: 194), that is, outside the *récit* narrative which frames the film as one long flashback, mobilised by Zorg's voice-over. The frame opens with Zorg alone cooking chilli for himself (prior to Betty's decision to move in with him) and closes with the same situation, and a repetition of the chilli pot image, shot from the same low angle. There are two essential differences: Betty is now truly absent, since Zorg has 'put her out of her misery' (although she maintains a partial, fantasy presence through the cat which 'speaks' to Zorg); and Zorg is truly a writer, involved in writing/narrating the story we have just seen, a story which has charted what the souvenir booklet in the box-set video describes as 'Betty's decline from "kooky" to crazy' (Constellation 1993: 8).

The film thus appears to conform strongly to the *récit* model. But this is to read the film as essentially 'masculine', monosexual in its appeal to the spectator. This reductive 'masculine' reading of the film as 'one of the ten great bonking movies of all time' (*Empire* magazine, November 1991, cited in Constellation 1993: 11) is indeed the established reaction to *37,2*. Describing the film as 'a male fantasy of the "supreme fuck,"' Susan Hayward fails to account for its appeal as a female fantasy, and therefore can only condemn for their false consciousness those female spectators who find pleasure in the film: 'the fact that it is much liked by many young female spectators' is 'a bit worrying' (Hayward 1993: 293). As Jackie Stacey remarks about canonical film theory in general,

'The reluctance to engage with questions of cinema audiences [...] has led to an inability to think about active female desire beyond the limits of masculine positionings' (Stacey 1994: 29). 'Active female desire' is in fact explored throughout *37,2* by means of the various problems and issues in Betty's life, with which the female spectator may strongly identify. This narrative identification with Betty is centred on her desire for Zorg and her desire for children, which results not just in her fantasised pregnancy but also (in a sequence restored in the 'version intégrale') her kidnapping of a small child. Such episodes testify to a more melodramatic element within the narrative, existing alongside the 'male sexual fantasy' which would construct Betty's body as a spectacle. The parallels with Isabelle Adjani's dual functioning (as narrative and as specta-cle) in *L'Été meurtrier* are clear. Adjani was of course a star at the height of her fame when she made that film, while Béatrice Dalle was an unknown who was subsequently touted as the French Mar-ilyn Monroe (Prédal 1991: 467). Iconic identification (whereby female spectators identify with the star in terms of appearance) is encouraged by *37,2* as much as by *L'Été meurtrier*. Both films use the image of the female protagonist for their poster design, while the English-language title of Beineix's film is of course *Betty Blue*. Betty is the focus of the film, but not as a silent or objectified premise, like the generic hairdresser Mathilde or the absent wife Marie in Leconte's work. Thus a more 'bisexual' trend of narrative and iconic functioning can be observed: the *récit* form mediated by melodrama, the male fantasy complemented by female desires.

Woman as subject

Writing on Susan Seidelman's *Desperately Seeking Susan* (1985), Jackie Stacey compares the relation between the female protagonists – desiring Roberta and iconic Susan – to that between female spec-tators and female film stars (Stacey 1987: 57). The narrative of the film is, she adds, 'propelled structurally by Roberta's desire' (Stacey 1987: 57). It is interesting to note that in interview (Root 1985), Seidelman has acknowledged the debt her own 'playful feminist' film owes to Jacques Rivette's *Céline et Julie vont en bateau* (1974). Rivette's film – shot in the same year as both *Emmanuelle* and *Les Valseuses* – focuses not on women as sexual objects but as the desir-ing subjects of the narrative. The two female protagonists do not conform to a male fantasy, rather it is their own fantasies which dynamise and direct the film they inhabit. In this regard it is impor-tant to stress that the film is a collaborative effort, co-written by Riv-ette, Edouardo Gregorio, and its three principal actresses: Juliet Berto, Dominique Labourier and Marie-France Pisier.

Céline et Julie vont en bateau: narrative as female fantasy

Like Godard and Truffaut, Rivette wrote for *Cahiers du cinéma* (see chapter 1) before making his own films. Despite the commercial failure of his first feature film, *Paris nous appartient* (1961) and the censorship of his second, *Suzanne Simonin, la religieuse de Diderot* (1965), he continued to make complex, often improvised films with immense running times, centring on the themes of theatre and fantasy. *Céline et Julie* was an avowed attempt to attract a larger and more mainstream audience through comedy, and to leave the ghetto of experimental cinema while still reflecting on the nature of the medium itself. For all its length – over three hours – and its low production values – it was shot in 16 mm rather than the usual 35 mm – the film was a success at the box office.

Julie, a librarian (Dominique Labourier) is sitting on a park bench in Paris, reading a book on magic. She tries out a spell and seems to conjure out of nowhere the mysterious Céline (Juliet Berto). Like the white rabbit in Lewis Carroll's *Alice in Wonderland*, Céline runs by, dropping belongings as she goes. Julie follows her, putting on the scarf and sunglasses that she discards, and tracking her to a hotel where she is registered as a magician. This silent opening sequence initiates the exploration of fantasy and identification which is essential to the film. By following Céline and donning her garments, Julie is in a sense behaving as a fan does towards a film star. But unlike, say, *Desperately Seeking Susan* (where Roberta puts on Susan's identity along with her jacket) *Céline et Julie* does not present a straightforward narrativisation of the female spectator's identification with an enigmatic icon. Thus the two sequences set in the magic club allow Julie, rather than simply imitating Céline's act, to enact a critique of its deference to the male audience. In Julie's revision of Céline's act, she addresses the male clientele (and also the spectator in the cinema), accusing them of leering at her and calling them (us) a bunch of 'perverted voyeurs' and 'cosmic pimps'. The comic element of her tirade does not detract from the significance of this attack on the male objectifying gaze and its role in constructing the female body as spectacle, be it in cinema, theatre or, indeed, this magic act. This episode is typical of Rivette's achievement in the film, whereby he both entertains the viewer and, with a light and absurdist touch, raises questions about the way that cinema functions.

Once Céline has moved in with Julie, the pair team up to form a female variant – rare in seventies French cinema at least – on the traditionally male buddy movie (see below). The mystery that they set out to solve together centres on an old house from which Céline has recently been ejected. Both women take it in turns to visit the house and investigate, but it is only through sucking on magic sweets that they can overcome their amnesia about what transpires inside the house. Piece by piece, the flashbacks that they 'see' along with the audience begin to unravel the mystery. This plot dynamises a crucial ambivalence, according to which Céline and Julie are at once active subjects whose desires and investigations structure the film and, in a more passive role, spectators watching the flashbacks brought on by the sweets. The parallel between the latter role and the position of the cinema audience is brought to the foreground by the composition of the sequences in which Céline and Julie suck their sweets simultaneously: sitting side by side like spectators in an auditorium, the two women directly face the camera and therefore the actual spectators of the film. This reflection of the audience's experience is compounded when, in response to the lengthy and repetitive nature of the flashbacks, Julie declares that it is time for the interval, during which she wants to smoke a cigarette. The narrative presented and repeated in these fragmentary glimpses concerns a perpetual day lived inside the old house. Whereas in *L'Amour fou* (1969) Rivette had distinguished between 'reality' and the film-within-a-film by shooting each in a different format (35 mm and 16 mm) here it is the décor, costumes and above all the dialogue and style of acting – the indications of genre – which set the theatrical spectacle apart. Based on stories by Henry James, the melodrama in the house concerns the rivalry between two women, Camille and Sophie (Bulle Ogier and Marie-France Pisier) for the love of Olivier, a widower (Barbet Schroeder). Céline and Julie are never purely spectators in this narrative, however, for each plays the part of 'Miss Angèle,' nurse to Olivier's young daughter Madlyn. Since their presence in the house implies a change of genre, they too assume a melodramatic delivery as they speak the nurse's lines. Towards the end of the film, however, they enter the house together, both playing the Miss Angèle role. It is during this joint visit that they play upon the theatrical nature of the melodrama – pausing in the wings between 'acts', accepting the applause of a hidden audience – before disrupting the eternal cycle in which Sophie poisons Madlyn. Céline's declaration 'On n'est plus dans le mélo' [we're not in a melodrama any more] heralds their rescue of Madlyn and the return of all three, Céline, Julie and Madlyn, to 'the real world.'

Julie's suggestion to Madlyn – 'On va t'emmener en bateau' [We're going to take you for a ride] – reflects on Rivette's knowing choice of title and introduces a concluding sequence which revises the film's opening. Asleep on a bench, it is Céline who wakes to see Julie hurrying past; when Julie drops her book of spells, Céline picks it up and chases after her. The fantastical cycle closes with the image of a cat staring enigmatically at the camera. By recasting the relation between the bearer and the object of the gaze – is Céline Julie's fantasy or vice versa? – the film's conclusion also asks whether cinema is the fantasy of the director or the viewer; throughout the course of the film, spectatorship has been associated not with passivity but with active identification (Céline and Julie identifying with Miss Angèle and playing her part in the melodrama that they are watching). The spectator participates in a conjuring trick which allows them to both desire and identify with the protagonists on the screen, to access a realm of fantasy which, as Rivette himself points out, is a child's dream of the cinema (Sadoul 1990: 58).

Social difference: *4 Aventures de Reinette et Mirabelle*

Eric Rohmer, like his *nouvelle vague* colleagues, wrote on cinema for *Cahiers* in the 1950s before shooting his own films (see chapter 1). During the sixties he worked in television as well as beginning the series of films that was to make his name, the six 'Moral tales'. Culminating in the popular trio of *Ma Nuit chez Maud* (1969), *Le Genou de Claire* (1970) and *L'Amour l'après-midi* (1972), the series was considered by Rohmer to constitute variations on a single theme: in each film, a man pursuing one woman inadvertently comes across another before finally returning to the first. But unlike the *récit* form, the 'Contes moraux' do not present authoritative male narrators. Although based on Rohmer's own first-person, male-narrated texts, the films tend to complicate or qualify the male protagonist's perspective. At the conclusion of *Le Genou de Claire*, for example, Gilles's supposed infidelity, a fact originally 'authenticated' by the camera's collusion in Jérome's point of view as he spies on Gilles through binoculars, and then corroborated as Jérome tells both Claire and Aurora his interpretation, is strongly qualified. Seen from Aurora's perspective, Gilles offers Claire an alternative explanation for his apparent infidelity. She believes him and the two are reconciled. The male point of view has proved false, or at least dubious: while Jérome is the 'titular narrator', he sees what he wants to see; Aurora, the 'real narrator' sees the truth (Rohmer 1980: ix). In the 1980s Rohmer shot a new series of six films, called 'Comédies et proverbes,' and then embarked on 'Contes des quatre saisons'. Both collections concentrate on women as desiring subjects, inverting the premise of the 'Contes moraux'. Rohmer's heroines during this period tend to embark on a rather melancholy search for a male object of desire, a search which is ultimately rewarded with a crucial revelation: Delphine's glimpse of the green ray in *Le Rayon vert* (1986), Léa's awakening to her emotions in the forest in *L'Ami de mon amie* (1987), Félicie's rediscovery of her child's lost father in *Conte d'hiver* (1992). Two factors distinguish *4 Aventures de Reinette et Mirabelle* (1986) from these films and from most of Rohmer's oeuvre: it stands outside a series and it does not present heterosexual desire, but rather a pairing of two women. The film is mobilised not by sexual difference but by the social difference between two girls, a country mouse and a Parisienne.

The first episode, 'L'Heure bleue,' introduces city-girl Mirabelle (Jessica Forde) into the rural milieu inhabited by Reinette (Joëlle Miquel). Reinette tells Mirabelle about the 'blue hour,' a moment between night and day when nature is completely silent. This moment, like the sighting of the green ray in *Le Rayon vert*, will render sacred a relationship: there between Delphine and the young man, here between Reinette and Mirabelle. Rohmer's construction of the moment is notable for the dramatisation of the looks which Reinette and Mirabelle offer each other. At once subject and object of the gaze, they are inter-related by Rohmer's editing, which relies on the traditional shot/reverse-shot technique. Five times in succession Rohmer switches from one girl to the other as they face each other in the garden. It is this moment of looking, as much as the silence of the blue hour which surrounds it or the embrace which follows, that inaugurates the friendship between the two.

Mirabelle is also shown Reinette's surreal paintings, which consistently present fetishised views of women's naked bodies. A typical example, shown in close-up, depicts a woman seen from the rear. As the camera dwells on the picture, Reinette explains to Mirabelle that she finds the behind the prettiest part of a woman's body, and therefore likes to place it in the centre of her paintings. Such an objectification of the female body raises questions about the representation of women in Rohmer's cinema, which in fact scrupulously avoids fetishised fragmentation, apart from the express exception of Claire's knee in *Le Genou de Claire*. In Reinette and Mirabelle's fourth and final adventure, 'La Vente du tableau,' the spectator's suspicions about the origin of Reinette's paintings is voiced by the gallery owner (Fabrice Luchini), who ascribes them to the fantasies of a mature, indeed old, man rather than to a young girl. This ironic characterisation of Rohmer himself questions the status of fantasy in the film – are the paintings Reinette's fantasies or are they, and Reinette and Mirabelle themselves, the fantasies of a middle-aged director? – and is only partially mitigated by the revelation in the closing credits that the paintings are the work of Joëlle Miquel, the actress who plays Reinette. The question raised by the paintings remains: the female subjects in this film, and indeed in any film by a male director, are necessarily male fantasies. Moreover, the role of woman as object is further brought to the foreground in the closing episode by Reinette's vow of silence. Her mutism in front of the gallery owner parallels the subordination of the (silent) actress to the (verbal) male director, and is particularly pertinent to Rohmer, whose adherence to his own scripts is well known. And yet *4 Aventures*, like *Le Rayon vert* and indeed Rivette's *Céline et Julie vont en bateau*, relies to a great extent on dialogue improvised by its principal actresses. It is this quality which allows all three films to authenticate female desiring subjects even as they dramatise the constraints imposed upon those subjects by the cinema as spectacle.

Merci la Vie as feminised buddy movie

Bertrand Blier's representations of sexuality often subvert the classic heterosexual *ménage à trois* or the male buddy movie. The latter form, combined with the traditionally macho sub-genre of the road movie, is used to depressingly conventional effect in Patrice Leconte's *Tango* (1992). One year previously, Blier himself had made what is undoubtedly his most complex film, *Merci la Vie* (1991), in which the assumptions of the buddy movie are challenged by feminising the form. Before the film was shot, Blier expressed a desire to leave behind the staple of the male duo and to build a film around two women (Haustrate 1988: 27), and also to return to the road genre after what he considered to be 'un film trop chic', *Trop Belle pour Toi* (1989). The key intertext for *Merci la Vie* is Blier's first successful film, *Les Valseuses* (1974), a fairly conventional, if sexually explicit, buddy movie, in which Pierrot and Jean-Claude (Patrick Dewaere and Gérard Depardieu) go in search of sexual adventures (see above). *Les Valseuses* is strongly alluded to in the opening sequence of *Merci la Vie*, both by the identical typeface used for the credits, and most obviously via the image of the shopping-trolley, which functions as a quotation from the earlier film: Camille pushes the passed-out Joëlle in a trolley just as Pierrot pushes Jean-Claude in the opening scene of *Les Valseuses*.

Camille (Charlotte Gainsbourg) finds Joëlle (Anouk Grinberg) dumped on the side of the road in a wedding dress. She takes her home to her parents' empty apartment in a deserted seaside resort (a setting familiar from *Les Valseuses*), and the pair begin a series of picaresque adventures, including a serious sub-plot in which Joëlle contracts Aids (see below). The strong characterisation of the two young women belies the accusations of misogyny and chauvinism which have dogged Blier throughout his career. During the early sequences, it appears that the two are as autonomous and carefree as the male buddies of *Les Valseuses*. But this is not simply a role-reversal buddy movie, for Blier is manifestly aware in *Merci la Vie* – as Rohmer is in *4 Aventures de Reinette et Mirabelle* – that women in cinema risk being submitted to male fantasies. As Joëlle asserts while in the resort, peeping Toms are everywhere. The position of the peeping Tom is occupied not only by two male directors who use the women, particularly Joëlle, in their films-within-the film, but also by Blier himself and by the spectator in the auditorium. In a typical scene, Joëlle, failing a screen test for the first film director encountered by the two women, and bursting into genuine tears, has her grief intruded upon: the film crew returns, the director calls for action, and the cameras roll. The primary effect of such self-conscious moments is to qualify the narrative function of Camille and Joëlle as desiring female subjects by exploring their relation to the male film crews and the camera itself. This self-consciously voyeuristic strain in *Merci la Vie* culminates with a doctor, Marc-Antoine (Gérard Depardieu), tracked by a film crew, running down a corridor to place an eye, torn from Camille's father Raymond (Jean Carmet), in Joëlle's vagina. The disembodied eye recalls Norman Bates's bulging eye in Hitchcock's *Psycho* (1960) as well as the finale of Georges Bataille's pornographic novel *Histoire de l'œil*. Raymond, from whom the eye is taken, is only the last in a long line of men in *Merci la Vie* who have desired Joëlle: he thus takes possession of her visually (scopophilia) before doing so sexually (at the railway station towards the close of the film). The discomfort aroused in the spectator by the eyeball scene, a discomfort not wholly mitigated by its farcical treatment, is redoubled by the climactic deportation sequence. Blier's film alternates between sepia and colour photography, between a contemporary setting and a recreation of the German Occupation (see chapter 2). In one of the sepia sequences, the Nazis deport Joëlle and Raymond. There follows a burst of machine-gun fire and the image of naked bodies falling from the train. Blier's use here of sepia photography, slow motion, and violins on the sound-track dares the viewer to enjoy this spectacle despite its horrific connotations. Blier is not interested in the 'destruction of pleasure' championed by feminist film theory (Mulvey 1975) but in the collusion between the pleasurable and the disconcerting. The deportation having broken up the female buddies, Camille finds herself back in the resort, and in a 'real world' of conventional family relations, with her mother and father and a boyfriend. Heterosexual structures replace the female pairing, and the horrific threats of Nazism and Aids give way to the normalised banalities which are Blier's usual targets.

Masculinities

In *Mensonge romantique et vérité romanesque*, Raymond Girard stated that all desire is triangular in form, and that rivals for a love object are as strongly bound to each other as to their common object. The implications of this theory for 'male bonding' and the buddy movie have been noted by Laura Mulvey (1975) and Naomi Segal (1988: 205). The one French film-maker who has made his name by exploring 'triangular' desire and the implicit homosexuality of the buddy movie is Bertrand Blier.

From *Les Valseuses* to *Tenue de soirée*: the permutations of masculine desire

Even within the rampant heterosexuality of *Les Valseuses* (1974), Blier reveals glimpses of the homoerotic foundation of Jean-Claude and Pierrot's friendship. This is most explicit in the sea-side resort sequence. With Pierrot (Patrick Dewaere) emasculated by a bullet-wound in the groin, Jean-Claude (Gérard Depardieu) makes advances to him in the intimacy of the deserted villa, washing his hair, drying him, and finally (in an elided scene) raping him. The reading of this situation by both men integrates the rape into the discourse of the conventional buddy movie, with Jean-Claude claiming that 'Entre copains, c'est normal' [It's normal between mates], and Pierrot generalising his humiliation to prove that the world is against him: 'Partout où je vais, je me fais enculer' [I get fucked over wherever I go]. The sequence concludes with the two reconciled, wrestling and 'bonding' on the beach. The representation of gay sex between buddies as explicit and unproblematic rather than implicit and repressed is central to Blier's revision of this straight/macho genre. A less overtly sexualised but equally significant feature of the film is the visual identification of the two men with each other. While the natural comic tensions between the melancholic Dewaere and the more convivial Depardieu are exploited throughout the film, in the pastoral sequence set by the

8   Patrick Dewaere and Gérard Depardieu in *Les Valseuses*

canal the two are equated through identical costumes (white flares, blue vest, straw hat) and synchronised gestures. This visual twinning of buddies is even more pronounced in Blier's Oscar-winning *Préparez vos Mouchoirs* (1978), which uses the same actors to great effect. The premise for the buddies to get together is here a shared love object, Solange (Carole Laure). By offering his wife Solange to Stéphane (Dewaere) as a gift, Raoul (Depardieu) initiates a relationship between himself and Stéphane which is fundamental to the narrative and rhythm of the film. Solange is merely the object of an exchange which inaugurates the buddy pairing. As in *Les Valseuses*, the men share not only a woman but also a stock of gestures and clothes, in particular an obsession with Mozart (an invisible buddy, whom they imagine paying them a visit and partaking of their *ménage à trois*) and a taste for identical jumpers knitted by Solange. Early on in the film Raoul shows Stéphane his open-plan apartment, declaring 'J'aime bien casser les cloisons, moi. Pas toi?' [I like breaking down walls, don't you?]. By the end, the barriers have been broken down and Solange herself, the very premise of their relationship, no longer matters as the two men walk off together into the night.

Blier's most sustained and remarkable exploration of the permutations of masculine desire is to be found in *Tenue de soirée* (1986). The film, initially conceived in response to the homophobic joking between Dewaere and Depardieu on the set of *Préparez vos Mouchoirs*, was to have starred that pairing again. After Dewaere's suicide Michel Blanc took the role of Antoine, rendering his character more vulnerable to the physical presence of Bob (Gérard Depardieu), and inspiring the celebrated final scene (Haustrate 1988: 81). The third member of the *ménage à trois* is Antoine's wife Monique (Miou-Miou, who played Marie-Ange in *Les Valseuses*). Just as the alienation of 'la zone' [slum belt] provides the setting for sexual adventures in *Les Valseuses*, urban poverty is the context for *Tenue de soirée*. Hence the film's concern with prostitution, and the central metaphor: burglary. Inviting himself into the lives of Antoine and Monique, Bob introduces them to the pleasures of housebreaking, pleasures that are overtly sexualised by his commentary on moistening locks and penetrating inside. Moreover, this activity seems to stimulate sexual desire, whether in the three thieves or in their victims, one of whom proposes a mixed orgy. It is after a break-in that Bob makes his first passes at Antoine, insisting that sex is natural between buddies. The presentation of these intentions as 'burglary' is furthered by the stereotypical attribution of Bob's homosexuality to his years spent in prison. Blier is on less conventional ground, however, as the film proceeds to map out a series of permutations within the *ménage à trois*. One of the trio is excluded in turn by the formation of a couple, at first straight (Antoine and Monique, Bob and Monique) and then gay, after Antoine has succumbed to Bob.

It is above all this pairing of Bob and Antoine which allows Blier to subvert heterosexual models and expectations. Thus Monique's dream of 'a house and kids,' and her mother's prediction that one day men would be at her feet, are both cruelly subverted when she finds herself cooking and cleaning for Bob and Antoine, and sleeping on the floor at the foot of their bed while they have sex. Betraying Monique as he earlier did Antoine, Bob sells her to a pimp and then casts Antoine as his 'wife.' This requires Antoine to act as a domestic drudge, and results in another inversion of heterosexual archetypes as he complains that Bob takes him for granted and never notices what he wears. The logical extension of this sequence is realised when Bob, having earlier promised to make Antoine his queen, turns him into a drag queen, buying him a dress and a wig and calling him 'elle' or 'Antoinette.' In an ironic variant on the opening scene (which finds Antoine and Monique at a dancehall) the two then go out dancing as a 'straight' couple. The subterranean sexual identities of the trio are charted further in the toilets under the dancehall, where Bob jilts Antoine for a gay pickup while Antoine, dressed as 'Antoinette,' discovers Monique working as a prostitute under the name 'Dolores'. Having stabbed Monique's pimp only to be shot and wounded by her in return, Antoine is framed in a series of mirrors as he picks up the pimp's gun. Once armed with this phallic weapon, he is in a position to impose on Bob a final, startling change of sexual roles. In another composition refracted by mirrors, Antoine forces Bob to put on the wig before shooting at the glass and thus destroying the reflected images of the two men. Feminised by the wig, dominated for the first time by the gun-toting Antoine, Bob too becomes a transvestite. The epilogue (which provided the film's poster, under the slogan 'Putain de film!')

shows Monique, Antoine and Bob, all dressed as female prostitutes, working the street. As they enter a café, they begin to talk about Pascal, Antoine and Monique's child, to whom Bob is 'godmother.' But even this heterosexual ideal is subverted: no image of Pascal is offered, and the playground sound-effects seem to confirm his status as a fantasy. Despite the evident shock value of Depardieu in a dress (played on by the poster), the film concludes with the image of 'Antoinette' in a miniskirt and heels, sitting at the bar and putting on lipstick. With a 'lascivious pan' so characteristic of the representation of women in heterosexual cinema, the camera moves slowly up Antoinette's legs and body and then shows his (her) face in close-up as he (she) pouts and smiles directly at the spectator, in a supremely confident gaze which challenges the objectification of sexuality.

La Cage aux folles and *La Cage aux folles II*: the queens of camp cinema

In *Now you see it*, Richard Dyer observes that 'lesbian/gay film has used many of the images and structures of non-lesbian/gay film, [...] for instance in the practices of camp or the use of traditional romance and adventure narrative structures' (Dyer 1990: 2). Although *La Cage aux folles* (1978) and its sequels are made by a straight director, Edouard Molinaro, the films occupy precisely this site between gay and straight imagery: the realm of camp. Adapted from Jean Poiret's popular stage play, *La Cage aux folles* is a French–Italian co-production starring one male lead from each country. Albin (Michel Serrault) and Renato (Ugo Tognazzi) are a gay couple whose lives revolve around the nightclub which lends its name to the film. Renato runs the club while Albin is the star attraction, the glamorous drag queen 'Zaza'. The plot concerns the farcical lengths to which the couple have to go in order to present this gay milieu as an ideal, heterosexual family unit in order not to jeopardise the wedding plans of Renato's son Laurent.

From the very first scene, the film investigates the functioning of camp, and more generally, of both gay and straight sexuality, as spectacle. The opening credits roll over images of the stage show at the club, ostensibly performed by women. When the credits finish, the 'women' on stage bow and remove their wigs, revealing themselves as men. As the camera moves backstage and follows Renato upstairs, the spectator is implicitly promised a similar 'unveiling' of Albin/Zaza, who is due on stage. The impatience of Renato and of the audience in the club is shared by the spectator in the auditorium. But the revelation is deferred through a suspense which is twofold: Albin/Zaza is playing hard to get, and will not let Renato see 'her' – nor will Molinaro let the spectator see 'her' yet. Our first sight of Zaza is of a figure in bed hiding under a sheet. 'She' shouts in a high, feminised voice at Renato, and throws a pair of high heels at him, without revealing herself. This visual foreplay is extended until Renato agrees to call the doctor, who persuades Zaza to let him (us) see her. Even when Zaza is finally revealed as a balding middle-aged man (that is, as Albin), the play-acting continues, with a prolonged complaint identical to one that Renato has tape-recorded the previous evening. Albin/Zaza is hence constructed as a queen, a hysterical prima donna in both sound and image. And throughout the film he (she) is always walking on stage or into shot (the star) or exiting from shots/rooms (the unwanted 'Other'). This is at once an act put on by a prima donna, and at a less explicit and comic level, a portrayal of the marginalisation of sexual identities (female and gay). Such is the drag queen's dual significance: to function as both a gay and a woman, to thereby embody 'the strategies of survival and resistance' against patriarchal sexual oppression (Dyer 1990: 83).

The plot of the film allows frequent cross-cutting between the theatrical, camp world of Renato and Albin (where the décor is kitsch and the 'maid' Jacob wears a wig and mules) and the austere, heterosexual patriarchy incarnated by Laurent's future father-in-law, Charrier (Michel Galabru). The Charrier household is an exaggeratedly repressive version of the heterosexual family, where Andrea (Laurent's fiancée), her mother and grandmother defer constantly to the authority of the *père de famille*. Images of this family tend to be gloomy and static, in contrast with the mobile, brightly-lit shots of Albin and Renato in their apartment, driving in cars, shopping for food. A farcical political edge is added to this portrait of the model family, since Charrier is the secretary of a reactionary party called 'L'Union pour l'ordre moral', whose leader has sensationally just been found dead in the arms of a black, underage prostitute. The threat of another marginalised element – camp homosexuality – to a man in Charrier's position will prove crucial to the plot. But the impending arrival of Charrier also requires that Renato and Albin 'normalise' their appearance and behaviour. Their attempts to conform to a heterosexual masculine ideal which Renato takes from John Wayne movies prove highly comic as well as suggesting that 'straight' identity is itself a culturally-constructed image. Renato does manage an approximation of virility, while in a motif from conventional farce, Albin cross-dresses as Laurent's 'mother'. With the apartment given a spartan new look, Albin and Renato are ready to entertain the Charriers, but of course their imitation of 'normal' family life collapses. Once Renato has acknowledged that Albin is really his transvestite lover, the camp spectacle that was temporarily banished returns as the cast of queens from the club burst into the apartment with a birthday cake. The film concludes with the comic reversal of accepted sexual images: the milieu of 'La Cage aux Folles' is more of a family than the disintegrating Charrier household, Charrier the arch-patriarch makes his escape from the press in drag (in a scene comparable to the ending of *Tenue de soirée*), and in the final image it is Renato and Albin, rather than the newly-weds Laurent and Andrea, who indulge in the affectionate bickering of the stereotypical married couple.

The film proved an enormous hit both in France and abroad, causing a sequel to be made by the same team. *La Cage aux folles II* (1980) was again popular, attracting nearly three million spectators to French cinemas (Prédal 1991: 402). International distribution followed, as did a second sequel; the three films have been shown together as a cycle at gay film festivals. What is notable about *La Cage aux folles II* is its cinematic status: although written by Jean Poiret, this is no stage play but an attempt to situate the original characters within a generic plot derived from the comedy thrillers so popular in France throughout the seventies and eighties (see chapter 5). Traditional narrative structures are employed in the original, namely farce (a theatrical model) and romance, but cinematic genres are largely absent. The sequel continues with the romance motif, which culminates in the reunion of Renato and Albin at the end, but has been criticised for its less successful appropriation of the espionage thriller. Although, however, the resultant plot is much more laboured, and the mood more uneven, than in the first film, *La Cage aux folles II* does gain from the thriller genre in one area: images of sexuality. The thriller form imparts swift editing, tense music and car chases; it also brings a distinctly macho image of masculinity, similar to the John Wayne ideal mimicked by Renato in *La Cage aux folles*. And it is to this virile image that Albin has to conform, in order to avoid being tracked down and killed by a gang of spies. Hence the scene in which Albin reinvents himself, not as Zaza but as 'Maurice' the macho window-cleaner, complete with deep voice and homophobic comments. When the action switches to Italy, in a pastoral sequence derived from thrillers such as Jacques Deray's *Borsalino* (1970) (see chapter 5), it is female roles which are questioned as Albin, disguised as a peasant woman, has to slave for 'her husband' Renato. Although cultural/racial stereotypes are in play here, none the less the film manages to explore through comedy the subordination of other sexualities by straight patriarchy. As a queen, Albin may represent 'the feminine principle' (Dyer 1990: 83), but as a gay man he is less valuable a commodity than women or children: consequently he has no exchange value as a hostage. However, it is this marginalised, ironically invisible status which allows the usually ultra visible Albin to escape from the siege at the close and reaffirm his relationship with Renato. The distinct pleasures of the film thus lie not in the uneasy juxtaposition of camp farce and comedy thriller, but in the interrogation of the sexual typing within these genres.

Gay cinema in France

Neither Blier nor Molinaro is a gay director. Films made by gays and lesbians about their own sexuality have generally existed only on the margins of French mainstream cinema (see also chapter 4). Gay film in France has at times been reliant on the more established field of gay literature, as in Jean Cocteau's film of his own play, *Orphée* (1950), or the various adaptations and derivations from the writings of Jean Genet, the most prominent of which is Fassbinder's Franco-German co-production *Querelle* (1982). After May 1968 however (see chapter 2), the creation of avant-garde gay film independent of mainstream cinema began to grow rapidly. Alongside the establishment of the Front Homosexuel d'Action Révolutionnaire (FHAR) in 1971 and the Groupe de Libération Homosexuelle (GLH) in 1974, the development of the 'home-movie' as a viable artistic medium enabled gay film-makers to express themselves in both personal and political terms (Dyer 1990: 223–4). According to Dyer, this new 'confrontational cinema' typically used montage in order to juxtapose erotic, comic and political images centring on the importance of drag, pornography and pederasty in homosexual desire. Drag, celebrated later in *La Cage aux folles*, was 'accepted as part of the revolutionary gay repertoire right across Southern Europe' in the 1970s, and featured in films such as Adolfo Arrieta's *Les Intrigues de Sylvia Couski* (1974) and Michel Nedjar's *La Tasse* (1977) (Dyer 1990: 224–5). Gay activism and 'cinéma différent' informed each other in the film festivals organised in 1977 and 1978 by the FHAR, and particularly in the work of Lionel Soukaz, a director associated with the revolutionary faction within the GLH. In addition to avant-garde confrontational cinema, a number of documentaries championing gay liberation were made in France in the late seventies, including Norbert Terry's *Homo-actualités* (1977) and Soukaz's own *Race d'ep!* (1979) and *La Marche gay* (1980). None the less, the 'films of Soukaz *et al.* remained highly marginal' (Dyer 1990: 227), and it was not until over a decade later that gay (or more precisely, bisexual) film finally became part of French mainstream cinema with Cyril Collard, whose work and whose death also brought the reality of Aids belatedly into the realm of French film.

Representing Aids

In 1986, Aids (known in French as 'le Sida') began to enter the cultural consciousness in France, and found its first forms of representation in French mainstream cinema. These forms were usually coded, metaphorical, even anonymous, and thus at one remove from lived experience.

Pseudonyms and metaphors: *Mauvais Sang, Tenue de soirée, Merci la Vie*

In its first manifestations, Aids in film appears almost as an afterthought, a topical allusion. This gratuitous status is exemplified in *Mauvais Sang* (1986) by Léos Carax (see chapter 6), where the thriller element of the narrative consists of a plot to steal a virus called 'le STBO'. It is through his role in this theft that Alex (Denis Lavant) meets Anna (Juliette Binoche). The function of the virus here recalls Hitchcock's use of an arbitrary element, known as the 'McGuffin,' as the pretext for each of his films. The exact nature of the 'McGuffin' was of no importance whatsoever. As regards *Mauvais Sang*, the virus adds a poignant tone to the doomed love between Alex and Anna. But although its effects are described as vomiting, blindness and eventually death, the disease itself is romanticised: it only infects those who make love without feeling. The reality of Aids, and in particular the disturbing fact that its transmission transcends moral judgement, has no place in the romantic, highly stylised world of *Mauvais Sang*.

Bertrand Blier's evocation of Aids in his film of the same year, *Tenue de soirée*, is also peripheral, but is more germane to both his subject – sexual identity, role-playing and transvestism – and to the style of the film, which is at least partially realistic. During the epilogue, which shows the three protagonists soliciting on the street, a cryptic mention is made of the 'new diseases' which constitute a threat to business. As in *Mauvais Sang*, the topicality of the reference is highlighted by the allusion to the newspapers which are breaking the story. The shooting of *Tenue de soirée* (which Blier had written in the late 1970s) coincided with the rise of interest in Aids and thus in the general question of sexuality (Haustrate 1988: 81). Blier attributed the positive reception of the film in the United States, particularly by the gay community, in part to this topicality (Haustrate 1988: 81). But film-makers, like politicians, were still slow to actually name the disease. It is only in *Merci la Vie* (1991) that Blier mentions – and engages with – 'le Sida'. If in *Tenue de soirée* there were hints that Aids was beginning to impinge upon the realities of daily existence, in *Merci la Vie* it is Aids which has come to characterise contemporary life. Hence the desire of the infected Joëlle (Anouk Grinberg) to escape from the nineties and return to a time when sex was innocent and safe. The conflation of past and present in the film renders the German Occupation and Aids, both 'diseases' of their time, metaphors for each other (see chapter 2). And it is through the metaphor of Aids as a new Holocaust that Blier raises the implicit question of fascistic responses to the disease, such as the deportation and incarceration of victims as practised in Cuba. By adding elements of pathos and melodrama to his usual back comedy, Blier here achieves a desperate portrayal of how Aids has changed sex forever. But because he is also, uncharacteristically, engaging with history, he does not present in *Merci la Vie* any sustained representation of Aids as an everyday reality. In contrast, *Mensonge* (1991) – the debut feature by François Margolin – is a serious attempt to portray the impact of the disease on an 'ordinary' family. Distinguished from the more fantastical narratives of Carax or Blier by its deliberate realism, the film derives a note of authenticity from the collaboration of Denis Saada, a psychiatrist used to working with Aids victims. It nevertheless demonises the bisexuality of the male protagonist, Charles (Didier Sandre), and presents Aids as a threat to the 'normal' heterosexual family.

Les Nuits fauves: from reality to *cause célèbre*

The suggestion that Aids can provoke not just fear or despair, but also emotional growth, is controversially dramatised in Cyril Collard's *Les Nuits fauves* (1992). Collard had previously worked with Maurice Pialat, a director specialising in films with a documentary tone (see chapter 5), and had written two novels, including the text adapted for the film. As well as directing *Les Nuits fauves*, Collard supplies some of the music and also plays the male lead, which had been turned down by Jean-Hugues Anglade, Hippolyte Girardot and others (*Cahiers du cinéma* 1992: 78). Set in 1986, the film recounts how Jean, a bisexual cameraman (Cyril Collard), contracts the HIV virus after a trip to Morocco. His struggle to come to terms with being HIV positive is complicated by his relationships with Samy (Carlos Lopez), a butch young man with sado-masochistic obsessions, and Laura (Romane Bohringer), an eighteen-year-old he meets at an audition. Although Collard dynamises a range of reactions on the part of the three principal characters, and uses a variety of aggressive visual styles (handheld camera, jumpcuts), he in fact consistently asks the question implicit in the ending of François Margolin's *Mensonge*: can Aids facilitate a form of emotional healing? A positive answer is given by both the Arab woman in Jean's Moroccan dream – 'Profite de l'épreuve de ta maladie' [Make the most of your illness] – and, towards the close, by his mother, who tells Jean that the virus can enable him to love. Between these two key scenes, the narrative veers from the clichés of heterosexual romance (the scenes between Jean and Laura, and her eventual descent into a hysteria reminiscent of the *récit* (see above)) to an anguished awareness of the imbrication of art and life, an interference which informs the film as a whole, since Collard was HIV positive at the time and had made this known publicly. It is not just the figure of Jean/Collard, but the use of sound and image that explores the relation between reality and fiction: in her audition for Jean, Laura uses lines of dialogue that she will later reprise when her jealousy of him becomes 'real' and not just acted. And from the outset, Jean's persistent use of the video camera to dramatise himself and what he sees not only replicates Collard's project, but establishes a flux between the video image and the 'real' film image. The photogenic images of Jean's suffering – driving too fast, getting drunk, singing a raging lament (penned by Collard) – are further complicated by the presence of the real virus in Collard's blood, and of real, visible liesons on his body, even while these images are parodied by Samy's imitation of suffering, as he cuts his body while looking at it in the mirror.

The idiosyncratic nature of *Les Nuits fauves*, and in particular the absence of any collective or political gay consciousness, attracted a degree of criticism. Despite the allusion to Genet's death early in the film, both Jean and Samy deny that they are gay. Collard himself acknowledged in interview that he was not interested in 'la militance gay,' and that he wanted to engage with the reality of Aids, not with ideology (*Cahiers du cinéma* 1992: 79). To this end, much of the film – including Samy's association with skinheads and fascists – was based on actual events or anecdotes. By contrast, the climactic scene, in which Jean prevents Samy and the skinheads from beating up an Arab by threatening them with his infected blood, was not in the original scenario and not based on fact. This is also the only scene which Collard acknowledged as symbolic: 'C'est un peu gros comme symbolisme, le sida contre le fascisme. Mais en même temps, pourquoi pas?' [The symbolism is a bit heavy: Aids against fascism. But then again, why not?] (*Cahiers du cinéma* 1992: 79). The naivety of this remark (in direct contrast with Blier's sinister conflation of Aids and fascism in *Merci la Vie*) suggests that Collard was wise not to embrace an ideological approach. And it is precisely the lack of ideology, the vibrant individualism, which made *Les Nuits fauves* such a popular success and, ultimately, a social as much as an artistic phenomenon. Praised by *Cahiers du cinéma* for disrupting the 'comfortable lethargy' of French cinema epitomised by 'official films' like *Un Cœur en hiver* and *Tous les matins du monde*, Collard's film was voted best film of 1992 by the *Cahiers* readership, and fifth best by the critics (*Cahiers du cinéma* 1992: 77, 12). Collard, in the meantime, was dying of Aids, a fact which may or may not have influenced the judging of the Césars (the French Oscars) for 1992. In any event, three days after Collard's death on 5 March 1993, *Les Nuits fauves* won four Césars, including best film. The television ceremony, an emotional response to Collard's death as much as to his film, heralded a general media celebration of Collard's work. Flammarion published *L'Ange sauvage*, journals written between 1979 and 1992, while the televising of the Césars by Canal Plus in 1994 was followed by 'Une Nuit fauve' consisting of Collard's entire film output: *Les Nuits fauves*, *Taggers*, his short films and video 'clips' (Strauss 1994: 20). But whether such activity presages a new awareness of Aids in the French media, or represents merely a cult of personality, remains to be seen.

References

Burch, N. (1979), *Correction Please, or How We Got Into Pictures*, notes to accompany the film.

Cahiers du cinéma (1992), Hors série.

Clover, C. J. (1992), *Men Women and Chain Saws: Gender in the Modern Horror Film*, London, BFI.

Constellation Productions/Cargo Films (1993), *37,2 le Matin*, souvenir booklet with box-set video.

Daney, S. (1992), Falling out of love, London, *Sight and Sound*, July 1992, 14–16.

Dyer, R. (1990), *Now you See it: Studies on Lesbian and Gay Film*, London and New York, Routledge.

Forbes, J. (1992), *The Cinema in France After the New Wave*, London, Macmillan/BFI.

Godard, J.-L. (1980), *Sauve qui peut ... Godard!*, Norwich, *Framework*, 13, 10–13.

Godard, J.-L. (1991), *Godard par Godard: des années Mao aux années 80*, Paris, Flammarion.

Haustrate, G. (1988), *Bertrand Blier*, Paris, Edilig.

Hayward, S. (1993), *French National Cinema*, London and New York, Routledge.

Irigaray, L. (1985), *Speculum of the Other Woman*, Ithaca, New York, Cornell University Press.

Klinger, B. (1988), In retrospect: film studies today, New Haven, CT, *Yale Journal of Criticism*, 2:1, 129–51.

Mulvey, L. (1975), Visual pleasure and narrative cinema, originally published in *Screen*, Autumn 1975, reprinted in C. Penley (ed.), *Feminism and Film Theory*, London and New York, Routledge, 1988.

Norienko, S. (1991), Philippe Djian: the character of the writer and the writer as character, Chalfont St Giles, Bucks, *French Cultural Studies*, 2:2:5, 181–97.

Penley, C. (1982), Pornography, eroticism, originally published in *Camera Obscura*, Autumn 1982, reprinted in R. Bellour and M. Lea Bandy (eds), *Jean-Luc Godard: Son + Image 1974–1991*, New York, the Museum of Modern Art, New York, 1992.

Place, J. (1980), Women in film noir, in E. A. Kaplan (ed.), *Women in film noir*, London, BFI.

Prédal, R. (1991), *Le Cinéma français depuis 1945*, Paris, Nathan.

Rohmer, E. (1980), *Six Moral Tales*, Lorrimer, Francombe.

Root, J. (1985), Céline and Julie, Susan and Susan, London, *Monthly Film Bulletin*, September 1985, 45.

Sadoul, G. (1990), *Dictionnaire des films*, revised and expanded by E. Breton, Paris, Microcosme/Seuil.

Segal, N. (1988), *Narcissus and Echo: Women in the French récit*, Manchester, Manchester University Press.

Stacey, J. (1987), Desperately seeking difference, Glasgow, *Screen*, 28:1, 48–61.

Stacey, J. (1994), *Star Gazing: Hollywood Cinema and Female Spectatorship*, London and New York, Routledge.

Strauss, F. (1994), Cyril Collard dans la nuit, Paris, *Cahiers du cinéma*, 476, 20.

Theweleit, K. (1987), *Male Fantasies, I: Women, Floods, Bodies, History*, Cambridge, Polity Press.

Williams, L. (1990), *Hard Core: Power, Pleasure and the 'Frenzy of the Visible'*, London, Pandora.

Williams, L. (1991), Film bodies: gender, genre, and excess, Berkeley, California, *Film Quarterly*, 44:4, 2–13.

Women film-makers in France   4

Feminism and film in France

Although film-making remains male-dominated in France as else-where, 'more women have taken an active part in French cinema than in any other national film industry' (Kuhn and Radstone 1990: 163). France claims not only the first woman film director – Alice Guy, whose career began in 1900 – but also the first feminist film-maker, Germaine Dulac, a pioneer of 'impressionist' cinema or 'the first avant-garde' in the 1920s (see chapter 1). Dulac, however, was the exception, and women were generally on the other side of the camera in classical French cinema. In the immediate postwar years, women – now granted the vote – were largely restricted to filming documentaries and shorts, although Jacqueline Audry specialised in literary adaptations during the forties and fifties, and Agnès Varda initiated the *nouvelle vague* with *La Pointe courte* in 1954 (see chapter 1). The year 1968 was a watershed for French feminism and consequently for women making films in France: 'The Events of May 1968 (see chapter 2) are usually considered to have provided the impetus for the development of the women's movement, [...] the creation of women's organisations and an upsurge in women's publications' (Forbes 1992: 77). Subsequently, in 1972, the French women's movement – the MLF – was launched, and in 1974 a women's film festival (in later years held at Créteil) was established. Many first features were made by women in this climate, such as Yannick Bellon's *Quelque part, quelqu'un* (1972) and Coline Serreau's *Mais qu'est-ce qu'elles veulent?* (1976), as well as militant documentaries on feminist issues, the most celebrated of which is Marielle Issartel and Charles Belmont's film on abortion rights, *Histoires d'A* (1973). But while the rise of feminism was reflected positively in Agnès Varda's *L'Une chante, l'autre pas* (1977), the response to the women's movement from male directors varied from a lucid account of male fears in Jean Eustache's *La Maman et la putain* (1973) to hysterical fantasies about the war of the sexes in Bertrand Blier's *Calmos* and Louis Malle's *Black Moon* (both 1976), and about lesbian vampires in Jean Rollin's sex/horror cycle of the early seventies (Weiss 1992: 85–90).

Although the 1970s generation of women directors included feminist themes in their work – the reversal of gender roles in Serreau's *Pourquoi pas!*, a denunciation of rape in Bellon's *L'Amour violé* (both 1977), a portrayal of lesbian desire in Diane Kurys' *Coup de foudre* (1983) – they tended to move towards less politicised, more popular genres in the 1980s. This move led to the comedy for Serreau, the thriller for Bellon and the heterosexual romance for Kurys (see below). By 1987 the Belgian film-maker Chantal Akerman was declaring that the idea of women's cinema was 'outdated'. The principal reason for this was that there was no longer any ideological difference in France between cinema made by men and by women, as 'feminism as a debate has vanished from the French cultural scene since the early 80s' (Vincendeau 1987: 4). Unlike the United States or Britain, France has not generated much feminist film theory, and has never shared in Anglophone feminist concerns with apparatus theory, the positing of a 'male' gaze and a 'female' object – a tendency which is in fact now being challenged by post-feminist critics such as Linda Williams and Carol Clover (Williams 1994). Several key female directors, including the most successful woman film-maker in France in the 1980s, Coline Serreau, have distanced themselves from feminism and questioned the significance of their gender in determining their work: 'Serreau: "*je ne suis pas une femme qui fait du cinéma*" [I am not a woman who makes films]; Diane Kurys: "*ça m'exaspère qu'on parle de films de femmes*" [it exasperates me that people should talk about women's films]; Issermann: "we resist any collective image or any attempt to make us into a school"' (Hayward 1993: 258). These women embrace a sense of diversity and individualism born not of feminism but of the *auteur* tradition in French cinema, 'a romantic tradition of humanist individualism which constitutes the bedrock of French critical approaches to film' (Vincendeau 1987: 7).

Avant-garde *auteurs:* Marguerite Duras and Agnès Varda

Two of the principal *auteurs* (see chapter 1) in French film since the 1960s, women whose idiosyncratic styles epitomise avant-garde *auteur* cinema, are Marguerite Duras and Agnès Varda.

India Song and 'the vanity of cinema'

For Marguerite Duras, literature and cinema are inseparable. The *auteurist* conception of film as a form of writing is taken to an extreme in her career – which spans thirty years and features novels, plays, and over a dozen films – and in her statements on cinema: each of her films is 'un livre sur de la pellicule' [a book recorded on film], while film-makers are described as writers whose

9   Delphine Seyrig (centre) in *India Song*

work is read and reread by the public (Duras 1989: 62). The two fields inform each other most dynamically in what has been termed her 'Indian cycle' of three novels – *Le Ravissement de Lol V. Stein*, *Le Vice-Consul*, *L'Amour* – and three films – *La Femme du Gange* (1974), *India Song* (1975), *Son Nom de Venise dans Calcutta désert* (1976) – which offer variations on a basic narrative and a single group of characters. In all of her films, Duras lays unusual emphasis on the function of sound, above all as an expression of women's experience: hence the 'resistant' silence in *Nathalie Granger* (1972) and the productive power of the woman's voice (her own) in the 1977 film *Le Camion* (Forbes 1992: 99–101). The general austerity of her work, which is almost devoid of the visual pleasures traditionally offered by cinema, has led the French feminist critic Françoise Audé to argue that 'if Marguerite Duras' characters are too intent on being engulfed in "submissiveness" for feminists to adopt them wholeheartedly ... they painfully endorse the destitution which is at the heart of the feminist protest' (Kuhn and Radstone 1990: 128).

India Song is set in Calcutta in the 1930s. It concerns the experiences of Anne-Marie Stretter (Delphine Seyrig), the wife of the French ambassador to India, principally in relation to three other characters: her lover Michael Richardson (Mathieu Carrière), the disgraced Vice-Consul (Michel Lonsdale) who is obsessed with her, and an unseen beggarwoman whose life in some ways runs parallel to her own. The film has a clear tripartite structure, consisting of a half-hour prologue, a central section of one hour, and a twenty-three minute epilogue. Both the prologue and the epilogue are obliquely narrated by anonymous voices which discuss the characters and the settings: in the former evoking the heat, leprosy and death associated with Calcutta, in the latter the historical events of 1937 as the characters gather at a hotel prior to Anne-Marie's suicide. Duras, whose voice is one of those narrating the film, has called them 'the authors ... the motors of the story' (Lyon 1988: 266). They are absent only from the central section, the reception given by Anne-Marie, and even here, the principle that all voices in the film are off-screen is maintained. The guests' dialogue is heard, but when they appear on screen, they are never seen to speak, so that their words, 'spoken by unmoving lips, unsettle the distinction between on-screen and off-screen' (Ropars-Wuilleumier 1980: 252).

As this summary indicates, Duras's textual conception of cinema here results in an unusual privileging of sound (the voices, the spoken word) over image. There is moreover a fundamental and sustained disjuncture between sound and image tracks. The two do not illustrate each other, but are autonomous, allowing Duras to use the same sound-track with a completely new image track for her subsequent film, *Son Nom de Venise dans Calcutta désert* (1976), where the Indian heat evoked by the voices contrasts with shots of wintry landscapes. Duras has even suggested that the two films should be seen one after the other, so that one could witness in *Son Nom de Venise* the destruction of *India Song* (Duras 1989: 64). The annihilation of visual pleasure in *India Song* – Duras was attempting to film 'the vanity of cinema' (Duras 1989: 65) – is achieved through the reduction of camera movement to a minimum, and the reliance on fixed tableaux which can last for minutes at a time. While most films comprise hundreds of shots, *India Song* has seventy-four in all, including repeated images such as the close-up of Anne-Marie's breast. The deathly stillness of these images, and their repetition, reinforces the thematic and structural importance of death in the film: the narrative returns compulsively to Anne-Marie's suicide, spoken of by the voices at the beginning and the end of the film, symbolised in the image of her photograph and possessions, and prefigured by the disturbing off-screen cries of the beggarwoman and of the Vice-Consul. The association between Anne-Marie and the beggarwoman is reaffirmed in the film's conclusion. Both, the voices in the prologue reveal, left Savannakhet in their teens to travel eastwards to Calcutta. After Anne-Marie leaves the frame (the implication is that she drowns herself) in the closing sequence, a slow pan across a map of Asia retraces the journeys of the two women from west to east, ending on Savannakhet: 'The trajectories of Anne-Marie Stretter and the beggarwoman, told in the present tense by the voices at the beginning of the film, are then retraced in reverse as history at its end' (Lyon 1988: 268). In the same way, conjured up by the anonymous voices in the prologue before she appeared on the screen, Anne-Marie now makes the reverse journey, leaving the on-screen space occupied by the living to enter the off-screen space where her death has long been evoked by the voices which control her story.

Tracking towards death: *Sans Toit ni loi*

Agnès Varda has declared: 'I make *auteur* films ... I am always very precisely implicated in my films, not out of narcissism, but out of honesty' (Kuhn and Radstone 1990: 411). Like Duras, she speaks of her work in literary terms, calling it *cinécriture*, a writing of films in which editing, camera angles, and the rhythm of the shoot are equated with the choice of words, sentences and chapters in the work of a writer (Murat 1994: 35). She also shares with Duras a concern for death as a central theme. Varda inaugurated the *nouvelle vague* with *La Pointe courte* in 1954 (see chapter 1), and cemented her reputation with *Cléo de 5 à 7* (1961). But the commercial failure of *Les Créatures* (1966) resulted in a ten-year gap before she made another feature film in France. She continued to work in the documentary field, however, and has combined fiction and documentary throughout her career. An avowed feminist, Varda's work reflects upon the women's movement, at times obliquely but nowhere more explicitly than in the feminist buddy movie *L'Une chante, l'autre pas* (1977). Consistently undervalued by American critics and feminists (Hayward 1987: 285), Varda was attacked in the American media for making a lyrically optimistic film about feminism: Pauline Kael found that in *L'Une chante, l'autre pas* 'Varda brings a Disney touch to women's liberation' (Heck-Rabi 1984: 349). Like her colleagues from the *nouvelle vague* – Jean-Luc Godard, Claude Chabrol and Eric Rohmer – Varda enjoyed a resurgence in the 1980s, although she continued to suffer more problems than her male counterparts in financing her films. *Sans Toit ni loi* (1985), her major critical and popular success of the decade, was initially refused the governmental funding known as the *avance sur recettes* (see chapter 7), before being granted direct aid from the Ministry of Culture. When released, the film was greeted with critical acclaim as a rejuvenation of *auteur* cinema, which had been perceived as flagging in the mid-eighties (Varda 1994: 271).

Varda's own voice introduces the episodic narrative of *Sans Toit ni loi*. Over the image of a woman's corpse found in a ditch in the middle of winter, she remarks: 'She had died a natural death without leaving a trace. [...] But people she had met recently remembered her. Those witnesses helped me tell the last weeks of her last winter.' But during the course of the film this woman proves to be an enigma. Mona (Sandrine Bonnaire) is a hitch-hiker who has been passing through the Midi region. In a complex series of flashbacks, the film records her journey, largely through the eyes of eighteen people she meets on the way. As these characters reflect on what they thought of Mona, they reveal as much about themselves – they come from various walks of life, and according to Varda represent 'la France profonde' (Varda 1994: 269) – as they do about the taciturn hitcher. Although there are long sequences concerning Mona's relations with Madame Landier (Macha Méril), a biologist, and Assoun (Yahiaoui Assouna), a Tunisian vineyard worker, she remains an enigmatic figure, resistant to easy interpretation. At the end of the film, exhausted and starving, she is caught up in an aggressive folk ritual before falling, dazed, into the ditch where she dies.

The synthesis of realism and mythical symbolism which characterises Varda's work is evident throughout *Sans Toit ni loi*. The primary myth alluded to is that of the goddess of love, Venus/Aphrodite, when Varda's voice-over – 'I know little about her myself, but it seems to me she came from the sea' – introduces an image of Mona emerging from a swim in the Mediterranean. The pictorial reference here is to Botticelli's painting of *The Birth of Venus*, an icon of classical female beauty. But, ironically, we soon learn that Mona is 'the opposite of the female [...] icon: she is dirty, unkempt, overweight, repulsive in her personal habits and her moral practices' (Forbes 1992: 93). The Venus/Aphrodite myth ties in with the folk ritual at the close of the film, in which Mona is attacked and daubed with wine dregs, since in legend 'the goddess [...] yields to Dionysus the god of the vine' (Hayward 1987: 290). Thus a mythical narrative underlies Varda's realistic depiction of the Midi region in winter, and her documentary-style observation of life on the road. The other major mythical structure underlying *Sans Toit ni loi* is that of the road movie. The narrative traces Mona's journey from her emergence out of the waves until her death. But Varda subverts the genre, since the road movie is a traditionally male form, and a variant on the buddy movie – as in Bertrand Blier's 1974 film *Les Valseuses* (see chapter 3) – while Mona is a woman, and alone. Viewed from the outside by those she meets, Mona makes no self-discovery, undergoes no rites of passage, and is unfathomable in terms of psychology. Even the temporary couple of Mona and David (Patrick Lepczynski) subverts generic expectations. Whereas the lovers on the run in Arthur Penn's *Bonnie and Clyde* (1967) or Terence Malick's *Badlands* (1973) are self-mythicising, Mona and David are self-effacing: when Mona writes their names in the dust David rubs them out, wanting to leave 'no trace' of their passage. Of course *Sans Toit ni loi* does rely heavily on the imagery of the road movie, and principally on the tracking shot. There are in fact fourteen tracking shots in *Sans Toit ni loi*, most of them accompanied by Joanna Bruzdowicz's bleak string music. But contrary to convention, 'in all these tracking shots [Mona] and the camera [...] move from right to left', so that her journey 'is filmed going backwards down the road' while providing a recurrent visual 'metaphor for both the flashback, and, even more significantly, death' (Hayward 1987: 290). The contrast with the left-to-right tracking shot – which usually denotes progression from the past to the future – is emphasised by the relation between the beginning of *Sans Toit ni loi* and the ending of François Truffaut's *Les 400 Coups* (1959). In that film, the young protagonist Antoine Doinel (Jean-

Pierre Léaud) escapes from a detention centre and, in a famous and lengthy left-to-right tracking shot, runs to the sea. The direction of the movement in this sequence signals that Antoine is embarking on a journey of self-discovery, and that further adventures await him (the story is continued in four more films about the same character, the 'Doinel cycle' (see chapter 3)). The first tracking shot in *Sans Toit ni loi* reverses this pattern, with Mona emerging from the sea and heading right to left towards no other destination than her own death (which has already been shown in the opening sequence of the film). Varda thus inverts the inherent optimism of the road-movie form, and of Truffaut's *nouvelle vague* vivacity.

Whereas the image and sound tracks in Marguerite Duras's films tend to be disparate (see above), in much of Varda's work sound and image are directly illustrative of each other. In particular, Varda's use of authorial voice-over tends to be 'pleonastic' (Forbes 1992: 95); in other words, what she says and what is shown on the screen are one and the same. Hence in *Jane B. par Agnès V.* (1987), a complex portrait of the singer and actress Jane Birkin, bizarre images are conjured up and authorised by Varda's voice-over. Her remark to Birkin 'I can see you as Ariadne' is immediately followed by a shot of the actress in classical costume in a labyrinth with a ball of thread. This self-consciousness, attacked in the *Cahiers du cinéma* review of the film (Philippon 1988), also entails a slow tracking shot from a cockerel to a donkey to illustrate Varda's use in voice-over of the idiomatic expression 'passer du coq-à-l'âne' [to jump from one subject to another]. *Jane B. par Agnès V.* is also notable for the filming of Birkin in several compositions derived from classical paintings, including one slow pan across her naked body which 'produces the woman's body as landscape, that field across which play multiple possible reflections about women's representation' (Flitterman-Lewis 1993: 315). Similarly in *Jacquot de Nantes* (1991), a portrait of her dying husband the film-maker Jacques Demy, Varda employs slow pans across the human body, here in extreme close-ups of his face, hands, hair, and eyes, 'comme s'il était un énorme paysage et qu'on s'y promène' [as if he were a huge landscape one was walking across] (Varda 1994: 279).

Popular cinema: Diane Kurys and Coline Serreau

Less radical, both ideologically and aesthetically, than Duras or Varda, Diane Kurys and Coline Serreau took women's film-making into the popular mainstream during the mid-1980s. In part because of their commercial success, both directors have been denied by critics the high cultural status of the *auteur*, while their declarations that they are merely film-makers who happen to be women has seen them often neglected by feminist criticism. Yet Kurys and Serreau have managed to explore personal concerns with issues of gender and sexuality within popular genres, while at the same time addressing millions of spectators.

Lesbian desire in *Coup de foudre*

Perhaps even more so than gay film (see chapter 3), lesbian film-making has occupied the margins of French cinema, from Germaine Dulac's avant-garde critique of marriage in *La Souriante Madame Beudet* (1923) onwards. The portrayal of lesbian desire did at times enter mainstream classical cinema in the form of the 'community of women' genre, exemplified by Jacques Deval's *Club de femmes* (1936) and Jacqueline Audry's *Olivia* (1951). Although made by a male director, the former was one of the first films to treat lesbianism in what the American lesbian journal *Vice Versa* called 'a sane, intelligent manner, rather than furnishing the usual subject for harmful propaganda or mere sensationalism' (Weiss 1992: 13). With the rise of the women's movement in the early 1970s, male-authored representations of lesbianism included the pathologising fantasies of Jean Rollin's vampire films, but this period also saw lesbian directors such as the Belgian Chantal Akerman beginning their careers. The major Francophone lesbian film-maker currently working, Akerman remains, for all the commercial success of *Golden Eighties* (1987), outside the mainstream. None the less many of the female *auteurs* who, since the 1970s have become increasingly active in French cinema, 'although speaking from a heterosexual (or unclear) position, provide very affirmative images of lesbianism, often seen as an enviable alternative to relations between the sexes' (Dyer 1990: 272). One of the most prominent and popular examples of this is Diane Kurys's *Coup de foudre* (1983).

Coup de foudre has clear *auteurist* origins, based as it is on Kurys's account – co-authored with Olivier Cohen – of her mother's life. The narrative centres on the friendship – which implicitly develops into a lesbian relationship – between Lena (Isabelle Huppert) and Madeleine (Miou-Miou). After a prologue set during the Occupation, the action switches to Lyon in 1952, where the two meet for the first time. The intensity of this meeting, evoked in a silent shot/reverse-shot of the faces of the two women, immediately suggests an emotional undercurrent which will run counter to the rather dull married lives that Lena and Madeleine have at this point. That undercurrent is, however, buried very deep, while Kurys's nostalgic attention to fifties costume and popular music, and above all her avoidance of the strident excesses of melodrama, ensure that *Coup de foudre* is for the most part merely a tasteful period piece. As Andréa Weiss has commented, 'the film's formal qualities – so dependent are they on the codes of art cinema – restrain the women's relationship as the narrative seeks to extend it', although as a consequence 'the shroud of ambiguity surrounding the exact nature of the women's relationship leaves space for the lesbian imagination' (Weiss 1992: 125). Once Madeleine has left her husband and moved to Paris to await Lena, the narrative pace quickens, with Lena first visiting her friend secretly and then attempting to secure the financial independence needed to join her by setting up a boutique. Fearing that she has been abandoned by

Lena, Madeleine has a breakdown, and it is in the emotional reunion of the two friends that the 'excessive' code of melodrama – signalled by tears (Williams 1991) – is first mobilised by Kurys. Although the tone becomes more measured again once Lena and Madeleine begin living together, their escape from Lena's jealous husband Michel is again signalled by tears, this time those of Michel himself, who finally accepts the situation with an appropriate 'feminine' response (weeping) rather than his previous inappropriate macho violence (destroying Lena's shop). As it has done throughout, however, the period music – here Perry Como – maintains a wistful and nostalgic note which characterises the film as a whole, and keeps the excesses of melodrama at arm's length, just as the image track assiduously avoids any direct representation of lesbian desire.

Kurys's subsequent film, *Un Homme amoureux* (1987), was a lush heterosexual romance filmed at Rome's Cinecittà studios with an international cast (Peter Coyote, Greta Scacchi, Claudia Cardinale, Jamie Lee Curtis and Vincent Lindon). The result is a largely predictable array of stereotypes, including the angst-ridden film star (Coyote) and the nagging wife (Curtis). *Un Homme amoureux* is mediated, like *Coup de foudre* and *Après l'Amour* (1992), by a female *auteur* figure, in this case Jane (Scacchi). Whereas the mother–daughter relationship underpinning *Coup de foudre* is only suggested in the final dedication, in *Un Homme amoureux* it is Jane's mother (Cardinale) who bestows on her daughter the narrative powers which result, in the closing scene, in her writing the story we have just watched as one long flashback. This framing device, although a cinematic staple, is usually associated with a male narrator (see chapter 3), and to that extent, its function in *Un Homme amoureux* is emblematic of Kurys's cinema in general: stylistically orthodox, but from a woman's point of view.

Maternal men in *Trois Hommes et un couffin*

Coline Serreau's *Trois Hommes et un couffin* (1985) is one of the greatest domestic box-office hits of recent French cinema. Over ten million people saw the film in the year of release, rising to twelve and a half million within three years, making it by far the most popular French film of the 1980s, and the most successful home product since Gérard Oury's *La Grande Vadrouille* in 1966 (Prédal 1991: 403–4). Moreover, the budget – recouped ten times over – was only 9.7 million francs, and the three leads – Roland Giraud, Michel Boujenah and André Dussolier – relatively unknown (Prédal 1991: 424). Serreau was subsequently asked to direct the Hollywood remake but pulled out, leaving Leonard Nimoy to direct *Three Men and a Baby* in 1989. In Serreau's film, three bachelor buddies – Pierre (Giraud), Michel (Boujenah) and Jacques (Dussolier) – live together in Paris. While Jacques is out of the country – he works as an airline pilot – Sylvia, an ex-girlfriend, sends him baby Marie to look after. Although Jacques is Marie's father, he is unaware of her existence. It therefore falls upon Pierre and Michel to act as surrogate fathers and, more pertinently, surrogate mothers too. Their attempts to care for Marie are complicated by a sub-plot involving stolen drugs which, like the baby, are thrust upon them. Jacques's arrival is followed by Sylvia's reclaiming of Marie but she proves a less able mother than the three men, and the baby is returned to Jacques, Pierre and Michel.

Serreau had considered the cultural difficulties fatherhood raised for men ten years previously in her first film script, *On s'est trompé d'amour*, which she resumed in feminist terminology as follows: 'On écrase les hommes sous leur propre phallus et on leur inculque qu'il est au-dessous de leur dignité de partager avec leurs femmes les préparatifs de la venue du bébé' [Men are crushed under their own phallus, and taught that it is beneath their dignity to share with their wives in preparing for a new baby] (Trémois 1993: 21). But by contrasting the caring male trio of *Trois Hommes et un couffin* with female examples of 'bad' motherhood, she gave rise to accusations from American feminist critics that the film was misogynistic, and subverted French feminist theory's emphasis on the importance of biological motherhood (Durham 1992). *Trois Hommes et un couffin* may not be a feminist film, but it does present – like much of Serreau's work – an optimistic response to a genuine social question (the role of men in bringing up children). The film also presents a fairly realistic picture of domestic routine – via the shots of nappy-changing, washing feeding bottles, and so on – which recalls the importance of representations of domesticity in feminist cinema, most famously in Chantal Akerman's real-time study of a house-wife's existence, *Jeanne Dielman, 23 Quai du Commerce, 1080, Bruxelles* (1976). Not only do Pierre, Michel and (eventually) Jacques thus inhabit a 'female' domestic space, and carry out 'female' domestic chores, they are feminised by their love for baby Marie which, as François Audé has observed, is maternal rather than paternal (Audé 1985: 70). This is most evident when Marie is temporarily taken away by Sylvia: in a drunken maternal fantasy, Jacques puts a cushion up his jumper, claiming that he is pregnant, and bemoans the sterility of men compared to the life-giving creativity of women. The question of gender roles also informs Serreau's manipulation of genre in the film, with the two plots deriving from genres traditionally encoded in gender terms: the drugs plot belongs to the 'male' thriller genre, the baby plot to 'female' domestic realism. The confusion between the two packages – the baby and the heroin – 'introduces narrative rivalry between a male story of [...] opposition to law and order, and a female plot of [...] compliance with societal norms and values' (Durham 1992: 775). The two plots are integrated when the baby herself (her nappy) is used by Pierre and Michel as a hiding-place for the drugs, and in a parody of the macho thriller genre, the archetypal set-piece in which bags containing drugs are switched involves not two brief-cases (serious, 'male', business-like), but two nappies. As in

10   Michel Boujenah and Roland Giraud in *Trois Hommes et un couffin*

Serreau's subsequent films, *Romuald et Juliette* (1989) and *La Crise* (1992), the apparently banal narrative of *Trois Hommes et un couffin* thus mobilises an examination of conventional roles and contemporary social problems. If in the latter it is gender typing which is addressed, in *Romuald et Juliette* it is racism and class snobbery, and in *La Crise* a crisis of masculinity in the face of divorce, unemployment and loneliness, while all three films are characterised by Serreau's use of parallelism in plotting and montage, and of frenzied, repetitious dialogue.

Late 1980s and early 1990s *auteurs:* Claire Devers, Claire Denis, Martine Dugowson

While Kurys and Serreau were prolific and popular throughout the 1980s, other female directors found it harder to attract funding. Catherine Breillat – co-writer of *Police* (1985) with Maurice Pialat (see chapter 5) – did not follow up her first film, *Tapage nocturne* (1979), for nearly ten years until *36 Fillette* was released in 1988. Caroline Roboh, whose *Clémentine Tango* (1982) was an early example of the *cinéma du look* style (see chapter 6), made no more films that decade. More successful was Aline Issermann, whose début film *Le Destin de Juliette* was well received in 1982, and whose subsequent work includes *L'Amant magnifique* (1986) and *L'Ombre du doute* (1992). The late eighties were to prove more fruitful for women film-makers, and 1986 – the year that Serreau's *Trois Hommes et un couffin* won Césars for best film and best screenplay – proved to be the watershed for a new generation. For the first time, several feature films by women were entered in the 'Perspectives du cinéma français' section at the Cannes film festival. Among the entries, and winner of the Caméra d'or award, was *Noir et blanc* (1986), the début film by Claire Devers. (Her second film, *Chimère* (1989), was an official selection for Cannes, but did not meet with the same critical acclaim.)

Noir et blanc: listening in on sado-masochism

Loosely based on a Tennessee Williams short story, and extended from her graduation film for IDHEC, the national film school, Devers's *Noir et blanc* is a compelling low-budget drama about the sexual and power relations between two men, a white accountant and a black masseur. Shot in monochrome in gloomy urban settings and with a disturbing sound-track, the film at times recalls *Eraserhead* (1976) by David Lynch, also a striking first feature which grew out of a film-school project. Antoine (Francis Frappat) is employed by a gym owner to go over his books, and meets Dominique (Jacques Martial), a masseur. What begins as a massage ends up as an increasingly violent sado-masochistic relationship, until Dominique breaks Antoine's arm and the gym owner throws them both out. Dominique sneaks Antoine out of hospital and the two spend the night in a hotel, before going to a deserted factory where Dominique ultimately kills Antoine.

Although *Noir et blanc* could be seen as a particularly dark satire on the 'body beautiful' exercise vogue of the 1980s, it functions above all as an exploration of male sexuality and of sado-masochism, 'voyeuristically presented from the female point of view' (Hayward 1993: 259). At times, the spectator is at least partially implicated in Dominique's point of view as he looks at Antoine, the camera placed just behind his shoulder. Thus in an early confrontation between the two, the camera focuses on Antoine uneasily trying out the new weights machine under the gaze of Dominique, who occupies the foreground of the frame and remains out of focus. This kind of composition, stressing Antoine's vulnerability and discomfort in the presence of Dominique, who remains blurred, silent and inscrutable, is repeated when the masseur looks for Antoine in the hospital. And a facial close-up of Antoine during this sequence shows Dominique's shadow looming across him. But if this framing of Dominique construes him as a sadist and a physical threat to Antoine (also playing upon implicit racial fears), a gradual shift occurs in which Dominique is characterised as a lover and protector rather than a torturer. After the tense hospital sequence, Dominique collects Antoine's clothes and walks through the dark streets in the snow to the rare sound-track accompaniment of choral music. When the two are together in the hotel, it is not Dominique's sadism but Antoine's masochism which is evoked. As Dominique asks 'What do you want from me?' and Antoine replies 'Hit me with all your strength', the composition of their first confrontation is reversed, the masseur facing the camera in clear focus, while the accountant – now a troubling figure

11　　　　　Francis Frappat and Jacques Martial in *Noir et blanc*

because he is articulating a taboo desire – assumes the blurred position in the foreground. The subsequent scene is that of Antoine's death.

But throughout *Noir et blanc* the sound-track actually carries more meaning than the image track. In other words, the violence that is central to the film (the breaking of Antoine's limbs, and his eventual killing) is not seen so much as heard. In visual terms, brutality and desire is either expressed obliquely with Antoine's face shot in close-up (a conventional index in cinema of female sexual pleasure), or elided, and implied later by the discovery of blood stains on the floor. Even when the gym owner, alerted by a scream, discovers Dominique roughing up Antoine, the two men are at first screened behind a curtain before it is pulled aside to reveal one strangling the other. The physicality of the sado-masochistic scenes is conveyed primarily by the loud noises of slapping and hard breathing, to which is soon added the sound of Antoine's cries. Speech is not favoured as a vehicle for the expression of desire except in the scene which precedes Antoine's death. Devers's privileging of sound over image is most evident in two late scenes: the first takes place in the hotel, with the noises of gasping and beating accompanied by banal shots of the desk, the stairs, the corridors. The second example is the final sequence, in which Dominique kills Antoine. Both the setting – a deserted factory which is never seen from the outside, and thus never situated visually within the dramatic space of the film – and the rumbling of machinery on the sound-track recall the *mise en scène* of *Eraserhead*. Once Dominique has chained Antoine and started the machine, Devers cuts to an image of turning cogs as Antoine begins to scream. The cessation of the screaming signals his death, while the sound of the machinery continues over the closing credits. The culmination of sado-masochistic desire in the film is thus not a visual horror, as has been suggested – Susan Hayward talks of the 'graphicness' of the scene, 'literally a ripping to pieces' during which one is devastated but 'keeps on watching' (Hayward 1993: 259) – but more troublingly an aural one, in which the spectator's own imagination is left to provide the images.

Chocolat and women's experience of the colonies

Whereas during the 1970s, films set in the French colonies tended to dwell on the military or the political (see chapter 2), it was only in the 1980s that 'the personal experience or semi-autobiographical recollection of an ex-colonial' became a common theme (Hayward 1993: 252). Many of these 'ex-colonial' films have been made by women, among them Claire Denis's *Chocolat* (1988) set in Senegal, Marie-France Pisier's *Le Bal du gouverneur* (1990) set in Nouméa, and Brigitte Rouan's *Outremer* (1990) set in Algeria. A singular precursor of these films is Marguerite Duras's oblique treatment of the female colonial experience in *India Song* (1975) (see above). Accused at the time of belonging to the wave of nostalgia for the thirties and forties known as *la mode rétro*, (see chapter 2), *India Song* transcended the empty stylisation of colonial history by evoking leprosy, madness, passion and death (Bonitzer 1975). Euzhan Palcy's altogether more conventional and popular representation of Martinique in 1930, *Rue Cases Nègres* (1983), considers the experience of the African work force rather than the European colonisers. What seems to characterise women's representations of colonialism is a critical perspective, but on a personal or domestic rather than a historical or epic scale. Frédéric Strauss has rather schematically contrasted the 'soft' films by Denis, Pisier and Rouan with 'hard' military accounts of colonialism by male directors such as Pierre Schoendoerffer, Régis Warnier and Jean-Claude Brisseau (Strauss 1990: 30). Certainly the marginal position of women in the colonies symbolises their marginality in society as a whole. Claire Denis has said of colonial wives and daughters that they represented France, but lived an empty and futile existence while their husbands and fathers lived a romanticised adventure closer to the world of Tintin (Strauss 1990: 32).

Claire Denis spent her early childhood in Senegal, and on her return as an adult found herself accused of being a mere tourist (Strauss 1990: 31). The question of identity raised by that experience is dramatised in the frame narrative of *Chocolat*, which presents a white adult narrator (Mireille Perrier), rather predictably called France, whose Senegalese childhood forms, in one long flashback, the main body of the film. As France drives (left to right) through the African landscape, the past is suddenly evoked in a tracking shot which reverses her direction, and leads us (right to left) into the past. France's point of view is thus no longer that of a French tourist but of a young girl who is part of colonial West

Africa. The narrative now centres on France's parents (Giula Boschi and François Cluzet), and in particular on her mother's unfulfilled desire for the black houseboy, Protée. The thematics of female desire, insufferable heat, and stifling convention are reminiscent of Duras's *India Song*, but *Chocolat* is far more conventional in form, and the constraints of the female colonial experience are tempered with an evident nostalgia for the period, the setting, and for child-hood. Nevertheless this impression is qualified in the epilogue, in which the adult France is told by a black American soldier that he has both an Afrocentric past and a future, while she, as an ex-colo-nial, has neither. Denis has stated that she was determined not to restrict herself to the story of her childhood, but intended in this conclusion to give a glimpse of Africa after colonisation (Strauss 1990: 31). Her two subsequent films, the quasi-documentary *S'en fout la mort* (1990) and the violent thriller *J'ai pas sommeil* (1994), continue this interest in contemporary society.

Mina Tannenbaum: self-conscious melodrama

The early 1990s saw a wave of impressive début films by women directors, which was represented in foreign distribution – at the 1994 Sarasota French Film Festival in Florida, 'seven of the twenty new features were directed by women' (Corliss 1994: 97) – as well as in the domestic market: the magazine *Télérama* claimed in late 1994 that half of the thirty young *auteurs* working in French cinema were women (Trémois 1995: 18). Moreover, the number of popular female-authored productions was seen as ending the his-torical marginalisation of women film-makers: 'Fini, le temps des "films de femmes!"' [The time of 'women's films' is over!] (Trémois 1995: 18). Among the major successes of 1993/4 were Marion Vernoux's *Personne ne m'aime*, Pascale Ferran's *Petits Arrangements avec les morts* and Tonie Marshall's *Pas très catholique* (all 1994), and Martine Dugowson's *Mina Tannenbaum* (1993).

Dugowson had previously worked as a scriptwriter on a televi-sion sitcom as well as making short films. *Mina Tannenbaum*, her first feature, has been categorised as both a Jewish film and a woman's film. Contrary to *Télérama*, Dugowson found that the crit-ical ghettoisation of women's cinema was continuing: 'This year there have been several first features by women in France, but we were all bunched together even though our films were very differ-ent' (Francke 1994). Unlike Vernoux's road movie or Marshall's thriller, Dugowson's offering is a melodrama. The narrative is set in a Jewish district in Montmartre, and follows the friendship between Mina Tannenbaum and Éthel Bénégui from their birth – in the same hospital, on the same day – in 1958 to Mina's suicide in 1991. In between, three episodes, set in 1968, 1974 and 1989, chart their changing attitudes to the world and to each other.

The story is narrated as a long flashback by Mina's cousin, although Mina and Éthel also contribute voice-overs, at times con-tradicting the principal narrator. This flashback narration is typical of the 'male' *film noir* genre (see chapter 5), but here the narrators are all female. Despite the self-deprecating humour of the early episodes which has seen Dugowson compared to Woody Allen, and the brief choreographed and fantasy scenes reminiscent of the Hollywood musical, the major generic influence on *Mina Tannenbaum* is the traditional melodrama or 'weepie': 'For me, the starting-point was those huge emotional canvases of movies such as *A Star is Born or Letter From An Unknown Woman*. [...] I wanted *Mina* to have the same visceral quality that exists in those great Hollywood melodramas' (Franke 1994). The wayward emotional relationship between the two buddies, Mina and Éthel, is reflected in the long, rambling narrative which changes tone frequently between humour and despair. The plot is also characterised by the classic temporal structure of the melodrama, the tendency for things to happen 'too late' (Williams 1991). Thus in the 1974 episode Mina and Éthel, both neurotic about their appearance, refuse to believe that their boyfriends really desire them until the boys move on. Their own friendship is littered with break-ups and reconciliations; the final tragic moment when it is too late to make up is all the more powerful, when it arrives at the film's conclusion, for having been deferred several times over. But as Ginette Vincendeau notes, the emotional development or revelation which characterises the denouement of the conventional melodrama is absent from *Mina Tannenbaum*: 'Whereas the genre leads us to expect both women to grow (as in Kurys' *Diabolo Menthe* or *Coup de foudre*) through their various traumas, Mina's tragic ending is not redeemed and her suicide is truly shocking' (Vincendeau 1994: 50). Éthel – always envious of her friend's talent as an artist, and implicated in her decision to kill herself – is not shown having learned anything from Mina's death, although the film does end with the sound of the two friends' voices as children, and an image of the painting which symbolised their relationship. Yet the self-conscious irony which has tempered the melodrama throughout qualifies even this scene, for the preceding sequence in which Mina's cousin, facing the camera, begins to cry (thus mirroring the anticipated audience reaction to the suicide) creates a sense of ironic distance: as the technicians close down the shoot, she is left alone on a darkened film set. A similar self-consciousness is evident in Dugowson's use of stylistic devices such as irises to close scenes, and bravura camera movements, which distance the spectator from the emotional events portrayed. These techniques are also cinephilic, recalling the work of other directors, and of François Truffaut in particular. Truffaut frequently used irises, while his famous circular tracking shot early in *Jules et Jim* (1962) informs the circling of the camera between the 1968 and 1974 episodes in Dugowson's film. Where Truffaut used Picasso's paintings as a rough chronological index for the setting of each episode in *Jules et Jim*, Dugowson uses French pop icons – Enrico Macias, Dalida, Serge Gainsbourg – to a similar effect throughout *Mina Tannenbaum*. Dalida's performance of the song 'Il venait d'avoir 18 ans' also functions – rather like the painting Mina gives Éthel to cement their friendship – as a melodramatic symbol, as 'their tune'. The song is first heard in the 1974 episode, where it is parodied and mimed by Éthel; in 1991, Mina, dropped by Éthel, watches Dalida perform the song on television before she kills herself. It is not only the memories of Éthel (visualised in a brief flashback) that the song evokes, but its emotive content (a woman of thirty-six loves a man of eighteen) which summons up the tragic 'too late' of the melodrama, immediately confirmed by Mina's suicide.

References

Audé, F. (1985), *Trois Hommes et un couffin*: Hommes d'intérieur, Paris, *Positif*, 297, 70–1.

Bonitzer, P. (1975), D'une Inde l'autre (*India Song*), Paris, *Cahiers du cinéma*, 258/9, 49–51.

Corliss, R. (1994), Toujours les femmes, New York, *Time*, 28 November, 97–8.

Duras, M. (1989), J'ai toujours désespérément filmé ..., Paris, *Cahiers du cinéma*, 426, 62–5.

Durham, C. (1992), Taking the baby out of the basket and/or robbing the cradle: 'remaking' gender and culture in Franco-American film, *The French Review*, 65: 5, 774–784.

Dyer, R. (1990), *Now you See it: Studies on Lesbian and Gay Film*, London and New York, Routledge.

Flitterman-Lewis, S. (1990), *To Desire Differently: Feminism and the French Cinema*, University of Illinois Press, Urbana and Chicago.

Flitterman-Lewis, S. (1993), Magic and wisdom in two portraits by Agnès Varda: *Kung-Fu Master* and *Jane B. by Agnès V.*, Glasgow, *Screen*, 34:4, 302–20.

Forbes, J. (1992), *The Cinema in France After the New Wave*, London, BFI/Macmillan.

Francke, L. (1994), French with tears, London, *The Guardian: G2*, 6 October, 8.

Hayward, S. (1987), Beyond the gaze and into *femme-filmécriture*: Agnès Varda's *Sans Toit ni loi*, in S. Hayward and G. Vincendeau (eds), *French Film: Texts and Contexts*, London and New York, Routledge, 285–96.

Hayward, S. (1993), *French National Cinema*, London and New York, Routledge.

Heck-Rabi, L. (1984), *Women Film-makers: A Critical Reception*, Metuchen, NJ, and London, The Scarecrow Press.

Kuhn, A., and Radstone, S. (1990) (eds), *The Women's Companion to International Film*, Berkeley, University of California Press.

Lyon, E. (1988), The cinema of Lol V. Stein, in C. Penley (ed.), *Feminism and Film Theory*, New York, Routledge/BFI, 244–69.

Murat, P. (1994), Le Temps des copains, Paris, *Télérama*, 2305, 34–6.

Philippon, A. (1988), Les Coquetteries d'Agnès, Paris, *Cahiers du cinéma*, 405, 12.

Prédal, R. (1991), *Le Cinéma français depuis 1945*, Paris, Nathan.

Ropars-Wuilleumier, M.-C. (1980), The disembodied voice: *India Song*, New Haven, CT, *Yale French Studies*, 60, 241–68.

Strauss, F. (1990), Féminin colonial, Paris, *Cahiers du cinéma*, 434, 28–33.

Trémois, C.-M. (1993), Vive les crises!, Paris, *Télérama*, 2243, 20–2.

Trémois, C.-M. (1995), Femmes de tête, Paris, *Télérama*, 2346, 18–19.

Varda, A. (1994), *Varda par Agnès*, Paris, Cahiers du cinéma/Ciné-Tamaris.

Vincendeau, G. (1987), Women's cinema, film theory and feminism in France, Glasgow, *Screen*, 28:4, 4–18.

Vincendeau, G. (1994), Mina Tannenbaum, London, *Sight and Sound*, October, 49–50.

Weiss, A. (1992), *Vampires and Violets: Lesbians in the Cinema*, London, Jonathan Cape.

Williams, L. (1991), Film bodies: gender, genre, and excess, Berkeley, California, *Film Quarterly*, 44:4, 2–13.

Williams, L. (1994) (ed.), *Viewing Positions: Ways of Seeing Film*, New Brunswick, Rutgers University Press.

The *polar*

The popularity of the *polar*

The first French thrillers date from the silent era, with Louis Feuillade's popular *Fantomas* and *Judex* series (between 1913 and 1918). Since World War Two, however, the form has often been associated with the American genres of the *film noir* and the gangster film (see below). The end of the war saw an influx of American crime novels published in France as the *série noire*, while a glut of Hollywood thrillers appeared on French screens, influencing the young critics of *Cahiers du cinéma* who went on to form *la nouvelle vague* (see chapter 1). For this reason the French thriller, also known as the *polar* or *film policier*, has been cited as 'the principal means by which the French cinema's relationship to Hollywood has been articulated' (Forbes 1992: 48). But the *polar* has also functioned in a variety of other ways, particularly in the years after *la nouvelle vague*. By the 1970s, 'the *polar* was naturalised as French' (Forbes 1992: 53), and proved a staple of the national cinema, diverse in format but always in demand. There remained a tradition of adapting American crime novels to the screen, from François Truffaut's *Tirez sur le Pianiste* (1960) to Jean-Jacques Beineix's *La Lune dans le caniveau* (1983). But the *polar* also functioned as a means of commenting on French society, whether it be urban decay in Alain Corneau's *Série Noire* (1979), colonialism in Bertrand Tavernier's *Coup de torchon* (1981), or drug dealing in Maurice Pialat's *Police* (1985) (see below). The popular revolt of May 1968 (see chapter 2) led to a vogue for political thrillers, such as Costa-Gavras's trilogy – Z (1969), *L'Aveu* (1970) and *État de siège* (1973) – starring the left-wing icon Yves Montand. The same period saw Jean-Pierre Melville's apolitical and heavily stylised trilogy with Alain Delon (see below). The breadth of the genre thus contributed to its popularity in the subsequent decade: a quarter of all French films made in 1981 were *polars* (Marsall 1992: 33), and many of those were box-office successes.

At the most commercial end of the market, two kinds of *polar* dominated in the 1970s and 1980s: the action-packed comedy-thriller and the stylised gangster format. These sub-genres were incarnated by the leading stars of the time, Jean-Paul Belmondo and Alain Delon respectively, so that Melville could declare, 'There are only two formats here: Delon and Belmondo' (Forbes 1992: 53-4). Co-stars in 1970 for Jacques Deray's *Borsalino* (see below), the two embodied the popular thriller in films by Deray, Henri Verneuil and Gérard Oury. Belmondo's action movies in particular attracted a large audience: four million spectators watched him in Georges Lautner's *Le Professionnel* (1981), five million in Oury's *L'As des as* (1982), and four and a half million in Deray's *Le Marginal* (1983). In the subsequent years Claude Zidi scored at the box-office with his cop comedies *Les Ripoux* (1984) and *Ripoux contre ripoux* (1990), each attracting over two million spectators (Prédal 1991: 402). But by the turn of the decade, in terms of domestic film, the *polar* was being out-performed by the *cinéma du look* – a genre none the less often reliant on the thriller for plot and characterisation – and by the heritage film (see chapters 6 and 7).

Voyeurism and the Hitchcockian thriller

In 1957 Eric Rohmer and Claude Chabrol, journalists on *Cahiers du cinéma*, wrote *Hitchcock*, the first serious critical work on this seminal director to be published. The primary importance of Hitchcock to the thriller genre, and indeed to cinema in general, derives from his obsession with voyeurism. As Rohmer and Chabrol noted of *Rear Window* (1954): 'let us merely say that the theme concerns the very essence of cinema, which is *seeing, spectacle*' (Rohmer and Chabrol 1992: 124). By positioning his protagonists as voyeurs, and filming what they see through recurrent point-of-view shots, Hitchcock encourages an identification between the cinema spectator and the voyeur. This is most explicitly the case in *Rear Window*, where a chair-bound photographer, played by James Stewart, is analogous with the spectator in the auditorium. As he watches the suspicious or banal actions carried out in the building across the yard, 'We wait, hoping along with him', and when it becomes apparent that a murder may have been committed, 'the crime is desired' both by the protagonist and 'by us, the spectators' (Rohmer and Chabrol 1992: 125). Rohmer and Chabrol conclude that what the photographer sees are 'the projections of his thoughts – or desires' (Rohmer and Chabrol 1992: 126). This model of the voyeur controlling what he sees – a model which Hitchcock uses to suggest in *Rear Window* the photographer's pleasure in watching his girlfriend in danger of being killed – is subverted in the complex plot twists of Chabrol's *Le Cri du hibou* (1987) and Patrice Leconte's *Monsieur Hire* (1989) (see below). Hitchcock's second major exploration of voyeurism, *Vertigo* (1958), released after the publication of Rohmer and Chabrol's study, was based on a French novel written by Boileau and Narcejac with the director in mind. It proved Hitchcock's most influential work in France, and not least on the film-makers of *la nouvelle vague*. The sequences of detective James Stewart following mysterious woman Kim Novak are echoed in numerous films, including Rohmer's own *Ma Nuit chez Maud* (1969) and *La Femme de l'aviateur* (1981), while the crucial clock-tower murder is reprised by Truffaut in *Une Belle Fille comme moi* (1972). But the French director whose cinematic voyeurism owes the greatest debt to Hitchcock is undoubtedly Claude Chabrol.

Framing the voyeur: *Le Cri du hibou* and *Monsieur Hire*

Of the various film-makers who initiated *la nouvelle vague* (see chapter 1), Chabrol is the one most closely associated with the *polar*. From very early in his career, he has combined a realist depiction of everyday locations with thriller narratives. *Les Bonnes Femmes* (1960), his fourth film and early masterpiece, is permeated with a general air of unease rather than any Hitchcockian suspense. The thriller plot – one of four shop assistants is followed and then murdered – is submerged under the neo-realist observation of Paris, and is shot from the point of view of the victim, not the voyeur. It thus contrasts with the voyeurism of *Rear Window*, *Vertigo* and many of Chabrol's own later films. In part because of the commercial failure of *Les Bonnes Femmes*, for much of the sixties Chabrol had to work on formula thrillers, and his subsequent work is dependent on the Hitchcockian models of voyeurism, tight plotting and suspense, commercial generic elements which were absent from *Les Bonnes Femmes*. The 'Hélène cycle' of the late sixties, featuring Chabrol's wife Stéphane Audran, included in 1969 his most famous film *Le Boucher* (see chapter 2). For the next decade, he specialised in psychological thrillers in which an apparent bourgeois harmony tends to be disturbed by an outsider or a voyeur figure. After working in television for a time, he returned to the *polar* with the popular *Poulet au vinaigre* (1984) and *Inspecteur Lavardin* (1986), films which spawned a television series based on the Lavardin character.

Le Cri du hibou (1987) is based on a novel by Patricia Highsmith, whose *Strangers on a Train* had been adapted by Hitchcock in 1951. Typically for Chabrol, the setting is provincial. In this case it is Vichy, a town with a guilty past, as Chabrol was to demonstrate in his Occupation documentary *L'Œil de Vichy* (1993) (see chapter 2). The provincial setting derives from a tradition which includes Henri-Georges Clouzot's poison-pen thriller *Le Corbeau* (1943) (see chapter 1). Hitchcock too shared 'this European perception of what may lurk beneath the surface of provincial respectability' (Buss 1994: 87). The disjuncture between a polished surface and the cruel depths beneath is essential to the action and *mise en scène* of *Le Cri du hibou*. The themes of surface gloss and inherent violence are embodied in the motif of the eagle's eye which recurs throughout the film, both in the protagonist's drawings and in Chabrol's use of lighting, whereby the characters' eyes glint yellow in the dark.

The glossy photography and plush décors seem anomalous given the increasing violence and melodrama of the plot, but in fact this seemingly reassuring aestheticism simply mirrors the deceptive public image of Chabrol's usual target, the bourgeoisie.

Le Cri du hibou stars Christophe Malavoy – previously the amateur detective in Michel Deville's playful and voyeuristic Péril en la demeure (1985) – as Robert Forestier, a divorced draughtsman. In this case, however, the urbane Malvoy is not long in control, but soon has to prove his innocence against a rising tide of coincidence and suspicion – again a theme favoured by Hitchcock. Forestier is a habitual voyeur, and at the start of the film has been spying on a young woman, Juliette (Mathilda May), for three months. Confronted by Juliette, he tells her that he was fascinated by the beautiful and reassuring image that she presented when knitting, watching television, or moving about the house. This reassuring picture, like Chabrol's rich mise en scène, is undermined by the cynicism and violence of what follows. As Forestier and Juliette rapidly become close friends, her fiancé Patrick spies on them in turn, proceeding to attack Forestier one night. After the struggle, Patrick disappears, and the police begin to suspect Forestier of his murder. Patrick has in fact fled to Paris, where he and Forestier's ex-wife Véronique plan to persecute the voyeur. The melodramatic last reel sees Juliette's suicide and the murder of a police doctor, deaths which again seem to point to Forestier. Ultimately, Patrick and Véronique decide to visit Forestier's house; here a brawl develops, in which both Patrick and Véronique are accidentally killed, leaving Forestier implicated in two more murders. The film thus concludes with the voyeur not only victimised by his enemies, but trapped by circumstance. Moreover, during the course of the narrative Chabrol reveals that the 'normal' bourgeois citizens apparently threatened by Forestier's behaviour in fact pay him back with violence and malice. This is true not only of Véronique and Patrick but of the entire community apart from Juliette, and is realised in the image of Forestier's neighbours pressing their faces against his window, staring at him as he lies wounded, shot by Patrick. This image, and indeed the film as a whole, enacts a reversal of the opening sequence in which Forestier is the prowler looking in. Earlier, he had plaintively informed the police that 'one has the right to look at people'. For exercising that right, the voyeur is punished by the hostile gaze of the community and the implacable gaze of Chabrol's camera.

A similar transformation from voyeur to victim is achieved in Patrice Leconte's Monsieur Hire (1989). Better known for his rather misogynistic sex comedies (see chapter 3), Leconte based his first and only polar on a psychological novel by Georges Simenon, but again Hitchcock is a dominant reference. If Rear Window informs the exposition, Vertigo is echoed in the denouement. Monsieur Hire (Michel Blanc) is a fastidious tailor who lives alone and spies on his neighbour Alice (Sandrine Bonnaire) every night as she undresses.

12   Michel Blanc in *Monsieur Hire*

When a young girl called Pierette is murdered in the vicinity, the investigating detective immediately suspects Hire. Meanwhile Alice apparently befriends Hire and he begins to entertain thoughts of a relationship with her. It transpires that the voyeur saw Alice's boyfriend kill Pierrette. When he promises silence on this matter if she will run away with him, Alice betrays Hire to the police, effectively framing him for the murder. Escaping across the rooftops, he slips and falls to his death.

The parallels with *Le Cri du hibou* are clear: demonised by 'normal' society for his solitary behaviour and strange, effeminate appearance, Hire – like Forestier – goes from being a peeping Tom to the object of a hostile collective gaze. In the reconstruction of the murder, he is forced to run the gauntlet under the eyes of a suspicious crowd; this public spectacle is repeated when he trips at the ice rink, and again at the moment of his death, when a crowd gathers waiting for him to fall. The Chabrolian disjuncture between soothing imagery and cruel actions is here too, Leconte filming this narrative of deceit and betrayal with a sedate, measured camerawork matched by Michael Nyman's baroque score. But unlike Chabrol, Leconte creates a mood of overwhelming pathos, derived in part from Nyman's music but also from the central relationship between the voyeur and the woman he watches. *Monsieur Hire* maintains an intimacy that *Le Cri du hibou* loses with Juliette's suicide, and most of Leconte's film concerns the shifting power relations between Hire and Alice. At first it was he who framed her with his gaze, staring at her through the window; by the film's close, she has asserted control by framing him for the murder. This question of framing remains in the foreground throughout the film through the iterative point-of-view shots and compositions using window frames, and culminates in the play of looks exchanged at the film's climax. As Hire falls to his death, the camera gives his point of view in a slow-motion pan down the side of the building, briefly capturing Alice standing at the window of his own apartment. Finally occupying the powerful position of the voyeur, Alice looks down on her victim even as the subjective camera allows him one last look at his betrayer.

Seeing and believing in *L'Enfer*

Chabrol's *L'Enfer* (1994) is based on a scenario written then abandoned thirty years earlier by Henri-Georges Clouzot, the director of *polars* such as *Le Corbeau* (1943) and *Les Diaboliques* (1954) (see chapter 1). Clouzot is of course one of Chabrol's major influences, and *Les Innocents aux mains sales* (1975) in particular refers to *Les Diaboliques*, both in terms of plot – a murder victim's body mysteriously disappears – and *mise en scène*, with Romy Schneider made up throughout the film to resemble Simone Signoret in the Clouzot thriller. *L'Enfer* considers the growing jealousy of Paul (François Cluzet), a hotelier, regarding his wife Nelly (Emmanuelle Béart). When she lies about the cost of a new handbag, he begins to wonder what else she is keeping from him. As Paul's jealousy develops he begins to follow his wife to town, and suspects her of sleeping with the local garage owner, Martineau (Marc Lavoine). Nelly denies the accusations and persuades Paul to forget them, but a home movie shown to the guests acts as a spur to Paul's jealousy. Eventually he accuses Nelly of sleeping with everyone in the hotel and proceeds to rape her. Nelly takes refuge with the local doctor but is persuaded to go back to her husband. In the final sequence, Paul locks her in the bedroom and appears to murder her. Or perhaps just fantasies that he does. While the plot is straightforward, its realisation is far from simple. This is because Chabrol questions the status of the sounds and images we are presented during the course of the film. Despite the scenes of Paul trailing Nelly – a reprise of Chabrol's own *L'Œil du malin* (1961) and Hitchcock's *Vertigo* (1958) – *L'Enfer* is not concerned with one man's voyeurism so much as with the destruction of a married couple who projected 'une trop belle image du bonheur' [a too beautiful image of happiness] (Taboulay 1994: 35). As in *Le Cri du hibou*, beautiful and reassuring images prove illusory. But here the process of shattering illusions is so violent as to destroy not only the family group – Paul,

13   Sandrine Bonnaire in *Monsieur Hire*

Nelly, their young son, Vincent – established in the idyllic early
scenes and parodied in the wedding and the family picnic glimpsed
later, but also the spectator's faith in the realist illusion itself.

At first Paul's jealousy is a controlled spectacle, viewed by the
spectator from the outside. Even when Paul follows Nelly, Chabrol
rarely uses the point-of-view shots favoured by Hitchcock, and does
not therefore encourage an identification between the spectator and
the jealous husband. What we see and what Paul sees are not at
this point one and the same. Sounds, not images, are in fact the first
subjective elements of Paul's delirium which the audience is offered,
beginning with the slightly amplified cry of baby Vincent, and
including the insistent roar of passing jets, the buzzing of flies and
Paul's own interior monologue, the voice of his paranoid delusion.
As the jealousy increases, Chabrol uses the subjective camera to
give Paul's perspective, not in 'reality' but in the first of half a dozen
fantasy sequences that punctuate the film: driving home from town
with Nelly, Paul imagines her meeting Martineau. From this point
on, Paul begins to create a 'film' about Nelly which is increasingly
hard to tell apart from the 'reality' of Chabrol's film. Thus at a given
point we see Nelly apparently kissing Martineau or vamping with
the guests: 'Paul *se fait* littéralement *un film* qui déboussole tout.
C'est le film d'un homme qui confine et change le monde par son
regard' [Paul literally *makes a film for himself* which disorients everything. It is the film of a man who confines and changes the world
with his gaze] (Taboulay 1994: 35–6.) This is made explicit in the
references to photography, slides and filming: Paul first disturbs
Nelly and Martineau together as they watch slides in the dark, and
when a guest shows his innocent home movie in the hotel, Chabrol

The *polar*

intercuts it with lurid scenes from Paul's imagination. Since no dissolves or obvious visual devices are used to encode such sequences as fantastical, it is largely their narrative contextualisation – usually via close-ups of Paul in a fit of rage – which signals that they are subjective. Chabrol does provide some aural clues, however, – amplified buzzing and roaring noises, or snatches of the song 'L'Enfer de mes nuits' – which suggest that certain scenes are wholly imaginary. Luis Buñuel had made a similar use of sound as an indicator of fantasy in the dream-like ending of *Belle de jour* (1967). But in the startlingly ambiguous final sequence of *L'Enfer*, Chabrol provides no hint as to whether Nelly's murder is fantasy or reality. In the first of what are in effect two alternative endings, Paul cuts his wife's throat; in the second, he seems to wake from a fantasy to find that Nelly is still alive. Ironically, in the former, Paul claims that he has changed, and is no longer jealous: 'ça se voit pas?' [can't you tell?]. In truth, it is impossible to tell. The principle that one can believe what one sees – the foundation of the spectator/voyeur identification – no longer holds.

American archetypes and the stylised thriller

The thriller genres of the gangster film and the *film noir* were initiated in Hollywood in the decades either side of World War Two. Both portrayed an urban nightmare, the down side of the American dream. The gangster film offered 'resonant myths of defeat' (Shadoian 1977: 59), in which organised crime confronted the forces of authority and lost, the charismatic gangster dying a tragic or melodramatic death. In *film noir*, in a sense, defeat has already happened: 'Frontierism has turned to paranoia and claustrophobia. The small-time gangster has made it big and sits in the mayor's chair. The private eye has quit the police force in disgust' (Schrader 1971: 86). The emphasis is no longer on violent action so much as a pervading tension, the hero's endeavour is solitary, not organised, and the morality is even more ambiguous. Both genres had some claims to realism – the gangster film began as a record of actual criminals like Al Capone and events like the Saint Valentine's Day Massacre of 1929, while the *film noir* consistently portrayed the alienation of life in the big city – but they were also heavily stylised, the gangster film in its choreographed shoot-outs, the *film noir* in its shadowy, expressionist *mise en scène*. This stylisation allowed French film-makers to exploit the iconography of both the gangster film – in the work of Jean-Pierre Melville and Jacques Deray – and the *film noir* – from Jean-Luc Godard's *A bout de souffle* (1959) to Edouard Niermans' *Poussière d'ange* (1987).

The gangster thriller was established almost single handedly in France by Jean-Pierre Melville, who filmed impassive loners caught in a cold *mise en scène*. Although *Le Doulous* (1962) starred Jean-Paul Belmondo, it was Alain Delon who went on to incarnate Melville's taciturn, solitary and increasingly abstract protagonists in

Le Samourai (1967), *Le Cercle rouge* (1970) and *Un Flic* (1972). This stylised trilogy sees 'the transformation of the actor's performance into a pure display of physical characteristics and metonymic objects such as the trench-coat and the hat' (Forbes 1992: 55). The short *Borsalino* series of the early seventies, produced by Delon and directed by Jacques Deray, knowingly combined the iconography of Delon's persona in these films with a nostalgia for the American gangster genre of the thirties.

Borsalino and the iconography of the gangster

Borsalino (1970) is set in Marseille in the 1930s. Two crooks – Capello (Jean-Paul Belmondo) and Siffredi (Alain Delon) – rise to power in the underworld by controlling the meat market. This power struggle is complemented by the romantic tensions traditional to the heterosexual buddy film (see chapter 3), with each man's infatuation for a dangerous or unattainable woman threatening the original friendship. Eventually, with the escalation of gang warfare and personal rivalry, the town is no longer big enough for both of them. At this point the light-hearted tone becomes melodramatic. The two gangsters decide to part before one of them kills the other, but after a false ending Capello is shot and dies in his friend's arms. Following Capello's death and Siffredi's disappearance 'never to be heard from again', the closing sequence presents still photographs of the two in a series of poses from the film.

Besides functioning as a straightforward buddy narrative, *Borsalino* pays a nostalgic and at times comic homage to the American gangster movies of the 1930s. It does so through the iconography of the genre – the urban setting, the sharp suits and hats, the cars – and also through Claude Bolling's score, which consists of thirties-style ragtime music. The film thus prefigures George Roy Hill's ragtime comedy *The Sting* (1973), as well as the films of *la mode rétro*, such as Francis Girod's *René la Canne* (1977) (see chapter 2). While several sequences in *Borsalino*, like the brawl between Capello and Siffredi when they first meet, are played for laughs, generic set pieces are also played straight, as with the pastoral interlude – a feature of arguably the last classical gangster movie, Raoul Walsh's *High Sierra* (1941) – when Capello hides out in the country. But as the final sequence suggests, Deray's film celebrates above all the iconic status of its stars. The characters played by Belmondo and Delon are images to themselves as well as to the spectator, and are regularly framed looking at themselves in mirrors. Delon in particular, via reference to his persona in Melville's *Le Samourai* (1967), is a self-conscious figure throughout the film: hence the recurrence in *Borsalino* of his trademark gesture, running his hand along the brim of his hat, and of the piano motif. Siffredi, like Costello – Delon's cold but vulnerable hitman in *Le Samourai* – is fascinated with the piano, and even plays the *Borsalino* theme just before Capello's death. And unlike Belmondo/Capello, Delon returns as star and producer of the sequel, *Borsalino et Compagnie* (1974): 'Delon as producer clearly set out to establish a series which, had it continued, might have stood comparison with the serials of the silent period such as *Judex* or *Fantômas*' (Forbes 1992: 58). Like those earlier heroes, Delon's gangster is 'more recognisable in his accoutrements than in his person' (Forbes 1992: 58), an objectified collection of symbols rather than a psychologically realistic character.

Starsky and Hutch in Belleville: *La Balance*

The American Bob Swaim's *La Balance* (1982) takes its inspiration from television rather than from cinema. As *Cahiers du cinéma* noted at the time, the film is in the mould of the American television series *Starsky and Hutch*. This influence is apparent in the characterisation of Paluzzi and Tintin, two wise-cracking police buddies, in the racial stereotyping and in Roland Bocquet's funky score. On a broader level it informs the thriller plot, which centres around the role of the police informer (a comic character in *Starsky and Hutch*, here a tragic one). After the murder of their usual informer, the Belleville *Brigade territoriale* need to find a new grass in order to catch underworld boss Roger Massina (Maurice Ronet). Detective Paluzzi (Richard Berry) decides upon Dédé (Phillipe Léotard), a former member of Massina's gang whose prostitute girlfriend Nicole (Nathalie Baye) once slept with Massina. The police harass Nicole and brutalise Dédé until the latter agrees to turn informer. Dédé sets up an art theft with Massina, but when the plan is changed at the last minute, the police ambush goes wrong. Amidst a chaotic shoot-out, Massina escapes to confront his betrayer. Dédé kills him and considers going on the run himself, before Nicole betrays him to Paluzzi for his own protection.

Despite the reliance on generic elements such as car chases and shoot-outs, and the frequent intertextual references to Hollywood thrillers – the *Dirty Harry* poster on the wall of the *brigade* headquarters, Dédé's allusions to Steve McQueen in *Bullitt* – the seedy Belleville locations lend the film a certain realism. And although the characterisation is largely dependent on the American archetype of the cynical cop, Dédé and Massina are coded as specifically French (via their obsession with cuisine), as are the Arab drug-dealers, albeit in a negative, racist sense. The tension in *La Balance* is generated by the clash between the violent police narrative and the romantic sub-plot involving Dédé and Nicole, which recalls the *film noir* as well as French poetic realism (see chapter 1), with its 'conventional underworld characters (sympathetic crook, affectionate prostitute) caught up in a story of doomed love' (Buss 1994: 145). This tension informs the film's imagery as well as its plot, and is notable in Swaim's use of slow-motion photography. In the opening sequence, the killing of the informer Paolo is realised in slow-motion, a convention of the thriller (and the Western) which dates back to the films of Sam Peckinpah, and is still in evidence in the *polar*, witness Luc Besson's *Nikita* (1989) and *Léon* (1994). The penultimate sequence of *La Balance*, however, presents a sexual image in slow-motion. Dédé and Nicole's love-making, however violent, is also a privileged, extended moment salvaged from the scheming around them, an escape from the thriller into the romance.

La Balance was an enormous success in France, winning Césars for best film, actor (Léotard) and actress (Baye), and attracting over four million spectators in the year of release (Prédal 1991: 402). The result was a spate of imitations, often with derivative titles, including Christine Pascal's *La Garce* – starring Richard Berry again – and Yannick Bellon's *La Triche* (both 1984). This was also a period of growing French interest in American television series. The 1980s in general was a decade of unprecedented expansion in French television, with a doubling in the number of channels and an increasing reliance on advertising revenues. As a consequence, rather than investing in expensive home-made drama the stations bought popular American imports, including police series such as *Starsky and Hutch* and *Chips*. The number of American series on French screens rocketed: in 1985, 73 million francs were spent by French channels on US television series; by 1987 the figure had grown to 613 million francs (Prédal 1991: 390). Hence *La Balance* can be seen to herald the popular demand for American drama series which the French television channels were to fulfil over the course of the decade.

Film noir and fantasy in *Poussière d'ange*

Edouard Niermans made his directorial debut in 1980 with *Anthracite*, a drama set in a Jesuit college in the early fifties. For the next six years he worked in television, before returning to the big screen with *Poussière d'ange* (1987), a seedy *film noir* mixing psychology, fantasy and realism. Inspector Simon Blount (Bernard Giraudeau) has been left by his wife Martine (Fanny Cottençon) in favour of a hotelier called Igor. Alcoholic, bitter and occasionally violent, Simon begins to look for his wife at night, while struggling with police work during the day. Asked to investigate thefts from a supermarket, he meets a mysterious young woman, Violetta (Fanny Bastien), who befriends him. While photographing Martine and Igor together in a hotel room, Simon inadvertently witnesses Igor's murder. From this point on, his investigation of the murder and his fascination with Violetta become increasingly interdependent. Despite the attempts of his boss Florimont (Michel Aumont) to have him transferred, Simon discovers that Violetta and her surrogate brother Gabriel are embarked on a series of murders to avenge the death of her prostitute mother, in which both Igor and Florimont were implicated. When Simon learns that Florimont is in fact Violetta's father, he confronts him and elicits a confession. Florimont is arrested, but in the violent conclusion Gabriel is killed escaping from the police. Simon helps Violetta to cross the border to

14   Bernard Giraudeau in *Poussière d'ange*

safety before an epilogue shows him reunited with his wife and daughter.

Film noir archetypes are evident throughout *Poussière d'ange*, in the *mise en scène*, narrative voice-over and characterisation as much as in the generic plot (rogue detective with morals uncovers corruption in high places). The consistently underlit or nocturnal *mise en scène*, the ubiquitous rain, and the seedy urban locations are all reminiscent of classic Hollywood *film noir*. But it is above all in the knowing characterisation of the detective hero that the genre is most evident. In both actions and appearance, Simon is a hyperbolic version of the crumpled private eye. He narrates his own story with the laconic humour typical of the genre. The traditional ambiguity of the *film noir* hero – is he a criminal or a lawman? – is epitomised in the scene where he wakes up in the drunk-tank in his own police station. His exaggeratedly dishevelled appearance – unshaven, clutching a bottle of whisky, wearing an overcoat and practically living in his beat-up car – identifies him with 'the earlier iconography of, say, Sam Spade or Philip Marlowe' (Hayward 1993: 289). In contrast with Godard's homage to *film noir A bout de souffle* (1959), where Michel (Jean-Paul Belmondo) is presented ironically for modelling himself on Humphrey Bogart, in *Poussière d'ange* there is no apparent critical distance between the director and the protagonist.

Deceit – a thematic preoccupation of *film noir*, where it is often personified by female protagonists – is fundamental to the characterisation of Violetta. But she is no *femme fatale*, rather a child of fantasy who encourages Simon to 'tell his life differently'. Violetta pretends to have a job at the museum and to have spent her childhood in Africa; she even hires actors to play her parents when

Contemporary French cinema

15   Fanny Bastien and Bernard Giraudeau in *Poussière d'ange*

Simon comes to dinner. Her central fantasy, however, is of vengeance for her mother's death. While this desire leads her to send Florimont taped death threats about a heavenly judgement on the whore of Babylon, Simon's equally violent revenge fantasy is enacted in terms of images, not sounds: his voracious photographing of Martine and Igor when together inspires a desire to kill them both, a desire enacted in part by Gabriel as his proxy. The recurrent fantasy motif in *Poussière d'ange* even contaminates the solution of the mystery at the film's close: Simon's showdown with Florimont takes place in the same empty house that Violetta populated with her artificial family, amid Florimont's accusations that the detective's theory is just another fantasy. To this extent, Niermans appears to qualify the formulaic ease with which Simon traps his corrupt boss. The rather perfunctory nature of this *film noir* ending is also challenged by the action sequence which follows. The violence and the driving score of the scene in which Gabriel kills Igor's lawyer before dying in a burning car at a police roadblock is far from the moody atmospherics of the rest of the film, and closer to the gangster movie or to Luc Besson's spectacular *Nikita* (1990) than to *film noir*. The influence of the *cinéma du look* is also apparent as regards plot and *mise en scène*, with the cassette implicating a police chief and the setting of an abandoned warehouse (where Violetta and Gabriel meet) recalling Jean-Jacques Beineix's *Diva* (1980) (see chapter 6). But there remains in *Poussière d'ange* a realistic portrayal of bleak Parisian locations, including a red-light district under the *boulevard périphérique*, which derives from a different tradition, that of the naturalistic *polar*.

The *polar*

The naturalistic *polar*

While the films of Henri-Georges Clouzot, like those of Claude Chabrol some years later, explored the underside of provincial communities, most *polars* in the 1950s tended to be set in an unspecified place and an approximate present, 'le contemporain vague' (Marshall 1992: 41). The *nouvelle vague* thrillers of the 1960s – notably Jean-Luc Godard's *Made in USA* (1966) – and the political *polars* of Costa-Gavras and Yves Boisset began to situate crime narratives in precise socio-political contexts, often as a critique of the French (or American) governments. It is to this tradition that the work of Alain Corneau and Bertrand Tavernier is related. Their careers have run in parallel – both made their first film in 1974 – and both are associated with the period drama (see chapter 7) as well as the *polar*. Their similarity of outlook extends to adapting the work of the same American crime novelist, Jim Thompson, and even to working on screen versions of the same novel, Thompson's *Pop. 1280* (Tavernier successfully, Corneau without result).

Thompson transposed: *Série noire* and *Coup de torchon*

Lately rediscovered by Hollywood – witness Maggie Greenwald's *The Kill-Off* (1989), Stephen Frears's *The Grifters* (1990) and Roger Donaldson's remake of *The Getaway* (1994) – Jim Thompson's bleak and brutal crime novels were part of the postwar American fare offered up to French readers in Gallimard's *série noire* range. Thompson had worked in Hollywood on Stanley Kubrick's *The Killing* (1956) and *Paths of Glory* (1957), and his novel *The Getaway* had first been filmed by Sam Peckinpah in 1972, but he died alcoholic and ignored. His rehabilitation in the eighties was in part sparked by his reputation in France, and by two French adaptations: Alain Corneau's *Série noire* (1979) and Bertrand Tavernier's *Coup de torchon* (1981).

Corneau worked with Costa-Gavras in the sixties, and his first two thrillers – *Police python 357* (1976) and *La Menace* (1977) – starred Costa-Gavras regular, and icon of the political *polar*, Yves Montand. *Série noire*, an adaptation of Thompson's *A Hell of a Woman*, is not a political thriller, but Corneau does achieve a naturalistic portrayal of alienation and poverty by transposing the action from Kentucky to *la zone*, the suburban wasteland surrounding Paris. Franck Poupard (Patrick Dewaere) is a door-to-door salesman making very little money. While looking for a client called Tikides, he meets an old woman who offers him her young niece Mona (Marie Trintignant) as payment for a dressing-gown, an offer Franck refuses. Having found Tikides and recovered the debt, Franck is none the less thrown in the cells when his boss, Staplin (Bernard Blier) accuses him of stealing on the sly. Franck is bailed out by Mona with some of her aunt's hidden savings. Franck begins to dream of stealing the money and escaping with Mona, particularly since his wife Jeanne has walked out. Having persuaded

16   Marie Trintingant and Patrick Dewaere in *Série noire*

17   Marie Trintingant and Patrick Dewaere in *Série noire*

Tikides to accompany him, Franck returns to the old woman's house, kills her, and steals the money, shooting Tikides and framing him for the crime. When Jeanne reappears and discovers the stolen money, Franck kills her too. Staplin, suspecting that Franck is the murderer, blackmails him and takes the money. In the final scene Franck, clutching an empty suitcase, meets Mona: they are finally ready to run away together.

The setting of *Série noire* is bleak and wintry: vacant lots and blocks of flats, deserted except for the central characters. Much of the film is shot in shabby interiors or in Franck's car, itself a restricted space from which he cannot seem to escape. The soundtrack adds to the sense of realism, comprising the rumble of thunder and traffic, and incessant pop music from the radios which are found in almost every scene. In the wretched world of *la zone*, pop songs offer a fantasy of escape which is at once cheerfully appealing and pathetically sad: when Mona strips for Franck in her dingy room, Boney M's 'Rivers of Babylon' blares from her radio. Music expresses above all Franck's futile hopes, as when he and Tikides achieve a drunken camaraderie while recalling their favourite songs. In the crucial scene of Tikides's murder, Franck pauses to remind him of the closing words of Gilbert Bécaud's 'Le jour où la pluie viendra' – 'Nous serons toi et moi les plus heureux du monde, les plus riches du monde' [You and I shall be the happiest, the richest in the world] – before shooting him dead. The fantasy expressed in the lyric belongs to Franck and Mona, no longer to Tikides, and remains their guiding obsession at the end of the film. While the pop music, from Sacha Distel to Sheila B. Devotion, also acts – like the setting – to situate the action in a precise everyday reality, there is one fantastical element in *Série noire* which qualifies the pervading naturalism: Georges Perec's script. Perec has Franck speak a mixture of French backslang (*le verlan*) and street slang, combined with Anglicisms and spoonerisms. As Corneau remarked: 'The challenge was to give an appearance of naturalism, but at all costs to avoid succumbing to it: we had to do something totally unrealistic.' Consequently, when Franck tries to express himself, he is at odds with reality, and in his mouth even the most banal language 'is turned around and used obliquely' (Corneau cited in Buss 1994: 122). Franck's monologues, uttered in despair or frenzy while imprisoned in his car, are his own attempt to talk himself away from *la zone*.

Bertrand Tavernier had used a specific socio-political context for his first film, *L'Horloger de Saint-Paul* (1974), a thriller adapted from Georges Simenon and featuring an analysis of the generation formed by May 1968 (see chapter 2), coupled with a naturalistic portrayal of the city of Lyons. In *Coup de torchon* (1981), Tavernier again enlisted screenwriter Jean Aurenche and actor Philippe Noiret to interpret a crime novel, but this time the transposition was more radical. Jim Thompson's *Pop.1280* is set in a small community in the deep south of the United States. Tavernier switched the action not to mainland France, as Corneau had done in *Série noire*, but to French West Africa at the end of the 1930s. The corrupt and murderous colonials embody the casual brutality of the French Empire, doomed by the imminence of World War Two, while the film's central metaphor – an eclipse of the sun – is an ironic reversal of the colonial symbol, a torch lighting up the dark continent of Africa. The violent narrative concerns the experiences of the local police chief Lucien Cordier (Noiret), who turns from a lazy do-nothing to a cynical murderer. Lucien is in fact the only policeman in the village of Boussarka; he has never arrested anyone, and turns a blind eye to racism and violence. Regularly abused by the local pimps, Léonelli and Le Péron, Léon finally snaps and shoots both men, dumping the bodies in the river. From this point on, he acts as a self-appointed vigilante: having killed the wife-beater Marcaillou, he embarks on an affair with the dead man's widow, Rose (Isabelle Huppert). When Vendredi, a black servant, learns of Marcaillou's murder, Léon shoots him too. Léon manages to deflect enquiries about the murders from Le Péron's brother and from the local colonel, until the declaration of war between France and Germany distracts the attention of the entire community. With the colonial way of life thus threatened forever, Léon confesses the murders to the schoolteacher, Anne, declaring that he himself has been dead inside for along time.

Léon is in fact present in practically every scene of the film, and operates as a guide to the colonial setting as well as a personification of corrupt imperialism. His wanderings around Boussarka allow Tavernier to introduce the seedy milieu, from the stinking privies to the corpse-ridden river. Moreover, by using a handheld camera to shoot these sequences, Tavernier lends them a documentary authenticity. While the images in *Coup de torchon* situate the film geographically, the sound-track of thirties jazz situates it temporally. A third form of contextualisation is provided by the official discourse of colonialism against which the narrative works. This is most evident in two sequences in which the African villagers constitute an audience for an imperialist spectacle: the film show and the classroom scene. In the former, the villagers gather to watch *Alerte en Méditerranée*, a French naval adventure which has to be translated to the audience by a bilingual African. A celebration of French imperial power, this black-and-white film is challenged by the lurid events around it in Tavernier's violent, naturalistic version of the colonial experience. A similar contrast between colonial myth and brutal reality is achieved when Léon writes his confession to the murders on the school blackboard. Realising that none of her African pupils can understand the written French, Anne tells them it is the words of 'La Marseillaise'. She then declaims the national anthem, which champions the glorious struggle against tyranny, while the text, visible behind her, ironically reveals the murderous consequences of French imperialism.

The naturalistic *polar* tends to illustrate Raymond Chandler's assertion that the ideal crime story would have no revelatory ending, but would concentrate instead on a series of discoveries about the nature of the society in which a murder is committed. Thus Corneau's *Série noire* is open ended – Thompson's novel ended with Mona's accidental death and the narrator's suicide – while in *L'Horloger de Saint-Paul* the motives for the central murder are never explained. *Coup de torchon* is similarly more concerned with an investigation into a particular community than with a psychological explanation for a series of killings. This tendency to privilege social observation over narrative closure is again evident in two naturalistic accounts of police procedures, Maurice Pialat's *Police* (1985) and Tavernier's *L.627* (1992).

Docu-drama in *Police* and *L.627*

In the 1980s, a new element was added to the urban setting characteristic of the *polar*: 'What does get introduced into this landscape as a signifier of Frenchness is the drug underworld almost always associated with an Arab "community"' (Hayward 1993: 291). This is true of Swaim's *La Balance* (1982) as well as the less overtly racist portrayal of an Arab drugs ring in Pialat's *Police* (1985) and of African drug users in Tavernier's *L.627* (1992). Both films use exactly the same setting as *La Balance* – the streets of Belleville – but are shot in a resolutely naturalistic manner.

Maurice Pialat trained as a painter, and began making films in 1960. Much of his work, including *Passe ton Bac d'abord* (1979) and *Loulou* (1980), is strongly influenced by documentary cinema, rejecting the theatrical values of *mise en scène* for shaky, dull-toned photography shot in real locations. Pialat has said of this naturalist aesthetic that 'perhaps because of my early career as a painter, I refused for many years to try to make my films pictorially interesting' (Forbes 1992: 220), although this subsequently changed in *Sous le Soleil de Satan* (1987) and *Van Gogh* (1991) (see chapter 7). *Police* is the last of Pialat's broadly naturalistic films: sound-track music is absent until the very end, there are no opening credits, the dialogue seems improvised, the camera work is often handheld and the locations naturally lit. Mangin (Gérard Depardieu) is a detective investigating a Tunisian drugs ring in Belleville run by Simon Slimane and his brothers. Mangin arrests both Simon and his girlfriend Noria (Sophie Marceau), but thanks to the efforts of the lawyer Lambert (Richard Anconina), Noria is released. Although Noria now starts seeing Lambert, Mangin's best friend, the detective falls for her too. With the disruption of the drugs ring, Noria steals the gang's money and is only persuaded to give it back by Mangin, with whom she has begun an affair. Mangin returns the money, and Noria leaves him.

The supposedly realistic portrayal of police brutality, racism and chauvinism which typifies most of the film has attracted more critical attention than its relation to the thriller form. But clearly some elements in *Police* are generic, above all the relationship between

Mangin and Noria. He, a widower, is the classic lone cop, while she is characterised misogynistically as a *femme fatale* who lies to get what she wants, seduces men, and breaks up the buddy relationship between Mangin and Lambert. The narrative is also analogous to the modern gangster film, particularly Martin Scorsese's *Mean Streets* (1973), in its thematic concern with redemption. Despite his betrayal of Lambert, Mangin ultimately returns the stolen money to the Slimane brothers (who were holding Lambert responsible), thus at once saving his friend and reaffirming his own position on the right side of the law. (The distinction between law and criminality is blurred throughout the film, with Mangin and Lambert accusing each other of 'crossing over to the other side'.) Mangin's action, and his acceptance of Noria's subsequent departure, is coded as an almost spiritual achievement by the burst of music – Górecki's Third Symphony – as he stands alone at the end of the film.

The title of Bertrand Tavernier's *L.627* refers to the legislation against dealing in narcotics. The film was co-written by Michel Alexandre, an investigating officer who had worked in a Parisian drugs squad for thirteen years. Alexandre is also the model for the protagonist, Lulu (Didier Bezace), a detective transferred to an underfunded and overworked drugs squad. What little plot there is concerns Lulu's relationship with Cécile, a prostitute and informer who is HIV positive, and his unfulfilled ambition to escape from Paris for a pastoral life in the Auvergne. But in the main the film is a docu-drama about police methods, and about attitudes to race, ranging from the relatively enlightened (Lulu) to the bigoted (Dodo). Although the action includes chases and arrests, there is also a degree of monotony and repetition, and the generic form of the crime narrative – the solving of a mystery – is absent: 'I needed a structure that did not seem "constructed", which would remain "accidental", raw' (Tavernier 1993: 253). Tavernier's aim was to integrate 'fictional elements and research materials, without recourse to a plot [...]. This approach gave rise to a whole series of reflections and questions about the relation between fiction and documentary, truth and realism' (Tavernier 1993: 253). Above all the film was to 'refuse all stylistic effects inherent in the thriller genre' and to subvert the audience's formal and ideological references, 'American references in particular: promotion of individualism, rejection of collective spirit, predominance of plot' (Tavernier 1993: 253: 254). To this end, Tavernier presents the police as a team working together; Lulu is not the traditional lone cop of *film noir* or of *polars* such as *Police*. A documentary atmosphere is achieved by the casting of little-known actors and the use of hand-held cameras to film in sometimes dangerous Parisian locations. The lighting is natural, and often gloomy. Unlike *Police*, however, *L.627* does feature a substantial amount of sound-track music, with Philippe Sarde's score mixing Western and African instruments.

Situating *L.627* in the tradition of the political *polar*, Tavernier has claimed that the film was an attempt to define the state of

French society (Sineux and Vachaud 1995: 25). The hostile reception it met with from the police authorities confirmed him in this belief. In September 1992, Interior Minister Paul Quilès, ordered that Tavernier's co-writer Michel Alexandre be investigated, declared that the film was an 'unjust and false caricature' of policing, and cancelled a public discussion due to be held after a screening in Lille (Tavernier 1993: 372, 376). More than two years later, Quilès's successor as Minister of the Interior, Charles Pasqua, demanded that all material relating to *L.627* be removed from an exhibition about films on police work (Sineux and Vachaud 1995: 26). All of which, combined with the increased ferocity of police operations in the area where the film was shot, led Tavernier to conclude that his didacticism was lost on the authorities: 'The boys at the Ministry have become like Dodo [the racist detective] in the film. And I had hoped they might follow the example of Lulu' (Tavernier 1993: 378).

References

Buss, R. (1994), *French Film Noir*, London, Marion Boyars.

Forbes, J. (1992), *The Cinema in France After the New Wave*, London, BFI/MacMillan.

Hayward, S. (1993), *French National Cinema*, London and New York, Routledge.

Marshall, B. (1992), National identity and the *film policier*: the moment of 1981, Chalfont St Giles, Bucks, *French Cultural Studies*, 3:1:7, 31–42.

Prédal, R. (1991), *Le Cinéma français depuis 1945*, Paris, Nathan.

Rohmer, E. and Chabrol, C. (1992), *Hitchcock: the First Forty-Four Films*, Oxford, Roundhouse.

Schrader, P. (1971), Notes on *Film Noir*, in K. Jackson (ed.), *Schrader on Schrader and Other Writings*, London, Faber and Faber, 80–94.

Shadoian, J. (1977), *Dreams and Dead-Ends*, Cambridge, Massachusetts, MIT Press.

Sineux, M., and Vachaud, L. (1995), Entretien avec Bertrand Tavernier: 'Comment montrer la violence sans en devenir complice?', Paris, *Positif*, 409, 25–30.

Taboulay, C. (1994), L'Enfer me ment, Paris, *Cahiers du cinéma*, 476, 34–7.

Tavernier, B. (1993), I wake up, dreaming, London, *Projections*, 2, 252–378.

The *cinéma du look* and fantasy film   6

Popularity and critical reception

The *cinéma du look* is a style of film-making which came to the fore in the 1980s and is still influential in French film in the 1990s. It is characterised not by any collective ideology but rather by a technical mastery of the medium, a cinephile tendency to cite from other films, and a spectacular visual style (*le look*). Beginning with Jean-Jacques Beineix's *Diva* (1980), the *cinéma du look* has had numerous popular successes, but has consistently been taken to task by the critical establishment in France, and even more so in Britain. The three main directors grouped together in this 'New New Wave' are Beineix, Luc Besson and Léos Carax. They have been bracketed as a movement because of a perceived similarity of visual style and, to a lesser extent, of subject matter (young lovers in urban or alienating surroundings). In France, populist cinema magazines like *Première* championed Beineix and Besson, who were notably more successful at the box office than Carax in the eighties (a situation not remedied by *Les Amants du Pont-Neuf* in 1991). The more intellectual and ideological *Cahiers du cinéma* tended to mount virulent attacks on Beineix and Besson while setting Carax apart as a film-maker closer to Jean-Luc Godard than to the *cinéma du look*. This is no surprise, since Carax – like Godard – once wrote for *Cahiers*. It is largely the *Cahiers* line that has been dominant in critiques of the *cinéma du look*: namely that it is superficial, and shows a complete absence of political and social concerns. Other common objections include attacks on the lack of plot and of psychological realism (the basis for the canon of 'great' French cinema from the thirties to the seventies). Comparisons to 'inferior' cultural forms like television, music video, advertising and the comic strip also abound. But it is the absence of ideology which is the central plank of attacks on Beineix, Besson and even Carax – an absence which is seen to stem from the fading of Marxism in France (and indeed

Europe), the electoral triumph of the Socialists in May 1981, and the growth of centrist 'consensus politics' in the decade that followed. Equating 'authentic cinema' with ideology, critics have tended to neglect the aesthetic importance of the *cinéma du look*. An important exception is Raphaël Bassan's essay, 'Trois néo-baroques français', which appeared in *La Revue du cinéma* in 1989. Bassan welcomes the *cinéma du look* as a break with the 'chronic naturalism' of French cinema, and values its synthesis of 'high' and 'low' art as well as its engagement with the problems of alienated protagonists who are outside any cosy familial structures (Bassan 1989).

Jean-Jacques Beineix

The eldest of the practitioners of the *cinéma du look*, Jean-Jacques Beineix worked as assistant to Claude Zidi, Claude Berri and René Clément in the 1970s. He also enjoyed a spell in advertising in the mid-eighties, his defence of which provides a fine summation of the debate surrounding the *cinéma du look*. Because it 'kidnapped colour', 'dispensed with stories' and 'captured youth', advertising ran counter to France's 'ageing' realistic, narrative cinema, while any film which privileged colour over narrative was attacked by the critics as being not cinema but advertising (Russell 1989: 45–6). Beineix made his film début, aged thirty-four, in 1980 with *Diva*. The 7.5 million franc budget was spent on producing the best possible image and sound rather than on stars, and gave the film highly visible production values. Initially distributed in only a few cinemas, and met by an ambivalent press reaction, *Diva* gradually became a cult hit, and in 1982 was a surprise winner of four Césars: for sound, music, photography and for best first film. It was subsequently redistributed and became a landmark in eighties cinema. The *cinéma du look* had arrived.

Diva: 'the first French postmodernist film'

The film's plot comes from a novel by Delacorta, and is notable only for the dual intrigue which allows Beineix to oscillate between the realms of obsessive love (*amour fou*) and urban thriller. Jules, a young postman (Frédéric Andrei), becomes involved in two narratives concerning tapes: he has made an invaluable bootleg of the opera singer Cynthia Hawkins (Wilhelminia Wiggins Fernandez) in concert, and has also come into possession of a message from a prostitute, Nadia, which incriminates police inspector Saporta in a vice ring. Pursued across Paris by villains in search of each of the cassettes, Jules is befriended by Alba (Thuy Ann Lu) and Gorodish (Richard Bohringer), thanks to whom Saporta is eventually killed. Finally, Jules returns the concert bootleg to Cynthia at the Opéra and is reconciled with her as they listen to the tape. The film thus has two plots from two different genres: the culturally 'low' thriller plot (Nadia's tape) meets the culturally 'high' opera film (Cynthia's

18   Frédéric Andrei and Thuy Ann Lu in *Diva*

tape). In between the two lies the romance, and Jules's infatuation
with Cynthia, played out in the nocturnal Parisian streets. The
cross-cultural address of the film is evident simply from the contrast
between the classical sound-track (Wagner, Catalani, Satie) and an
image track that many have compared to television advertising.
Beineix's use of blue to create a calming mood (Gorodish's clothes
and apartment) prefigures Besson's *Le Grand Bleu* (1987), while
stylised interiors feature throughout the film: Jules's flat, Gorodish's
apartment, the lighthouse, the abandoned warehouse. *Diva* also
suggests the importance that the *métro* was to assume as a key setting for the *cinéma du look* – in *Subway* (1985), *Mauvais Sang*
(1986), and *Les Amants du Pont-Neuf* (1991). The importance of set
design in the film, and in the *cinéma du look* in general, recalls the
poetic realism of the thirties and forties (see chapter 1). On the other
hand, the cartoon-strip villains who are comic as much as menacing derive from *la nouvelle vague*, especially François Truffaut's *Tirez
sur le Pianiste* (1960). This juxtaposition of contradictory cinematic
schools is characteristic not just of Beineix but also of Carax and
Besson, who again fall between the influence of *la nouvelle vague*
(mixing of genres and of high/low culture, symbolic use of colour,
intertextuality) and that of forties production values (increasingly
large budgets, sumptuous sets, studio rather than real locations,
attention to *mise en scène*).

Press reaction to *Diva* was divided, with attention centring on its
undoubted aesthetic appeal. Comparisons were drawn with
Magritte and surrealism, as well as with comic strips. More recently,
Christophe Gans has offered a persuasive reading of the film's rela-
tion to advertising imagery and consumer society. Noting that
Beineix achieves the advertising ideal of combining 'chic' culture

with a young image, Gans finds that the film as a whole replaces unique objects with manufactured reproductions: hence Cynthia's reluctant agreement to submit her voice to disc, and Gorodish's blowing up of his vintage Citroën only to produce an exact replica (Gans 1991: 3-4). Similarly, Fredric Jameson concludes that the fetish for technological reproduction in *Diva* is integrated success-fully into the plot – in the form of Cynthia's attitude to recording and Nadia's recorded testimony – and is therefore not merely a superficial or self-conscious gloss (Jameson 1990: 62). Thus although the style of *Diva*, and in particular the knowing mixture of disparate cultural references, make it 'the first French postmod-ernist film' (Jameson 1990: 55), this quality is integrated into the narrative drive rather than detracting from it.

Between fantasy and naturalism: *La Lune dans le caniveau, 37,2 le Matin, Roselyne et les lions*

The success of *Diva* led Gaumont to grant Beineix the largest French film budget of 1983 to adapt David Goodis's low-life novel *The Moon in the Gutter*. The international cast featured Gérard Depardieu, Nas-tassia Kinski and Victoria Abril, and filming took place at the Cinecittà studios in Rome. The production's sumptuous sets derived from the poetic-realist tradition, especially Marcel Carné's *Les Visi-teurs du soir* (1942) and *Les Enfants du paradis* (1945), while the stylisation of décor and colour recalled Godard's *Le Mépris* (1963) and Fassbinder's *Querelle* (1982). And where Carné, Godard and Fassbinder used setting, colour or *mise en scène* to launch explo-rations of the psychological functioning of their characters, Beineix also attempted this. In the judgement of critics and public alike, however, his attempt failed. Attacked by the press, booed at Cannes and ignored at the box office, *La Lune dans le caniveau* (1983) was even savaged by Depardieu, who called it 'a thriller preoccupied with its own navel' (Buss 1994: 185). But the film, dynamised like the novel by social difference and the tension between the real and the ideal, is in fact a clear expression of the conflict between natu-ralism and fantasy, essential to the *cinéma du look*.

William Kerrigan (Depardieu) is a stevedore who lives with his stepfamily on the wrong side of the tracks. He is tormented by the recent death of his sister, who committed suicide after a sexual assault by an unknown assailant. When he meets Newton Chan-ning, a rich slummer, and his sister Loretta (Kinski), Kerrigan at once suspects the former, while falling in love with the latter. Throughout the film, Kerrigan is torn between the brutal but famil-iar environment of the streets – embodied by his degenerate brother Frank and his voluptuous stepsister Bella (Abril) – and Loretta's up-town allure. The idealised world outside his experience is repre-sented not just by Loretta, but by the billboard slogan which tempts him to 'Try another world'. Unable to solve the mystery of his sister's death, and despite having married Loretta in a dream-like

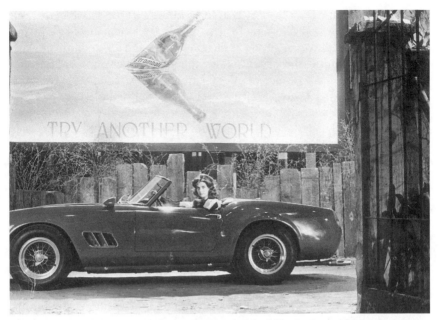

19   Nastassia Kinski in *La Lune dans le caniveau*

ceremony, Kerrigan finally returns to Bella and the way of life he
has always known.

What is striking about the film is not so much the representation
of Loretta and Bella as emblematic of their own milieux, but rather
the means by which the tension between realities and dreams per-
meates both image and sound tracks. While there is a naturalistic
tone to the shoplifting sequence in *Diva*, naturalism and fantasy are
never expressly juxtaposed in that film. Their juxtaposition is the
very subject of *La Lune dans le caniveau*. The realistic dock sequences
and the exaggerated squalor and violence of the bar and street
scenes contrast with luscious sunsets reminiscent of *Querelle*, spectacular photographic tricks using mirrored ceilings and unusual
angles, and even an animated link between shots (the jet of liquid
which becomes a line of light under Kerrigan's door). Loretta is the
embodiment of spectacle in the film: often framed in mirrors, she is
distorted in the multiple refractions of a camera lens; she is an idealised commodity like the sportscar she drives or the drink adver-
tised on the billboard she parks beside. The casting of Nastassia
Kinski as Loretta plays on her roles as a fantasy figure in Francis
Ford Coppola's studio-bound musical *One from the Heart* (1982),
and as the romantic heroine in Roman Polanski's *Tess* (1979).
Loretta/Nastassia is thus an icon of Hollywood fantasy, a creature
from 'the dream factory' for the audience as well as for Kerrigan.
Loretta is idealised through sound as well as imagery, with overly
lush, romantic music bursting out whenever she appears. Indeed,
Beineix thereby parodies the romantic and idealised role of the classical sound-track in *Diva*. Generic parody also dominates the wedding sequence, which replaces the novel's sordid ceremony in a

shack with a fantastical Gothic scene in a Disney-style cathedral. There are also allusions to Jean Vigo's *L'Atalante* (1934) – in the scene of Kerrigan eating a block of ice – and to Godard's technicolour films of the sixties in the symbolic use of colours. In *Le Mépris* (1963), for instance, Godard expresses the conflict between a screenwriter (Michel Piccoli) and his wife (Brigitte Bardot) by pitting reds against blues with yellow as a neutral tone. More conventional codes of sexual representation are evoked in *La Lune dans le caniveau*: Loretta usually wears red, and drives a red sportscar (not grey as in the novel), symbolising her sexual threat to Kerrigan, but her appearance in white also associates her with the purity of Kerrigan's dead sister.

La Lune dans le caniveau is probably the single film most emblematic of the *cinéma du look*. But it was a commercial flop. Beineix responded with his most profitable film to date, the hit movie *37,2 le Matin* (a.k.a. *Betty Blue*) (1986). This is also one of his most naturalistic and least fantastical films, although one which does mobilise certain narrative and sexual fantasies (see chapter 3). Where *La Lune dans le caniveau* dynamised the conflict between the naturalistic and the spectacular, in *37,2* there is a more surreptitious infiltration of Phillipe Djian's broadly realist narrative by photogenic images. These images seem to function independently of the rest of the film, and present a series of consumable moments familiar from advertising: a minor character pausing to play the saxophone at dusk, a blue seascape with distant sailing boat. Nevertheless the urgent and rather simple narrative drive of the film, to which such moments are rarely integrated as they are in Beineix's previous work, captured an enormous international audience. As for the borrowing of images from other directors, this is not as disruptive of the narrative in *37,2* as it is, say, in Léos Carax's *Mauvais Sang* (1986) (see below). The relation between spectacle and narrative is crucial to Beineix's fourth film, *Roselyne et les lions* (1989). The vast majority of the film, which tells the story of Roselyne (Isabelle Pasco) and Thierry (Gérard Sandoz), a young lion-taming duo, is shot in an uncharacteristically flat, naturalistic style which matches the small-time beginnings of the protagonists. Once the couple are hired by a high-tech German circus, Beineix begins to frame his shots in a more stylised fashion, but full cinematic spectacle is saved until the finale of their first major show which, complete which dry ice and slow motion, presents Roselyne and Thierry's routine with the lions. Beineix has stated that the film is a satire on the film industry, and it is interesting to note the defence of *le look* which emerges, particularly in Thierry's nationalistic championing of French 'style' against the demands of (German) efficiency. The film is ultimately a discourse on itself, in which 'style' finally wins out in the overblown, spectacular ending.

IP5: the pastoral *look*

The reception of *IP5* (1992) in France was clouded by the death, on the last day of filming, of the actor Yves Montand. What scandalised some about Montand's death was not so much that Beineix's zealous direction (requiring the star to swim in a cold lake) might have contributed to it but, more insidiously, that Montand – '*the* fetish star' of '1970s authentic cinema' (Hayward 1993: 296) – should end his illustrious career in a film by Beineix rather than a classic by Costa-Gavras or Godard. In *IP5* (subtitled *L'Ile aux pachydermes*, and numbered because it is Beineix's fifth film) Montand plays Léon Marcel, an old man who has escaped from an asylum to wander in the woods in search of a past love. He is joined by a pair of reluctant companions, a graffiti artist called Tony (Olivier Martinez) and his young black friend Jockey (Sekkou Sall). Unexpectedly, the film engages with the French countryside, personified by Montand's holy fool. Although *37,2* features a number of rural sequences, Beineix's work – and the *cinéma du look* in general – is usually confined to an alienating urban setting. *IP5* begins in this familiar territory, introducing Tony and Jockey in a threatening Parisian environment. Beineix mixes bleak naturalism – the scenes with Jockey's alcoholic father – with hip-hop music, dayglo colours and cartoon-style violence. The film portrays skinhead thugs as cardboard cinematic villains reminiscent of *Diva* or *Tirez sur le Pianiste*, but the use of colour derives from graffiti art. If in *Diva* painting occupies a cultural middle ground, represented by the murals in Jules's flat, in *IP5* painting is both 'high' and 'low' art, the two brought together when Tony gives Jockey a book on Michelangelo. Where French art cinema considers classical painting – witness Jean-Luc Godard's *Passion* (1982) or Agnès Varda's *Jane B. par Agnès V.* (1987) – Beineix appropriates both the Renaissance and graffiti to his own populist medium.

The film enters its pastoral section as Tony and Jockey drive towards Toulouse in search of Gloria, a nurse Tony has fallen in love with. When their stolen car crashes and explodes, Léon comes to the rescue, and there follows a prolonged generational and cultural confrontation, not only between the characters but between the cinematic styles that they embody. In this regard, Montand represents at once the ostensible wisdom of age and the iconic power of French cinema in the three decades preceding the *cinéma du look*. Moreover, he constantly chastises Tony in terms which recall the usual critiques of Beineix's work, calling him an 'empty shell' and informing him that the woods surrounding them are no film set. A more conventional narrative would simply settle for a rite-of-passage movie in which Léon would educate his young charges. Beineix, however, after initially portraying Léon as a mystical figure at one with nature, slyly explores the deceit and despair beneath the old man's benign façade, thereby both eschewing sentimentalism and calling into question the mythical status of past French cinema. The romantic plot may end in a predictable manner, with Tony and Gloria reunited, but the spectacular closing sequence in the Pyrenees includes a psychological characterisation and an emotion which have been considered lacking in the *cinéma du look*. The mountain scenery is not just a spectacular sight, but a backdrop to Léon's poignant death. The film closes, not with a slow-motion spectacle as in *Roselyne et les lions*, but on a freeze-frame of Jockey crying out in grief. The allusion to the still image at the end of Truffaut's *Les 400 Coups* (1959) is perceptible, but totally secondary to the emotional impact of this ending. A comparison with the critical and popular impact of Carax's *Les Amants du Pont-Neuf* a year previously (see below), however, suggests that the pastoral look of *IP5* does not signal a general turning away in the nineties from the usual urban concerns of the *cinéma du look*.

Luc Besson

Luc Besson is the *look* director who has received the most sustained ridicule from the critics while proving a consistent hit with the public. Despite the increasingly large budgets for his films, he continues to work with friends, always casting Jean Reno and using a score by Eric Serra. At the age of twenty-five he directed *Le Dernier Combat* (1983), a black-and-white, low-budget post-nuclear piece short on dialogue but strong on atmosphere. The film won prizes at the Avoriaz festival for science fiction and fantasy film, but more significantly it opened Besson to the accusations of cinematic autism that were to dog his later work, *Le Grand Bleu* especially.

Subway: pastiche, celebration, pessimism

On its release in 1985, *Subway* was attacked in *Positif* for its meagre scenario and lack of characterisation. Described as a three-minute 'clip' (music video) over-extended to feature film length, it was compared unfavourably to Besson's television advert for Dim tights (Tobin 1985). Certainly, the plotting in *Subway* is both derivative and perfunctory: Fred (Christophe Lambert) steals some documents from a powerful crook whose wife, Helena (Isabelle Adjani), eventually finds him hiding in the depths of the Paris *métro*. Their mutual attraction is doomed by the closing-in of both the police and the crook's men, one of whom ultimately kills Fred. But setting has more importance here than plot, and Besson's excellent choice of milieu structures the claustrophobic narrative. Much of the film involves Fred discovering the service tunnels behind the *métro*, and then exploiting them to keep one step ahead of his pursuers. As with Beineix's *La Lune dans le caniveau* (1983), the sets recall poetic realism: *Subway*'s set designer was in fact Alexandre Trauner, who had designed the *métro* station set for Marcel Carné's *Les Portes de la nuit* (1946) (see chapter 1). This underground environment is populated by a gallery of minor characters, drop-outs from Parisian society. In a rather lame subplot, Fred persuades some of them to form a rock band with himself as manager. This does allow Fred/Besson to stage a finale in which middle-aged 'high' culture – a Brahms recital – is replaced by the pop culture of the Anglophone

20   Christophe Lambert in *Subway*

rock band, whose audience of the young, marginal and trendy
apparently mirrors Besson's own target audience.

The subplot concerning the rock band also overtly, one might
say defiantly, aligns *Subway* with music video. Critics have tended
to see both music video and the *cinéma du look* as postmodern, and
hence as characterised by pastiche, that is, by uncritical imitation,
what Fredric Jameson has called 'blank parody' (Jameson 1990).
But this pessimistic diagnosis ignores 'the extent to which the phenomenon [of pastiche] is also one of *celebration*' (Goodwin 1987:
47). Where Goodwin writes 'music video' one can read the *cinéma
du look* as a whole: 'Much music video "pastiche" is actually a celebration of popular culture that has nothing at all to do with
parody' (Goodwin 1987: 47). By playing to the cineliterate nature
of its target audience, *Subway* pays homage to previous films and
generic models without wishing to launch any critique of them. The
opening car chase initially places *Subway* within the thriller genre,
but when the cars pass under the elevated metro line it pays specific homage to the celebrated chase scene in William Friedkin's
Oscar-winning *The French Connection* (1971). There is a brief quotation from George Lucas's *Star Wars* (1977) when Fred, lost in the

bowels of the *métro*, picks up a piece of fluorescent tubing to use as a torch and is momentarily recast as a Parisian Luke Skywalker. And Besson's ending is based on the shooting of Michel Poiccard at the conclusion of Godard's *A bout de souffle* (1959). Celebratory cinephilia is also emphasised by the lyrics sung (in English) by the band during this finale: 'Just one glance and love had hit me/ Just like being in a movie'. Meanwhile in melodramatic slow motion, Helena finds Fred in the concert crowd only for him to be shot dead as she reaches out to him. Besson qualifies any tragedy in Fred's death by emphasising the surrounding spectacle: *Subway* ends with the crowd cheering the band. There remains, however, a covert bleakness about the film, emphasised in Bassan's reading of *Subway* as a pessimistic view of eighties society. The apparently seductive elements of the film – the neon lighting, the costumes, the hairstyles – are, he claims, signs of death rather than of well-being; although looking like an advert for youth and for 'Paris by night', *Subway* is in fact a desperate vision of stifled individuals (Bassan 1989: 48). *Subway* is indeed dynamised by both a celebration of popular culture and, less overtly, by a romantic/social despair, tendencies which characterise the *cinéma du look*, reaching their apogee in Carax's *Les Amants du Pont-Neuf* (1991).

Le Grand Bleu: a French *E.T.*?

Besson's third film, *Le Grand Bleu* (1988) is at once his most successful to date and the least favourably received by the critics. Attracting nine million spectators in the year of release, it was second among home-produced films only to Jean-Jacques Annaud's *L'Ours* (Prédal 1991: 403). When Besson only agreed to show the film at Cannes if it opened the festival, *Cahiers du cinéma* predicted that the director was intent on creating a global phenomenon, 'une planète Besson', which threatened to eclipse French cinema (Strauss 1988). This alarmist prognosis has been partially borne out by Besson's subsequent American project *Léon* (1994), and by the commercially successful marketing of *Le Grand Bleu*. Without the direct tie-ins of the marketing for *Batman* or *Jurassic Park*, the film nevertheless inaugurated a trend in France for the consumption of loosely-associated products: dolphin posters, blue lamps, a vaguely ecological, 'new age' style. The '*Grand Bleu* generation' was even the subject of a French television documentary in September 1991 (Daney 1993: 364).

Consistently privileging spectacle over narrative, *Le Grand Bleu* is pure *look*, and is as close to televised sport or natural history programmes as it is to any cinematic genre. The film concerns the rivalry between two 'free divers', Jacques Mayol (Jean-Marc Barr) and Enzo Molinari (Jean Reno), and follows them to various spectacular locations as they compete for the world title for unaided descent into the ocean. The central relationships are thus first between the two comrades/rivals and second between each man and the sea. Although this dangerous obsession is the crux of the film, Besson does not have the courage of his convictions: for all that Jacques keeps a photo of a dolphin in his wallet, a limp romance is introduced between him and an American journalist, Johana (Rosanna Arquette). Stereotypical and poorly played for comedy, the romantic subplot is only a pause in the long exposition of Jacques's fascination with the ocean, which concludes with Enzo's death and then his own, a marine suicide which leaves the pregnant Johana widowed. Besides the rather banal Freudian implications of Jacques's behaviour, the film has no narrative impulse. Jacques is asked by his uncle why he doesn't ask any questions: the implicit answer is that he – like Besson, and perhaps like the audience – is not interested in origins or explanations. The subject of *Le Grand Bleu* being essentially the length of time a man is able to spend underwater without breathing, Serge Daney concludes that the film is constructed as a speechless promo video, 'le *clip de l'aphasie*' (Daney 1993: 101). Yet it is precisely this aspect of the film – the iterative sequences of Jacques and Enzo diving, or of dolphins swimming – which constitutes its box-office appeal. As Daney himself notes, we are close here to the anthropomorphism of Annaud's *L'Ours* and Spielberg's *E.T.* (Daney 1993: 99). Besson largely neglects human relations, mediated by speech and narrative, in favour of an episodic exploration of marine spectacle. He also focusses on the 'authentic' nature of the experience, alluding in the title to the blue screen behind cinematic special effects (Katsahnias 1988). Besson's own blue screen is the ocean, and his effects are special because organic. To this extent at least, the film encapsulates the apolitical but environmental concerns of its audience, engaging not with society but with Nature (and, unlike Beineix's *IP5*, doing so without a trace of irony). The elevation of the film to the status of a quasi-mystical experience – exemplified by the scenting of Le Grand Rex cinema with sea-air for showings of the extended version – was noted by *Paris-Match*, which concluded that: 'The absolute is no longer in the depths of space, nor in the thoughts of Chairman Mao: it is in the blue' (Reader 1989: 5–6). This tendency seems to have led naturally to Besson's marine documentary, *Atlantis* (1991).

Gender and genre in *Nikita* and *Léon*

The opening shots of *Nikita* (1990) and *Léon* (1994) parody Besson's own camera work in *Le Grand Bleu*, but here the camera glides over the tarmac of a Parisian street or the water of the New York seafront rather than the surface of the ocean. *Nikita* is essentially an urban thriller, although like *Subway* it also inhabits a set of conventions drawn from other genres, principally the romance. Moreover, Besson's use of a female rather than a male protagonist allows him to play on the gender roles associated with genre in a manner absent from his earlier work. Nikita (Anne Parillaud, Besson's partner) is the only woman in a gang of young junkies who becomes involved in a gun battle with police. When she shoots and kills an officer at point-blank range, she is condemned to death and then given a reprieve which furnishes the film with its basic plot: the State will let her live in order to train her as an assassin. The resultant narrative is divided almost exactly into two halves: the first relating Nikita's transformation during three years in a secure training centre; the second her life 'outside', her subsequent missions and eventual desertion.

In *Le Mensuel du cinéma*, John Badham's US remake, *Point of No Return* a.k.a. *The Assassin* (1992) was preferred to *Nikita* (Verkindere 1993). Besson's already 'Americanised' film was seen as functioning only on a personal level while Badham explored the chaotic nature of American society, and its rejection by the heroine. This is doubly ironic, since the scenario for the remake was written by Besson himself, and since the original, like much of the *cinéma du look*, in fact concerns an alienated individual within a fragmented and threatening society. Besson has said of this strand in his films: 'Je suis guidé par une préoccupation: la société moderne crée un grand déséquilibre familial, un manque affectif chez les jeunes' [I am guided by a single preoccupation: that modern society creates a familial crisis, and an emotional lack for young people] (Gandillot 1994: 53).

At the outset, *Nikita* is presented as belonging to the thriller form, a male-dominated genre derived in part from American gangster movies and *film noir* (see chapter 5). The opening shoot-out includes an allusion to Mervyn Le Roy's seminal gangster movie *Little Caeser* (1930), while Besson's manipulation of lighting – blue, green and infra-red – recalls Godard's more overtly symbolic use of colour filters in *Le Mépris* (1963) and *Pierrot le fou* (1965). When Nikita is shot and wounded by her mentor, Bob (Tcheky Karyo), the slow-motion photography is also generic, reminiscent of thriller/Western director Sam Peckinpah and many others since. In these early sequences, Nikita herself is coded as male, through her androgynous name and appearance and her monosyllabic, abusive, and violent behaviour. Subsequently, she is trained not only in computing, martial arts and target practice, but also in the construction of a new and 'feminine' identity. No longer dressed in her leather jacket, trousers and Doctor Marten's, Nikita is provided with a wig, lipstick, and a little black dress. After she dances outlandishly to the Mozart sound-track, Bob pins a poster of a Degas ballerina on her graffiti-covered wall: Besson seems to be presenting the autocratic State as a purveyor of both gender stereotyping and of 'high' culture. The State also supplies an artificial familial structure: the surrogate mother Armande (Jeanne Moreau, herself a cinematic icon of femininity) teaches Nikita to use make-up, while Bob, the substitute father, normalises Nikita's origins by pretending to be her uncle and inventing stories of an idealised girlhood. The feminising process is concluded by her renaming (as 'Josephine' and also 'Marie'), and is realised visually in a series of facial close-ups and mirrored compositions. Nikita no longer spills out of the frame, she fits the screen as an amenable spectacle. Thus reconstituted as a 'feminine' ideal, a beautiful nurse – and also, in the supermarket sequence, a parodic housewife – Nikita gains a perfect cover (who would suspect a nurse of being a killer?) and a new generic role, no longer as a 'male' outlaw but as the predatory *femme fatale* of *film noir*. Hence the rather perfunctory love interest with Marco (Jean-Hugues Anglade), which recalls *Le Grand Bleu*; in each film, the romance serves as a norm against which the extraordinary destinies of the protagonists are measured. In *Nikita*, this means that sex is deferred – most explicitly in the Venice hotel room – by the demands of Nikita's role as assassin. If the film combines the macho thriller with 'feminised' romance, it is always the former which wins out.

The narrative also functions at a mythical level, retelling the Pygmalion story and the plot of Jean Cocteau's *La Belle et la bête* (1946), which informs Nikita'a transformation from beast to beauty. In the final reel, Besson unleashes the violence of the thriller genre with farcical brutality. In response to the absurd machismo of Victor the 'cleaner' (Jean Reno), Nikita assumes a submissive position, first foetal and then hysterical. The reassertion of orthodox gender roles here – Nikita is no longer the cool assassin, she is merely Victor's sidekick – is brought centre stage, with Victor a ludicrous parody of the macho hit man of convention. Serge Daney has associated Victor with advertising's obsession for images of cleaning (Daney 1993: 237), but 'le nettoyeur' also has a cinematic resonance, as the American director Quentin Tarantino has realised: Harvey Keitel, the cleaner in Badham's remake, reprises the role for laughs in Tarantino's *Pulp Fiction* (1994), alongside more established stereotypes like the *femme fatale*. Besson himself subsequently based *Léon* entirely around the character of the cleaner, who was again played by Jean Reno, after Robert de Niro refused the role. Filmed in New York and entirely in English, *Léon* – like *Nikita* – is built on generic foundations: here Besson uses the violent Mafia thriller, complete with taciturn hit man, corrupt cop (Gary Oldman), and knowingly exaggerated shoot-outs. But again the macho generic form is modified, here by the central relationship between Léon (Reno) and twelve-year-old Mathilda (Natalie Portman). Coded as father and daughter from their first encounter – he tells her not to smoke, and later when her family is murdered they stay at hotels together as father and daughter while he teaches her his trade – Léon and Mathilda engage in an emotional narrative of loss and reunion. Besson conflates family melodrama and violent thriller as the two are reunited in slow motion under hails of gunfire, or forced to part in the final doomed shoot-out. Again, the question of gender roles within the thriller genre is raised, with Léon telling Mathilda that 'little girls' cannot be hit men, yet subsequently explaining to her the tricks of the trade while Björk's 'Venus as a boy' plays on the sound-track. Ultimately, *Léon* presents a Hollywood-inflected narrative of emotional growth and family ties, in which the hit man – like his houseplant – finally puts down roots through meeting Mathilda. Interviewed about the film's reception, Besson noted that in America *Léon* was considered typically French, while in France it was considered truly American (Besson 1995). Either way, it was a success in both countries, attracting three and a half million spectators in France (more than the number that saw *Nikita*) and grossing twenty million dollars within three weeks of its American release (Pascal 1994: 61).

Léos Carax

By some years the youngest film-maker of the *cinéma du look*, Léos Carax – real name Alex Dupont – has tended to be singled out for praise by a press generally antagonistic towards Besson and Beineix. Having studied cinema at Paris III university, Carax wrote a number of articles for *Cahiers du cinéma* in 1979–80 before releasing a short – *Strangulation Blues* – the same year, thus repeating the career pattern of the *nouvelle vague* critics-turned-directors (see chapter 1). This parallel also extends to his infatuation with silent cinema which Carax – like Godard, Rohmer and Truffaut before him – first encountered at the Cinémathèque française. His first feature, *Boy meets girl* (1984), made when he was only twenty-three, was a critical success notable for its stark black and white photography and allusions to other films. What distinguishes Carax from his peers is the eclectic and sometimes disruptive nature of his cinematic references and the autobiographical thread in his work. The latter tendency is enhanced by the presence of an alter ego called Alex – played by Denis Lavant – as the male protagonist in *Boy Meets Girl*, *Mauvais Sang* (1986) and *Les Amants du Pont-Neuf* (1991).

Sound and image in *Mauvais Sang*

In the manner of Jean-Luc Godard's *A bout de souffle* (1960) and *Pierrot le fou* (1965), *Mauvais Sang* mingles the generic conventions of the thriller – heist, car chase, murder, double-cross – with an intense and doomed romance, articulated most strongly in a long bedroom scene. The plot concerns a young card-sharp and ventriloquist, Alex (Denis Lavant), who is paid to replace his late father as the safe-breaker for a heist run by Marc (Michel Piccoli). Leaving behind his girlfriend Lise (Julie Delpy), Alex joins the gang and falls in love with Marc's lover Anna (Juliette Binoche). In the build-up to the job, Alex and Anna spend a night of revelations and confessions together, but without sex. The heist – to steal the virus which causes 'le STBO', a romanticised form of Aids (see chapter 3) which kills those who have sex without love – goes wrong and Alex is pursued and shot. Marc kills the pursuers before Alex dies, leaving Lise to ride away distraught, chased by Anna.

What is most striking about the film is not the narrative, but the sounds and images which convey it. Carax's symbolic use of colour – red and black – in décor and costume derives from Godard's *Le*

Mépris (1963), and also reflects upon the films' title. *Mauvais Sang* is punctuated by Godardian extreme close-ups, especially of newsprint and text, while the use of illuminated news flashes on city hoardings is a direct reference to *A bout de souffle*. But although Godard is the primary influence here, there are others, in particular Jean Cocteau – who is supposedly spotted in a café, and whose *Orphée* (1950) provides the prototype for Lise's role as an angel of death on a motorbike – and Jean Gremillon, whose work *La Petite Lise* (1930) is glimpsed briefly in the film. If Binoche's appearance throughout apes Anna Karina and Louise Brooks, the physicality and clowning of Lavant's performance recalls not only Chaplin and Keaton, but the beginnings of film as a circus-like 'cinema of attractions'. The sound-track is characteristic of the *cinéma du look*, mixing as it does 'high' classical music with 'lower' forms, such as contemporary pop and the theme from Chaplin's *Limelight* (1952). But far from being dynamised by this furious cinephilia, *Mauvais Sang* tends to bear the allusions rather heavily. Carax's stylised photography, notably the recurrent and lengthy facial close-ups – which prompted Binoche to ask Carax never again to film her as 'the Madonna' (*Cahiers* 1991: 93) – proves exhausting and ultimately tedious, while the slow pace of the narrative is not aided by the rather claustrophobic sets. It is in the rare mobile sequences that the film excites, such as the final car chase or the vibrant tracking shot of Alex running down the street to the sound of David Bowie's 'Modern Love'. Such scenes generate the basic cinematic pleasure of rhythmic motion, the 'smile of speed' sought by Alex, and attained in the final shot by the accelerated image of Anna running towards the camera.

Les Amants du Pont-Neuf: neorealism meets artifice

According to Carax, *Les Amants du Pont-Neuf* (1991) concludes a trilogy begun with *Boy Meets Girl* and continued in *Mauvais Sang* (*Cahiers* 1991: 97). Originally a tight personal project like its two predecessors, the film mutated into the most expensive in French cinema history, taking three years to complete. Part way through, the crew had to cease shooting on the Pont-Neuf in Paris and a replica bridge and surrounding sets had to be built in the south of France. This change of location in fact simply enhances the interplay between realism and artifice which runs throughout *Les Amants du Pont-Neuf*. Carax integrates the expected elements of spectacle and fantasy with a portrayal of the harsh realities experienced by the Parisian homeless, achieving an intermittent documentary quality far removed from the usual concerns of the *cinéma du look*.

The narrative centres on the romance between Alex (Denis Lavant) and Michèle (Juliette Binoche), she a painter who is slowly going blind, he a down-and-out who lives on the bridge. The two first meet in the brown-toned neorealist section which opens the film, Michèle witnessing Alex being run over, and sketching what she supposes to be a dead man. The beatific close-ups of Binoche in *Mauvais Sang* are here replaced by images of Lavant's battered and filthy face. Subsequently, we follow Alex to a shelter in Nanterre where he and a group of homeless people are filmed with a hand-held camera and grainy film stock in a strikingly raw documentary sequence. This is Paris by night as a bleak reality rather than as the throw-away spectacle provided by Beineix's *Diva* (1980) or Eric Rochant's *Un Monde sans pitié* (1989). And yet Carax's film also features a nocturnal Parisian fantasy so exaggerated as to at once parody and celebrate the most spectacular offerings of the *cinéma du look*, namely the celebrated spectacle of Michèle and Alex water-skiing on the Seine as a waltz plays, fountains gush and fireworks explode. These two sequences – the neorealist and the fantastical – illustrate the breadth of Carax's achievement in *Les Amants du Pont-Neuf*. That they can successfully coexist is due to a consistent social concern with the dual function of Paris, the site of public spectacle and also of personal suffering. If the bicentennial celebrations are the embodiment of the one, Alex and Michèle's story exemplifies the other. Hence the juxtaposition of Alex's dangerous yet exhilarating firebreathing with the tricolour vapour trails of the jets passing overhead, or the cross-cutting between parading soldiers and Michèle's flight after she has shot Julien. In this context, the water-skiing sequence is both an ironic exaggeration of the bicentennial fireworks (and of the *cinéma du look*'s reliance on the spectacular) and a desperate escape fantasy on the part of the protagonists, who have already escaped Paris once for the lyrical interlude on the coast.

In terms of genre, the film moves between the poles of neorealism and fantasy, encompassing the exaggerated perspectives of expressionism – the shot of Michèle and Alex lying drunk next to enormous wine bottles and fag ends – the photogenic imagery and cultural mix of the *cinéma du look* – the coast at sunset, a soundtrack running from Public Enemy to Shostakovich – and the studio-bound lyricism of poetic realist film. Even the bicentenary imagery is in a sense intertextual, deriving from Godard's use of Eisenhower's visit as the backdrop to *A bout de souffle* (1959). Given the sustained nature of this cinephilia – including a borrowing from Bresson's *Pickpocket* (1959) for the prison sequence and an allusion to Truffaut's *Les 400 Coups* (1959) in Alex's first sight of the sea – it is no surprise when Carax's protagonists themselves escape into cinema, namely into a scene from Jean Vigo's *L'Atalante* (1934), by jumping into the Seine and being rescued by a barge heading for Le Havre. As Keith Reader has noted, 'It is almost as though one filmic intertext of escape alone were not enough to free Alex from the attachment that is clearly destroying him' (Reader 1993: 414). And yet it is ultimately the romantic narrative, rather than the intertextuality, which carries the film. In terms of the elemental symbolism which runs throughout *Les Amants du Pont-Neuf*, the couple's escape from Paris by river is only the last example of how

21 Denis Lavant in *Les Amants du Pont-Neuf*

their romance depends on the agency of water. Where the Seine has already carried away all threats to that romance (in the form of Michèle's diary, the money that could restore her sight, and even the old tramp Hans), now it carries away the lovers themselves.

Fantasy outside the *look*

The *cinéma du look* is not quite confined to the films of Beineix, Besson and Carax, the three neo-baroque 'wonder boys' (Bassan 1989: 45). Caroline Roboh's camp cabaret *Clémentine Tango* (1982) belongs to the genre too, as does Virginie Thévenet's *La Nuit porte jarretelles* (1985), which led *Cahiers du cinéma* to coin the phrase 'style Forum des Halles' (Vincendeau 1987: 15), and prompted an attack from *Positif* on the quality of the narrative, acting, and portrayal of sexuality. Part of the press reaction to the *cinéma du look* which such critiques exemplify can be attributed to the dominance of the realist aesthetic within French film, whose consequence is the 'chronic naturalism' Bassan speaks of. Besson, Beineix and Carax all brought elements of fantasy back into French cinema, elements which had been marginalised for decades, and which when evident were often subordinated to a generally realist project, as in the influential genre of poetic realism. The privileging of director over genre in French film criticism – most explicitly in the *politique des auteurs* (see chapter 1) – has mitigated against the habitually formulaic genres that make up fantasy film: horror, melodrama and science fiction. (The thriller is formulaic and yet realist, and has thrived (see chapter 5).) Moreover, despite the pioneering work of Georges Méliès, and later, of surrealist cinema, the fantastic has been perceived as a principally Anglo-Saxon form, epitomised by

German expressionism, Hollywood melodrama and Hammer horror. French film-makers associated with the fantastic – notably Jean Cocteau and Georges Franju – were perceived as mavericks. Cocteau in particular, like the perpetrators of the *cinéma du look*, faced constant attacks from critics schooled in psychological realism and narrative cinema, but was appreciated by an enthusiastic youth audience. It is ironic that at the end of his own career Cocteau should write of Franju's horror movie *Les Yeux sans visage* (1959) that it had been 'a long time since we last experienced the dark poetry and the hypnotic effect of the macabre' (Cocteau 1991: 121), for it was at this point that the French fantasy film began to fade from sight, to be represented only intermittently in the two decades before the *cinéma du look* by New Wave interest in science fiction and the musical (see chapter 1), by Walerian Borowczyk's erotic fantasies and by Jean Rollin's low-budget vampire films. Yet French companies continued to finance co-productions, from the Franco-Italian Jules Verne adaptations of the 1960s to the Franco-American hit *Stargate* in 1994, while the French fantasy film lay dormant. This is partly because American imports have been commercially successful, and partly because French fantasy has had a particular national outlet: the *bande dessinée*. The rise of BD – which comprises comic strips and cartoon books – as a repository of the fantastical for an adult audience began in 1959 with the launch of *Pilote* magazine (Starkey 1990: 95), and paralleled the decline of fantasy in the French cinema during the sixties and seventies. There has tended to be little interaction between the two media, despite some formal similarities. The most celebrated live-action film of a French BD fantasy, *Barbarella* (1967), although a Franco-Italian production, was made in English. In the wake of the *cinéma du look*'s challenging of psychological realism, however, the horror film has been reinterpreted in Christian de Chalonge's *Docteur Petiot* (1990) (see chapter 2), while certain BD-influenced fantasy films have been released, including Henri Xhonneux's Sadean animated feature *Marquis* (1988), the cartoonist Enki Bilal's *Bunker Palace Hôtel* (1989), and most successfully, Jeunet and Caro's *Delicatessen* (1991).

The Occupation as comic fantasy in *Delicatessen*

Delicatessen (1991) is the début feature by the pairing Jean-Pierre Jeunet and Marc Caro, whose subsequent project, *La Cité des enfants perdus*, was released in 1995. *Delicatessen* is set in a decaying city of the future, where nothing grows and food is so scarce that the local butcher (Jean-Claude Dreyfus) has started to sell human meat. In order to keep his trade going, he employs young men and then murders them, but is also prepared to slaughter his neighbours in the crumbling apartment block. Stan Louison (Dominique Pinon), a vegetarian circus performer whose chimpanzee partner has recently been killed and eaten, arrives at the butcher's shop looking for work. As Stan goes about his odd jobs he meets Julie (Marie-Laure

Dougnac), the butcher's short-sighted daughter, and they fall in love. When her pleas to her father to spare Stan are rejected, Julie stumbles upon 'les Troglodistes', an underground network of vegetarian terrorists, and enlists their help. Ultimately, after a climax involving fire, flood and mayhem, the butcher is killed, and Julie and Stan are rescued by the underground, allowing them to start a new life together.

As well as being an inventive and futuristic comedy, *Delicatessen* also functions as a fantasy version of the German Occupation of France during the Second World War (Daney 1993: 295), a historical subject which French cinema continues to reinterpret, notably in Christian de Chalonge's *Docteur Petiot* (1990) and Bertrand Blier's *Merci la Vie* (1991) (see chapter 2). Both of those films might be said to inform *Delicatessen*, the former in terms of plot – an evil protagonist incarcerates and murders his victims – and the latter in the use of sepia photography. The central figure in *Delicatessen* is the butcher, a grotesque character who is not only a monster derived from the horror genre, but also the embodiment of the term applied during the Occupation to war criminals such as Klaus Barbie, 'the Butcher of Lyons'. The narrative presents several further parallels with the war period in France: an underground resistance movement, clandestine radio messages, the collaboration of the neighbours with the tyrannical butcher, rationing, the black market, and general deprivation. The *mise en scène*, moreover, evokes the 1940s not only in the décors, the costumes, and the persistent brown tones, but also in the primordial role of poetic realism as an overall influence on the look of the film: hence the impressive set design, expressionist lighting, nocturnal effects and ubiquitous vapour clouds, as in Marcel Carné's *Quai des brumes* (1938) (see chapter 1). Unlike poetic realism however, *Delicatessen* has a purely fantastical aesthetic, partly derived from BD, featuring crazy camera angles, facial contortions and bulging eyes, and a cast of bizarre minor characters including a man who lives in a slime-filled room full of snails and Aurore, a woman who keeps failing spectacularly in her suicide attempts. Pinon as Stan is a softer and more charismatic version of the acrobat played by Denis Lavant in Léos Carax's films (see above), and his circus tricks are a source of visual humour in the film, as are the slapstick gags involving the myopic Julie and the unfortunate Aurore. There is also a superbly orchestrated sequence of sound gags in which the bed springs squeaking under the butcher and his wife set off an orgasmic crescendo of noises throughout the building, including mat-beating, cello-playing and tyre-pumping. Even in the furious action of the finale, however, there are moments of lyricism, such as the underwater embrace between Stan and Julie and the tender final scene on the rooftop (both scenes incidentally recalling films by Jean Vigo, one of the idols of the *cinéma du look*).

Les Visiteurs: time-travel comedy

The most popular French fantasy film ever, indeed one of the most successful French films of all time, is Jean-Marie Poiré's *Les Visiteurs* (1993). In a year when Spielberg's *Jurassic Park* dominated cinema on a global scale, *Les Visiteurs* beat it into second place at the French box office, attracting more than double the audience, with an astounding 13.6 million spectators (Robinson 1995: 127). Poiré had already directed hit comedies developed from the *café-théâtre* vogue of the seventies, including in 1983 *Papy fait de la Résistance* (see chapter 2). *Les Visiteurs* features Poiré regulars Christian Clavier (who also co-wrote the screenplay), Valérie Lemercier and Marie-Anne Chazel. While Poiré certainly uses farce to send up the bourgeoisie in a manner derived from *café-théâtre*, he also presents a time-travel fantasy which pits a medieval knight and his servant against the modern-day world. Poiré claims to have written the basic scenario at the age of seventeen, intending to make a short science-fiction drama which ended when the two protagonists arrived in modern times (Nevers and Strauss 1993: 85). This remains the crux of the film, which transports the chivalrous Godefroy de Montmirail (Jean Reno) and the oafish Jacquouille (Clavier) from 1123 to 1993. Having mistakenly killed the father of his betrothed, Frénégonde (Lemercier), Godefroy drinks a magic potion hoping to travel back in time and undo his deed. Instead, he and his servant Jacquouille find themselves in modern-day France, where they meet their respective descendants, the kind-hearted upper-class twit Béatrice (Lemercier again, in her usual role) and the pompous *nouveau-riche* snob Jacquart (Clavier again). Jacquart, having changed the family name from the vulgar-sounding Jacquouille (which contains the French word for 'balls'), is running Godefroy's former castle as an overpriced hotel, while Béatrice and her dentist husband live in a gentrified cottage. Finding an ancient spellbook in the castle dungeon, Godefroy drinks a second potion and returns to his own time. Jacquouille, however, wishing to stay in the 1990s with friendly bag-lady Ginette (Chazel), drugs Jacquart and sends him to the Middle Ages in his place. The film ends with Godefroy and Frénégonde reunited and their lineage assured.

Whereas in *Delicatessen* (1991), Jeunet and Caro satirise the Occupation through a futuristic setting, in *Les Visiteurs*, Poiré and Clavier satirise the present through two characters who embody the feudal past. The persistent misunderstandings arising from Godefroy and Jacquart's arrival in the twentieth century generate both slapstick humour (Jacquart washing his face in a toilet bowl, or attempting to roast a leg of lamb on a spit made from an umbrella) and a commentary on present-day France which is vaguely ecological (the two express revulsion at the ugliness, pollution and noise around them), and politically anti-Revolutionary (Godefroy is disgusted to learn that his lands have been shared out democratically and that his castle is now owned by a peasant). On a narrative level, these two concerns are integrated in the finale: Godefroy's

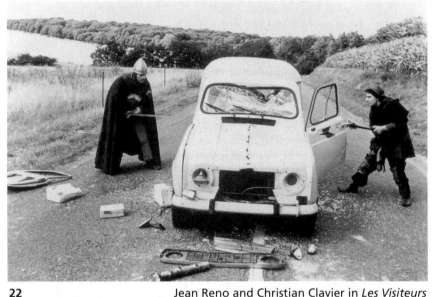

Jean Reno and Christian Clavier in *Les Visiteurs*

return to the Middle Ages is dependent on the castle dungeons remaining intact, that is to say, neither dismantled by the Revolution nor modernised by developers. The culture clash between 1123 and 1993 is most succinctly expressed in a sequence which shows Godefroy on horseback competing vainly against first a motorway, then a train, then an aeroplane. As well as giving rise to physical violence, as when Godefroy and Jacquouille attack a postvan thinking it is the devil's chariot, this comic conflict is also linguistic. Godefroys' anachronistic vocabulary and Old French verbs clash with Béatrice's sloane-speak and Ginette's coarser slang, which Jacquart learns in order to stay with her.

Les Visiteurs is related to three other genres besides popular comedy: fantasy cinema, poetic realism and the heritage film. The former connection is manifest above all in the time-travel plot, the Gothic scenes concerning the Witch of Malcombe, and the action sequence in the dungeon, which recalls Steven Spielberg's *Raiders of the Lost Ark* (1981). The medieval scenes in *Les Visiteurs* also tend to pastiche the historical settings of such poetic realist films as Jacques Feyder's *La Kermesse héroique* (1935) and of more recent heritage dramas like Jean-Jacques Annaud's *Le Nom de la rose* (1986). Praising the smelly and dirty Middle Ages of *Les Visiteurs* as a subversion of the ornamental portrayal of the medieval in *Le Nom de la rose*, a *Cahiers du cinéma* review even proposed that Godefroy's inadvertent killing of Frénégonde's father symbolises Poiré's overturning of Annaud, an interpretation apparently suggested by the fact that Godefroy sees his victim in the form of a bear, representing Annaud's 1989 film *L'Ours* (Nevers 1993). More persuasively, *Cahiers* contrasted the film's vigorous but culturally low humour with the high culture of the expensive décors and the historical setting. High production values and the trappings of the prestigious heritage genre are presented in the opening sequences before being assaulted later when chaos and destruction tear through the castle (Nevers 1993). The film in fact begins by conforming precisely to the conventions of the historical drama (see chapter 7), with period costume, spectacular landscapes shot from high and wide angles, lush music and an authoritative voice-over which situates the action in 1123. First undermined by the loutish violence of the English soldiers in the credit sequence, the heritage code is placed under increasing strain by the burlesque energy of the subsequent scenes. *Les Visiteurs* thus engages in combat with the values of Claude Berri's *Germinal* (1993), its major French box-office competitor (see chapter 7), and with all those 'cultural' projects which Poiré and Clavier protest are better supported by the State, easier to finance and easier to cast than popular comedy (Nevers and Strauss 1993: 86).

References

Bassan, R. (1989), Trois néo-baroques français, *La Revue du cinéma*, 449, 45–53.

Besson, L. (1995), Interview for *Le Journal*, France 2 television.

Buss, R. (1994), *French Film Noir*, London, Marion Boyars.

Cahiers du cinéma (1991), Hors série: Carax, *Les Amants du Pont-Neuf*.

Cocteau, J. (1991),The art of cinema, compiled and edited by A. Bernard and C. Gauteur, Marion Boyars, London.

Daney, S. (1993), *L'Exercice a été profitable, monsieur*, Paris, POL.

Gandillot, T. (1994), Luc Besson le professionnel, *Le Nouvel Observateur*, 1558, 52–3.

Gans, G. (1991), *Diva*, dix ans après ..., *L'Avant-Scène Cinéma*, 407, 3–4.

Goodwin, A. (1987), Music video in the (post) modern world, Glasgow, *Screen*, 28:3, 36–55.

Hayward, S. (1993), *French National Cinema*, London and New York, Routledge.

Jameson, F. (1990), *Signatures of the Visible*, London and New York, Routledge.

Katsahnias, I. (1988), L'Écran bleu, Paris, *Cahiers du cinéma*, 409, 5.

Nevers, C. (1993), Les Visiteurs font de la résistance, Paris, *Cahiers du cinéma*, 465, 83.

Nevers, C., and Strauss, F. (1993), Entretien avec Jean-Marie Poiré et Christian Clavier, Paris, *Cahiers du cinéma*, 465, 84–9.

Pascal, M. (1994), Les Cinéastes de l'an 2000, Paris, *Le Point*, 1163, 61–2.

Prédal, R. (1991), *Le Cinéma français depuis 1945*, Paris, Nathan.

Reader, K. (1989), 'L'Air du temps' – three recent popular French films, paper given at Warwick University Conference.

Reader, K. (1993), Cinematic representations of Paris: Vigo/Truffaut/Carax, *Modern and Contemporary France*, NS1:4, 409–15.

Robinson, D. (1995), *The Chronicle of Cinema, 5: 1980-1994*, London, *Sight and Sound*.

Russell, D. (1989), Two or three things we know about Beineix, London, *Sight and Sound*, 59:1, 42–7.

Starkey, H. (1990), Is the BD 'à bout de souffle?', Chalfont St Giles, Bucks., *French Cultural Studies*, 1:2, 95–110.

Strauss, F. (1988), La Planète Besson, Paris, *Cahiers du cinéma*, 409, 4.

Tobin, Y. (1985), *Subway*, Paris, *Positif*, 292, 79.

Verkindere, S. (1993), Nom de code: Nina, *Le Mensuel du cinéma*, 9, 42–3.

Vincendeau, G. (1987), Women's cinema, film theory and feminism in France',
Glasgow, *Screen*, 28:4, 4–18.

7

The heritage film

Filming and funding the heritage genre

The quality costume drama of the 1980s and 1990s has been termed the 'heritage film' (Higson 1993). In France it is a genre closely related to la *tradition de qualité* (see chapter 1), although chronologically it parallels the British trend for nostalgia initiated by *Chariots of Fire* in 1981. Classical in form, historical or literary in inspiration, the heritage genre tends to place a premium on high production values, often relying on international co-productions and famous stars in order to ensure a large audience. Although spectacle is clearly fundamental to the heritage film, it is always a supposedly authenticated spectacle, legitimised by claims to historical accuracy or cultural sources; hence the number of literary adaptations, biopics of forgotten figures, and reappraisals of revolution and empire. If the form is classical, following a straightforward linear narrative, so is the music: the theme from Claude Berri's *Jean de Florette* (1986) is derived from Verdi, while baroque music provides both subject and score in Alain Corneau's *Tous les Matins du monde* (1992) and Gérard Corbiau's biopic of a seventeenth-century castrato, *Farinelli* (1994). A measure of the dominance of visual pleasures over narrative ones in the heritage genre is the privileging of the visual arts as a subject. Moreover, the generic camera style is pictorialist: 'crane shots and high-angle shots divorced from character point of view, for instance, are used to display ostentatiously the seductive *mise-en-scène* of the films. [...] The effect is the creation of heritage space, rather than narrative space' (Higson 1993: 117). As regards framing, the genre demonstrates 'a preference for long takes and deep focus, and for long and medium shots, rather than for close-ups and rapid cutting' (Higson 1993: 117). François Truffaut made a similar point when he vowed that after the 'picturesque' period drama of *Les Deux Anglaises* (1971), he would never again film *une guinguette* (an open air café) or a carriage drawing up in front of thirty extras in costume, electing to cut the landscape, extras and sky out of the nineteenth-century narrative *L'Histoire d'Adèle H.* (1975), so that only cropped frames, claustrophobic interiors and the face of Adèle (Isabelle Adjani) should remain (Truffaut 1988: 331). This unusual attention to private suffering rather than public spectacle, via intimate framing of the protagonist's face, is echoed in Corneau's *Tous les Matins du monde* (see below).

Historical and mythical subjects are of course susceptible to a treatment outside the heritage genre: witness Robert Bresson's *Lancelot du Lac* (1974) or Eric Rohmer's *Perceval le Gallois* (1978). The bare demythologising of Arthurian legend in Bresson's film is achieved largely via ground- and body-level camera angles and a general absence of sound-track music. In Rohmer's *Perceval le Gallois* the spare yet evident artifice is the antithesis of the supposedly authentic period realism of the heritage film. All of the music and sound effects are provided by visible musicians, with the film shot in a studio against flat metal backdrops. In contrast, Daniel Vigne's medieval heritage film *Le Retour de Martin Guerre* (1982) features detailed and extensive exterior locations, numerous extras, rich photography and sound-track music. This drama, based on a sixteenth-century court case which passed into legend, declares its legitimacy from the outset by including in the opening credits the contribution of Natalie Zemon Davis as historical consultant. Moreover, the introductory voice-over of the investigating judge assures the spectator that this is no adventure or fantasy but 'a pure and true (hi)story'. In clear contrast with the fundamentally cinematic aims of Rohmer and Bresson, Vigne's film 'offers innumerable validations of its own authenticity, of its capacity to document' the period in question (Pauly 1993: 41).

While some seventies works – such as André Téchiné's *Les Sœurs Brontë* (1979), or the period dramas of Truffaut and of Bertrand Tavernier (see below) – prefigured the genre, the 1980s was clearly the decade of the heritage film, and 1982 the break-through year, featuring not only *Le Retour de Martin Guerre* but also the international co-productions *Danton* and *La Nuit de Varennes*. François Mitterand's presidential victory of the year before was fundamental to the development of the heritage film as a coherent and successful genre in the eighties, for two reasons. First, the victory of the Socialists in May 1981 stimulated a nostalgia for the 1930s, a time of left-wing government by the Front Populaire and, in terms of French cinema, the golden age of poetic realism. As the greatest French film-maker of that era, and one moreover associated with the Front Populaire, Jean Renoir became an important touchstone for the heritage film; in particular, his evocation of impressionism in *Une Partie de campagne* (1936) exerted a direct influence on films by Tavernier and Pialat (see below). Second and more significantly, the Socialists began to target for funding a particular brand of French film, prestigious but popular 'cultural' cinema. The result was 'la "nouvelle qualité française"' (Sainderchin 1982: 18), the filming of France's historical and cultural past as a form of national education, aiming to provoke 'le retour du grand public au cinéma' [the return of the general public to the cinema] (Le Péron 1982: 20), and funded or promoted by Jack Lang as Minister of Culture and later of Education.

Set up in 1959, the system of *avance sur recettes* is an advance loan made by the French government to film-makers, to be repaid from subsequent takings at the box office. During the 1980s, Jack Lang refined this funding mechanism and used it to support work by young directors like Besson and Beineix as well as by established *auteurs* such as Duras, Varda, Resnais and Bresson. The culturally respectable heritage genre, however, was the major beneficiary. The first year of Lang's influence, 1982, saw funding granted for the international co-productions of Wajda's *Danton* and Schlöndorff's adaptation of Proust, *Un Amour de Swann* (1983). This tendency to favour prestigious international projects characterised government subsidising of the cinema throughout the Lang years of the early and mid-eighties. After an unexpectedly populist funding round in 1984, Lang chose the publisher Christian Bourgois as head of the *avances sur recettes* for the next year, with a brief to target 'culture' once more (Prédal 1991: 384). This tactic enabled Claude Berri to film his expensive yet hugely successful Pagnol diptych, *Jean de Florette* and *Manon des sources* (both 1986), which epitomised Lang's vision of a cultural/popular French cinema (see below). When in the late eighties the Socialists were briefly out of power, Lang's successor François Léotard pointedly suppressed aid for 'artistic' films, but on his return to office Lang continued as before, and introduced a supplementary form of direct aid for ten to fifteen 'high quality' films per year (Prédal 1991: 388). Again, it was largely – though not exclusively – the heritage film which profited. The 'Langist' conception of film as high culture for the masses ensured that cinema now belonged to the new arena of the heritage industry, or in Lang's phraseology, 'les industries culturelles' (Toubiana *et al.* 1986: 27).

Revolution and empire

In the months following his election victory in May 1981, President Mitterand was faced with 'a declining franc, an escalating arms race, a crisis in the Middle East, and trouble everywhere on the home front'. But in the autumn of 1983 'the crisis that he placed at the top of his agenda was the inability of the electorate to sort out the themes of its past' (Darnton 1984: 19). Launching a reform of the French curriculum, Mitterand implicitly attempted to take control of French history, and in particular the founding moment of republican France, the Revolution of 1789, since to control the image of the Revolution 'is to exert political power, to stake out a position as the authentic representative of the left' (Darnton 1984:

23). This might also be seen as an attempt to challenge the reading of the Revolution myth presented in Andrzej Wajda's *Danton* (1982) (see below). According to *Cahiers du cinéma* in an A to Z of Lang's years as Minister of Culture, far from constituting a new left-wing cinema, political films such as *Danton* were in fact supplanted over the course of the eighties by evocations of cynical self-interest reflecting Lang and Mitterand's own opportunism and drift towards the centre (Toubiana *et al.* 1986: 27). As for representations of French history, over the decade the focus switched from revolution to imperialism and ultimately – with Socialist power declining and Mitterand's presidency clearly doomed – to decolonisation and the end of the Empire: witness in 1991 *Indochine* (see below) and in 1992 *Dien Bien Phu* (see chapter 2).

Relating 1789 to 1981: *La Nuit de Varennes* and *Danton*

Two mythical periods for the French left, the Revolution of 1789 and the Front Populaire government of the 1930s, came together in Jean Renoir's film *La Marseillaise* (1938), an evocation of the Revolution made under the auspices of the Front Populaire. A similar attempt to relate republican history to the society of the day, resulted, immediately after Mitterand's victory, in Andrzej Wajda's *Danton* and to a lesser extent Ettore Scola's *La Nuit de Varennes* (both 1982). These prestigious international co-productions were viewed by *Cahiers* as 'official' left-wing projects, underwritten by the Socialist government, and *Danton* was indeed funded in part by the Ministry of Culture (Daney 1982; Toubiana 1983), although the subsequent interpretations of the film proved resistant to government control (see below).

Although *La Nuit de Varennes* is not overtly politicised, its director had over the previous decade made several militant films for the Italian Communist Party, thus strengthening the association between himself and Renoir, who had overseen the Front Populaire/Communist campaign film *La Vie est à nous* (1936). A joint production financed by French and Italian television companies, *La Nuit de Varennes* was attacked in *Cahiers* for being merely a sumptuous exercise in televisual history (Daney 1982). Set in June 1791, it concerns the attempted escape from France of Louis XVI and the royal family. In Scola's fantastical version of history, they are pursued across country by a coach containing not only the lady-in-waiting Comtesse Sophie de la Borde (Hanna Schygulla), but also the cultural celebrities of the period: the legendary lover Giacomo Casanova (Marcello Mastroianni), the English revolutionary Thomas Paine (Harvey Keitel), and the libertarian writer Restif de la Bretonne (Jean-Louis Barrault). *La Nuit de Varennes* is hence as much an anthology of eighteenth-century culture as it is a historical account of the Revolution. As *Cahiers* noted at the time, political history is presented as literary history through the eyes of idealised witnesses who – along with the spectator – remain at a safe distance from the proletariat (Daney 1982). In a gesture typical of the heritage genre, Scola privileges cultural references of all kinds, and in particular literary forms, whether through direct quotations from contemporary texts or through the emphasis on written communication – messages, maps, articles and decrees – which is the motor behind the plot. The central narrative – the king's flight from Paris – is moreover framed by the self-conscious device of the puppet show, which first enacts revolutionary events prior to the king's disappearance, and ultimately closes with his execution. The theatrical theme is continued throughout by Scola's *mise en scène*, which stages the celebrities' coach and the inns at which they pause as dramatic spaces where the characters endlessly argue opposing cultural or ideological viewpoints (Pauly 1993: 55). Because the spectator travels with the pursuers, the king and family are never seen. Even when they are finally caught at Varennes, their faces are not visible, and the image of the king's body with his head outside the frame predicts the result of his return to Paris. Finally, after the return to the puppet show, the camera follows Restif de la Bretonne as he climbs up to the streets of Paris in 1981, a sequence one critic has interpreted as 'suggesting that the revolutionary creature beneath the surface can rise again any time from the *pavés* so often used as weapons by the people' (Pauly 1993: 60). On release, the reception of the film in France was however far more cynical with Serge Daney concluding in *Cahiers* that the heavy-handed final sequence epitomised a didactic gimmickry prevalent in 'official' historical dramas. He added that Restif should have emerged not in Paris but in Cannes as Scola's press agent for the film festival, since such a resolutely 'cultural' work was bound to win a prize (Daney 1982). As it turned out, *La Nuit de Varennes* won nothing.

After three decades of film-making in Poland, Andrzej Wajda left in 1980 when the Communist authorities declared a state of emergency in response to the growing support for the banned trade union Solidarity. He came to France and filmed *Danton*, at once a dramatisation of the French Revolution and an urgent commentary on the political situation in Poland. The narrative follows the manœuvrings of the charismatic man of the people Danton (Gérard Depardieu) and the harsh ideologue Robespierre (Wojciech Pszoniak, dubbed) during the Reign of Terror, and concludes with Danton's trial and execution, on the orders of Robespierre, in April 1794. The film's power derives from a series of contrasts between Danton and Robespierre on the level of characterisation and staging as much as ideology. The conflict is most evident when the two men confront each other in claustrophobic and enclosed spaces, particularly during the aborted supper in Danton's private apartment. In such scenes the theatricality of the dialogue, rendered all the more artificial by the dubbing of Pszoniak, is at odds with Depardieu's more relaxed and gestural performance, which recalls the more enigmatic power of the silent cinema (Toubiana 1983: 55). The political conflict between the two is underlined not just by the contrast in styles of performance, but also by Wajda's *mise en scène*, so that Danton's clothes and rooms are red, Robespierre's blue. This simple colour scheme is complemented by the use of white, which both symbolises revolutionary purity and completes the republican tricolour. In the ironic final sequence which takes place after Danton's death, the deathly pale Robespierre, having concluded that the Revolution has mutated into a dictatorship, passively listens to a young boy reciting the revolutionary creed. A close-up of the boy's face dissolves into a blank white screen, suggestive of the revolutionary purity that has been lost in the Terror. The irony is underlined by Jean Prodromides's discordant, wailing music, the sound-track of the Terror, which drowns out the boy's idealistic words.

A Franco-Polish co-production, the film was based on the Polish play *The Danton Affair*, written in 1935 by Stanislawa Przybyszweka and staged by Wajda himself in the late seventies and early eighties. Abel Gance's *Napoléon* (1927) and Renoir's *La Marseillaise* (1938) were also points of reference, but the Polish resonances dominated the film's critical reception: 'The film is a triple parable for its Polish audiences, of Tadeusz Kosciuszko's role in fighting the Russians in 1794, of conditions in Poland during the 1930s when the play appeared, and lastly of Poland's situation in 1981, when Lech Walesa and Solidarity were struggling to free the nation from dominance, by a stale soviet bureaucracy and its secret police' (Pauly 1993: 93). According to the latter reading, the most prevalent in the press despite Wajda's disavowals, Danton was identified with Lech Walesa and Robespierre became General Jaruzelski. Interpretation of *Danton* in relation to French politics was far more problematic, and entailed a struggle over the film's meaning which again concentrated on the portrayal of the two protagonists. Historically associated with the victory of 'republican France against the combined forces of feudal Europe', and hence with the birth and identity of the modern state, Robespierre remained an iconic figure for the French left (Darnton 1984: 20). Hence the delight of the Gaullist opposition and the dismay of both Communists and Socialists, including Mitterand, at the characterisation of Robespierre as a tyrant and Danton as a sympathetic pragmatist: 'The persona of Danton created by the immensely popular Gérard Depardieu [...] elicited a conservative bourgeois image in France, was even labelled Gaullist. Thus the implications of the film in Poland and France were reversed' (Pauly 1993: 94). Faced with a 'Gaullist' Danton, Mitterand and Lang, despite being 'the champions of socialism with a human face' (Darnton 1984: 19), were obliged to identify with Robespierre, and thus to fall foul of a revision of accepted republican history which they had in effect financed themselves.

Fort Saganne: handing down the imperialist adventure

The tendency to recreate a 'televisual' slice of history which certain critics had detected in *Danton* and *La Nuit de Varennes* was rendered explicit two years later in Alain Corneau's *Fort Saganne* (1984), a hybrid production which was sold as an international television mini-series before being released at the cinema (Prédal 1991: 389). A director who had made his name in the thriller genre (see chapter 5), Corneau made the transition to the heritage film with great success, *Fort Saganne* attracting over two million spectators in France and thus proving the eighth biggest-grossing French film of 1984 (Predal 1991: 403). This is unsurprising when one considers that the film united Gérard Depardieu and Catherine Deneuve, perhaps the two most powerful and popular French stars today.

Beginning in 1911, *Fort Saganne* is essentially an epic adventure story following the career of Charles Saganne (Depardieu), an army officer stationed in the Sahara. In keeping with the heritage genre's claim to historical, cultural, or geographical authenticity, the opening credits reveal that the Saharan sequences 'were shot in and around the historic towns of Chinguetti and Ouadane'. The exotic locations, numerous extras and imperialist subject are all comparable to the sub-genre of the British heritage film which concerns the Raj – as in David Lean's *A Passage to India* (1985) or the eighties television series *The Jewel in the Crown* – while the precise setting and epic military narrative recall Lean's *Lawrence of Arabia* (1962). As in these British productions, social class is a crucial theme: Saganne, who is of peasant stock, falls in love with Madeleine (Sophie Marceau), a daughter of the *haute bourgeoisie* and cousin of the President. The narrative concerns Saganne's rites of passage in the Sahara – where, he discovers, a man is judged by his actions and not his social origins – first under the tutelage of Colonel Dubreuilh (Philippe Noiret), a paternalistic figure described at one point as 'a medieval lord', and then in confrontation with the war lords of the desert. It is only when Saganne has learned a kind of chivalric 'nobility' – and won the Legion of Honour – that he can marry Madeleine and accede to a powerful social status. During the course of this military and social education, Saganne faces a sexual interlude in Paris with Louise (Deneuve), a predatory journalist. As a cool seductress, Louise manipulates Saganne as only men (his superior officers) have managed to do thus far in the film, exercising an ambiguous sexual power which Depardieu identified when he said: 'Catherine Deneuve is the man I would have liked to be' (Vincendeau 1993: 47). Deneuve's presence in *Fort Saganne* is not however limited to the role of *femme fatale* or, later, of nurse to the troops. She also functions as an icon of France, the mother country which Saganne and the empire-builders are defending (she makes her first appearance as he gives a speech about the need to protect France in the Sahara). This symbolic function, reprised in 1991 in Régis Warnier's *Indochine* (see below), is accentuated by Deneuve's iconic power outside cinema, whether as 'a semi-official ambassador for French fashion' and indeed for French womanhood as constructed by the advertising industry or, since October 1985, as the model for official images of Marianne, the personification of the

French Republic (Vincendeau 1993: 46, 41). But although France is embodied by a woman in *Fort Saganne*, ultimately it is in the masculine arena of war and through the male line of descent that the continuity of the empire is assured. Hence no sooner is the threat of World War One announced to the spectator (in the form of the subtitle 'July 1914') than it is obviated by a sex scene between Saganne and Madeleine, in which a son is conceived. Even as Saganne lies dying on the Western Front, Madeleine is pregnant, and the imperialist adventure is thus guaranteed for one more generation. This is confirmed in the final sequence, set in 1922: young Charles Saganne junior accompanies his mother at the ceremonial naming of Fort Saganne, and is initiated into the ways of the desert by his father's ally, a Saharan war lord. With Madeleine excluded, and World War One forgotten, the 'noble' rites of passage and the masculine tradition of empire can continue.

The aftermath of war: *La Vie et rien d'autre*

Like Corneau, Bertrand Tavernier is equally adept at the heritage film and the thriller (see chapter 5), and in both genres he is associated with a return to the narrative and psychological values of the postwar *tradition de qualité*. Hence his frequent literary adaptations, and his collaborations with Pierre Bost and Jean Aurenche, scriptwriters popular during the 1950s before their rejection by *la nouvelle vague* (see chapter 1). Along with François Truffaut, Tavernier represents the first stirrings of the heritage film in France after *la nouvelle vague*; his costume dramas of the seventies – *Que la Fête commence* (1974) and *Le Juge et l'assassin* (1976) – were followed by *Un Dimanche à la campagne* (1984) (see below), *La Passion Béatrice* (1987), and *La Vie et rien d'autre* (1989). A film critic before he turned director, Tavernier is deeply influenced by classical Hollywood cinema, and his medieval frontier story *La Passion Béatrice* has been credited with 'doing for French history what the Western did' for American history (Forbes 1992: 168). His painterly style, sweeping camera movements and humanist themes also owe a debt to Jean Renoir, and have rendered Tavernier probably the most consistent heritage film-maker in France, producing a popular yet bourgeois left-wing cinema, humanist in tone yet conservative in form, emblematic of the Mitterand years (Prédal 1991: 285).

Despite the director's previous successes, *La Vie et rien d'autre* proved difficult to finance because its subject was considered 'morbid, uninteresting and sinister' (Tavernier 1993: 266). Set in 1920, the film portrays the aftermath of the First World War and its attendant traumas, an area elided in *Fort Saganne* by the gap between Saganne's death and the inauguration of his monument. As with his other heritage films, Tavernier's evocation of period is detailed and his cinematography fluid, while the enormous sets and the hordes of extras prefigure Claude Berri's realisation of the coal mine in *Germinal* (1993) (see below). The plot concerns the efforts of Major Dellaplane (Philippe Noiret) to identify the bodies of thousands of missing men, and also to choose those to be entombed under the Arc de Triomphe as France's 'unknown soldiers'. The wider question of unearthing the horrors of the war before they can be buried again links the film with Tavernier's subsequent project, the Algerian War documentary La *Guerre sans nom* (see chapter 2), of which he said: 'I have a sense of continuing *La Vie et rien d'autre*, taking a historical fact and studying its effects and consequences' (Tavernier 1993: 267). Dellaplane specialises, moreover, in the art of photography and thus his activity throughout the film parallels that of Tavernier himself: excavating the past by means of a camera. Rather as in *Le Juge et l'assassin*, Tavernier combines costume drama with a detective narrative, in this case via a subplot concerning two women looking for the same man, a dead soldier who was the lover of one and the husband of the other. Dellaplane meets both women and falls for the widow, Irène de Courtil (Sabine Azéma). In a crucial speech which reflects not just on history but on its filmic representation – in *Fort Saganne* or in the war film generally (see chapter 2) – Irène attacks the masculine discourse of war and its perpetuation in all-male clubs and gatherings. She concludes that Dellaplane is afraid of women and hence of life. This is followed immediately by the ritual entombment of Dellaplane's unknown soldiers in a cold, patriarchal ceremony. Dellaplane seems to have chosen death over life. Characteristically, Tavernier concludes with an elegiac epilogue and a lyrical tracking shot reminiscent of Renoir. As Dellaplane walks alone through his vineyard, his letter to Irène is read in voice-over; just as he evokes the enormity of the loss of life in the war, the camera tracks from right to left to reveal rows of vines like so many war graves.

Indochine: Mother France and melodrama

In contrast with the patriarchal genealogy of imperialist power in *Fort Saganne*, Régis Warnier's Oscar-winning *Indochine* (1991) presents the decline of the French empire as a tragic, matriarchal narrative. In other words, *Indochine* is, unusually for a heritage film, a melodrama. Set in Indochina in the 1930s, Warnier's film conveys the loss of the colony not as military history – like Pierre Schoendoerffer's *Dien Bien Phu* a year later (see chapter 2) – but as a family history, in which the central relationship between a French mother and her adopted Indochinese daughter explicitly symbolises the colonial power structure. By choosing melodrama, Warnier also subordinates the heritage genre's inherent nostalgia for another period and an exotic setting to a more primal desire, traditionally addressed by melodrama: the spectator's desire for union with the mother. According to Steve Neale, the spectator watching a melodrama wishes for 'the union of the couple' in order to satisfy 'a nostalgic fantasy of childhood characterised by union with the mother: a state of total love, satisfaction, and dyadic fusion' (Neale 1986: 17). What is notable about *Indochine* is that 'the couple' here includes not only various personal relationships between a mother and her daughter, her lover and her grandson, but also the political relationship between France and Indochina. To this end, the film casts Catherine Deneuve in the role of Éliane, the French mother. As Corneau did in *Fort Saganne*, Warnier plays on Deneuve's status as an icon of French womanhood, able to 'signify a constellation of traits – career woman who remains feminine, determined but tragic mother, strong-willed but vulnerable lover – that allude to the changing roles of French women, but at the same time confine them to this precisely symbolic function' (Vincendeau 1993: 48). While the narrative of *Indochine* casts her in each of these roles at one point or another, it is her function as a tragic mother which combines with her extra-filmic role as Marianne, the personification of France, to portray the French empire as a mother who has to reconcile herself to the loss of her colonial child.

Like Jean-Jacques Annaud's *L'Amant* (1992) (see chapter 3), the film is shot in authentic oriental locations and is conveyed by a female narrator, in this case Éliane. Her voice-over states the film's melodramatic premise early on, declaring that in her youth she believed that the world was made up of inseparable dyads, 'men and women, Indochina and France'. If as a colonial rubber plantation owner Éliane embodies France, her adopted daughter Camille (Lin Dan Pham), a teenager gradually finding a sense of her own identity, embodies Indochina. The two are doomed to separation by the rules of melodrama as much as by political history. A tender and tragic mother to Camille, Éliane is portrayed as a cruel maternal figure – a kind of imperialistic career woman – in relation to her Indochinese workers, and as a seductive yet maternal lover to the young officer Le Guen (Vincent Perez). It is when Camille and Le Guen embark on an affair that the mother–daughter dyad is broken and the narrative takes on an epic sweep: Éliane has Le Guen transferred to a remote northern outpost, only for Camille to leave in search of him. In sequences reminiscent of Bertolucci's epic heritage film, *The Last Emperor* (1987), Warnier presents a brief panorama of the poverty, hunger and social unrest which are generating rebellion against French colonial power. Melodrama is privileged over history however, as Camille, captured by slave traders, is rescued by Le Guen. The reunited lovers are separated again during the uprising, but not before Camille has given birth to a son, Étienne. At this point the narrative frame allows us to glimpse that it is to the adult Étienne that Éliane is telling the story of the film. With the death of Le Guen and the imprisonment of Camille, the child is brought up by Éliane, functioning once more in a maternal role. But the division of mother and daughter (and hence of France and Indochina) is ironically confirmed at the moment of their reunion: released from prison, Camille has become a communist rebel – 'the red princess' – and therefore rejects her mother and imperialist power simultaneously. Her words to Éliane here sum up the pattern of melodrama: 'C'est trop tard, maman; je ne peux pas revenir en arrière' [It's too late, mother; I can't go back]. In melodrama, notes Neale, 'pathos is the product of a realisation that comes too late' (Neale 1986: 10). But the pleasure of melodrama derives from the possibility that the desired reunion may simply be postponed or modified: the fantasy of oneness with the mother 'can be re-engaged, re-articulated, perhaps finally fulfilled in the next film, the next melodrama (or the next episode of a soap opera)' (Neale 1986: 21). In *Indochine*, the reunion is achieved in the superb final sequence: having lost her lover and her daughter, and at the precise moment that Indochina's independence from France is declared, Éliane is finally granted the love she deserves and craves. The sequence takes place in Switzerland in 1954; Éliane has given Étienne the chance to be reconciled with his mother Camille, who is a member of the Indochinese delegation to the Geneva Conference on the future of the ex-colony. By refusing this reunion, Étienne enacts another, telling Éliane that she alone is his mother. Camille, belonging to the realm of politics, has lost her place in the melodrama. Warnier concludes *Indochine* with a shot of Éliane looking at her own motherland, France, in the distance beyond Lake Geneva. The image is held in a sepia freeze-frame, signalling that what was melodrama has become history, as confirmed by the closing text, which reveals that the French empire is over: 'On the following day, 21 July 1954, the Geneva Conference closed, putting an end to fifteen years of divisions and sealing the partition into two distinct states of what would henceforth be known as Vietnam.'

Filming the arts

The heritage film often takes its subject or source from the 'culturally respectable classicisms of literature, painting, music' (Higson 1993: 113). Painting is obviously the most important of the three in determining the imagery of the genre, usually by means of the static tableau shot. In Eric Rohmer's mannerist *La Marquise d'O* (1976) the *mise en scène* replicates Fuseli's painting 'The Nightmare', later imitated in Ken Russell's *Gothic* (1986). Outside the heritage format, Jean-Luc Godard and Agnès Varda deconstruct the tableaux of famous classical paintings in *Passion* (1982) and *Jane B. par Agnès V.* (1987) respectively. But the essential precursor for the painterly images of the genre is Jean Renoir. Renoir's homage to impressionism began with the short, unfinished masterpiece *Une Partie de campagne* (1936), set in the 1880s, in which a Parisian family spend a day in the country. In this film – and later in *French Cancan* (1954) and, to a lesser extent, *Le Déjeuner sur l'herbe* (1959) – Renoir founds his imagery on the impressionist paintings of Monet, Manet, Degas and his own father, Auguste Renoir. Within the heritage genre of the eighties and nineties, impressionism is evoked in a similar manner in Bertrand Tavernier's *Un Dimanche à la campagne* (1984) and Maurice Pialat's *Van Gogh* (1991).

Mobilising the tableau in *Un Dimanche à la campagne* and *Van Gogh*

Based on a novel by Pierre Bost, *Un Dimanche à la campagne* details a day in the life of an elderly painter at the turn of the century. But the film is clearly a homage to the cinema of Jean Renoir as much as to the paintings of Monet or Renoir *père*. The opening sequence, like the title, establishes an analogy with *Une Partie de campagne* which runs throughout the film. Renoir had characteristically made use in *Une Partie de campagne* of the depth of field and painterly frame afforded when a window is opened to reveal action in the background (in this case, the impressionist scene of two women on the swings in the café garden). Tavernier begins *Un Dimanche à la campagne* with a similar composition, although mediated by a slow tracking shot (another device typical of Renoir). The camera moves slowly from a shadowy interior towards a sunlit garden, framed in a doorway. Crossing the frame, the camera reveals the garden bathed in the morning light, before the screen fades to black. This simple painterly sequence initiates the narrative as a story of changing light, from morning to nightfall (an impressionist concern) and of varying depths of field (a Renoirian concern). It is moreover repeated at the film's close, and thus acts as a frame for the narrative.

Monsieur Ladmiral (Louis Ducreux), a widower and painter who lives in the country, receives a visit from his son, daughter-in-law and grandchildren. They are joined later in the day by the old man's favourite, his daughter Irène (Sabine Azéma). During the course of the day, family conversations and arguments are punctuated with flashbacks as Monsieur Ladmiral and others recall idyllic family scenes from the past, to a sound-track which features elegiac music by Fauré as well as occasional passages from Bost's novel read in voice-over by Tavernier. After his visitors have gone, Monsieur Ladmiral's impending death is heralded by nightfall, and thus the opening (and closing) sequence functions as a microcosm of the film's narrative: the movement from morning to night, from life to death. Nostalgia, the basic emotion of the heritage genre, dictates the nature of the film in four ways: on a narrative level, as the family's nostalgia for the past (when Madame Ladmiral was alive), and also as Tavernier's three-fold nostalgia, historical (for the turn of the century), painterly (for impressionism), and filmic (for Renoir). During the course of the film, Tavernier repeats the camera movement that reveals the garden through a doorway or window frame, a composition suggestive of Matisse as well as of Jean Renoir. But the most explicit reference to impressionist art is made when Irène and her father dance at a riverside café – a *guinguette* – which recalls Auguste Renoir's paintings 'The Luncheon of the Boating Party' and 'Dance at Bougival'. Knowingly, Irène even tells her father that he should have painted the scene. The image of the dancers is, unusually for Tavernier, a fixed shot and one viewed from the front in a classic tableau format. (Maurice Pialat includes a very similar image in *Van Gogh*, but one mobilised by a camera which dances with the characters (see below).) Typically in Tavernier, as in Renoir, the tableau is not static but explored by a moving camera. Most often in *Un Dimanche à la campagne* this involves a slow tracking shot into the painterly image, be it the garden, a portrait of Madame Ladmiral, or the white tablecloth spread like a blank canvas on the grass. In *Van Gogh*, meanwhile, Pialat varies between fluid camera movements and lingering, still tableaux to reproduce almost exactly Van Gogh's last paintings.

Such a painterly concern marks a development in Pialat's work, which has been more notable for the use of improvised dialogue, handheld camera and seedy locations to create a documentary style, as in the urban love story *Loulou* (1980) and *Police* (1985), a naturalistic thriller (see chapter 5). The commercial success of the latter allowed Pialat to use bigger budgets and consequently to modify his style, paying more attention in his next two films to production values and establishing a stylised *mise en scène*. *Sous le Soleil de Satan* (1987), taken from a novel by Georges Bernanos and influenced by Robert Bresson's *Le Journal d'un curé de campagne* (1950), is a rather uneasy combination of naturalism and spectacle. The interior shots in the church, especially the image of Mouchette's body on the altar, are lit and framed like sumptuous tableaux. In *Van Gogh* (1991) the composition of tableaux at times detracts from a lengthy account of the final months of the artist's life. By far the most expensive film Pialat has made, it was perhaps fittingly (given the subject) a commercial disaster.

The subject of numerous biopics in the United States and Europe, Van Gogh also inspired Alain Resnais and Gaston Diehl's black-and-white documentary *Van Gogh* (1948), in which 'camera movements across the surfaces of canvases were increased in speed until the paintings became unreadable, focus was also pulled to create blurs, and montage was accelerated as the film neared its end', such distortions aiming to symbolise the artist's growing mental turmoil (Walker 1993: 181). Pialat's representation of the paintings is by contrast tame imitation, but he does integrate them with the circumstances of Van Gogh's life by including compositions in the course of the narrative, ostensibly by chance, and sometimes in the background. The film begins with the arrival of Van Gogh (Jacques Dutronc) in Auvers-sur-Oise in May 1890, and follows his deteriorating relations with his host, Doctor Gachet, Gachet's daughter Marguerite, and his own brother, Theo. Drinking heavily and in despair, the artist shoots himself in the chest and dies two days later. Photographed largely in melancholic blue tones, although at moments imitating the palette of Van Gogh's canvases, the film is reminiscent of Pialat's earlier work in the unsteady, restless camera movement and the absence of sound-track music. Although the seemingly improvised dialogue and the harsh, unsentimental tone are far from the conventions of the heritage film, the composition of impressionist tableaux demonstrates a desire to reproduce the 'authentic' which is fundamental to the genre. Among the paint-

23   Sabine Azéma and Louis Ducreux in *Un Dimanche à la compagne*

ings by Van Gogh reproduced here are the portraits of Gachet and
of Marguerite and the views of wheatfields and of boats on the Oise;
Renoir *père* and Degas are also alluded to in the long Parisian
cancan sequence and the scene at the riverside *guinguette*. And
again, Jean Renoir's *Une Partie de campagne* and *French Cancan* are
visible influences on this painterly enterprise.

Private space in *Camille Claudel* and *Tous les Matins du monde*

Like *Van Gogh*, Bruno Nuytten's *Camille Claudel* (1988) is the
lengthy biopic of a troubled artist, but a biopic watched by three
million spectators (Prédal 1991: 403). The popularity of the film is
above all attributable to the presence of Isabelle Adjani and Gérard
Depardieu as the leads. For Adjani this was a personal project,
directed by her ex-partner Nuytten and co-produced by herself amid
accusations that she had abused her position as president of the
commission d'avances sur recettes (Reader 1989). The film may also
have benefited from the publicity surrounding Adjani at the time,
whose public declaration that her father was Algerian and her
mother German was followed by a rumour in the press that she was
dying of Aids (Andrew 1995: 24). As she noted later, the two
events were not unconnected: 'the French have long regarded for-
eigners as an infectious body within the nation, and of course that's
like Aids. So to the right-wingers like Le Pen, I became a good
target' (Andrew 1995: 25).

   Camille Claudel has been termed 'the climax of a long period of
art-historical rehabilitation' inspired by feminist reassessments of

cultural production (Walker 1993: 79). The sculptor had previously been known, not as an artist in her own right, but as pupil, assistant and mistress to Auguste Rodin in the 1880s and 1890s, and also as the sister of the poet Paul Claudel, who was in fact responsible for her incarceration in an asylum for the last thirty years of her life. Three biographies of Camille Claudel had been published in France in the early 1980s, initiating a revision of this reductive image. Anne Delbée, having written a play and a biography about Camille which were critical of her treatment by her family, planned to make a film too. This project was scuppered by the Claudels, who granted access to personal documents and letters to Nuytten and Adjani instead, since their version was based on a much more favourable biography by Camille's grandniece Reine-Marie Paris (Reader 1989). The resultant film relates how Camille (Adjani), an ambitious young sculptor aged nineteen, meets Rodin (Depardieu) in Paris and becomes his model and assistant, ultimately subordinating her own work to his so that he even signs what she has sculpted. Despite her family's disapproval, and the fact that Rodin has a long-term partner, Camille becomes his mistress. Later she leaves him and tries to establish an independent career, which is jeopardised by her drinking and an increasing paranoia about Rodin. After a disastrous exhibition at which she appears drunk, she destroys many of her sculptures, and on her father's death her mother and brother have her taken to an asylum.

Authentic in terms of setting – as in the shot of a half-built Eiffel tower – and costume, the film is less persuasive as an account of the creation of art, which is seen 'only in snatches, so the drawn-out sequence of steps from concept to finished work [...] is never fully documented' (Walker 1993: 87). This could be said of Pialat's *Van Gogh* and of the heritage genre's approach to art in general, and is in contrast with the extensive exploration of the creative process in Jacques Rivette's *La Belle Noiseuse* (1991). As one might expect from a cinematographer turned director, Nuytten shoots *Camille Claudel* effectively in brooding nocturnal colours and with intricate camera work. But although Rodin's visit to the Claudels' house in the country is the cue for an impressionist-inspired *mise en scène*, the compositions are often intimate and gloomy, and thus unusual for a heritage film. The predominance of interiors over public spaces can be related to Paul Claudel's definition of his sister's art as an 'interior' sculpture, 'proscribed from public square and open air' (Walker 1993: 88), but also to François Truffaut's claustrophobic period drama *L'Histoire d'Adèle H.* (1975), a clear influence on *Camille Claudel*. Adjani received Oscar nominations for both performances, each time for her role as a troubled woman seeking independence from a dominant father figure only to end up in an asylum. Unlike *L'Histoire d'Adèle H.*, however, *Camille Claudel* does at times feature those clichés of the costume drama – such as carriages pulling up in front of houses – which Truffaut had excised from his film, making it altogether shorter, sparer and more

24   Jacques Dutronc (centre) in *Van Gogh*

psychologically convincing than Nuytten's.

If in *Camille Claudel* Nuytten fails to fully match his *mise en scène* to the 'interior sculpture' of his subject, in *Tous les Matins du monde* (1992) Alain Corneau achieves a perfect integration of theme and form, of private music and private space. The film reunites the co-stars of Jean-Paul Rappeneau's *Cyrano de Bergerac* (1991), Gérard Depardieu and Anne Brochet, and like *Cyrano* a year before, won numerous awards at the Césars. Marin Marais (Depardieu) is a seventeenth-century court musician. It is he who narrates the action of the film proper, in which the young Marais (Guillaume Depardieu, Gérard's son) is schooled in the art of the viol by the brilliant but puritanical Sainte-Colombe (Jean-Pierre Marielle), who has retreated into solitude since his wife's death. Marais and his teacher's eldest daughter, Madeleine (Brochet) fall in love, but when Marais leaves her to marry an aristocrat and enter the court, and her child by him is still-born, Madeleine hangs herself. The remorse-filled Marais is finally reconciled with Sainte-Colombe as the two men play music together in memory of Madeleine.

For all the apparent melodrama of such a plot, *Tous les Matins du monde* is in fact a melancholic film which always privileges *mise en scène* over narrative. As impressive as the seventeenth-century music is the photography by Yves Angelo, who went on to direct his own heritage film, *Le Colonel Chabert*, in 1994 (see below). The use of colour filters, based around a simple red/blue opposition with pastoral green as a neutral tone, replaces the conventional naturalism of the historical drama with an emotional symbolism as effective in conveying passion and conflict as Godard's famous colour scheme in *Le Mépris* (1963). Throughout the film, warm red interiors, reminiscent of Rembrandt's paintings, contrast with cold blue nocturnal exteriors. The *mise en scène* – lighting, décors and costumes – is an index of the tension between spirituality and materialism, between Sainte-Colombe's suffering and creativity and the cold indifference of the wider world, Marais and the court. The luminous but narrow palette of the *mise en scène* is complemented by the austere framing – which makes great use of facial close-ups – and is only relieved in the rare court sequences where public space is represented by a wider frame and a diversity of colours typical of the heritage genre. The theme of austerity is invoked from the start of the film, when the aged Marais, in a red close-up, evokes the memory of Sainte-Colombe. After this spare opening sequence, the main body of the film comprises a flashback. Sainte-Colombe's withdrawal into his music on the death of his wife is realised in repeated facial close-ups, lit in red, as he plays or composes. When the young Marais asks to study under Sainte-Colombe, his red costume relates him both to the musician and to the dead wife. Corneau's *mise en scène* divides the screen when the two men meet, with the left-hand side, occupied by Marais, coloured red, and the right, where Sainte-Colombe sits resisting the appeal of human contact and of music-making, coloured blue. This painterly composition is reversed near the end of the film when the two men are reconciled: Marais, 'a man fleeing palaces in search of music', stands in the blue darkness outside the cabin where Sainte-Colombe, bathed in red light, grieves and plays his viol. In between these two crucial scenes the romance between Marais and Madeleine is played out, ending with the bleak, blue-toned scenes of her decline and suicide. Corneau's privileging of painterly images and beautiful music in *Tous les Matins du monde* takes the heritage film's usual aesthetic concerns to their limit. But the result is resolutely austere rather than spectacular, and the music melancholic and repetitive, illustrating Sainte-Colmbe's comment to Marais that 'music is not for kings', but for the expression of private sorrow.

The Pagnol phenomenon

A successful film-maker and novelist whose career stretched from the 1930s to the 1950s, Marcel Pagnol was famous for his evocation of the Provence region of France. Filmed in Provence, his comedies and melodramas are notable for the poetic dialogue and genuine southern accents. But whereas Pagnol's representations of the south were always of the moment – *Toni*, directed by Jean Renoir and produced by Pagnol in 1933, was based on the newspaper report of a crime – the heritage films derived from his work are doubly picturesque, 'doubly exotic, temporally as well as spatially' (de la Bretèque 1992: 61). Perhaps because of this potent nostalgia for another time and another place, the Pagnol adaptations of the eighties and nineties were extremely successful at the box office. In 1986 more than 6 million people saw Claude Berri's *Jean de Florette* and more than 4 million the sequel *Manon des*

25   Jean-Pierre Marielle and Gérard Depardieu in *Tous les Matins du monde*

Gérard Depardieu in *Tous les Matins du monde*

sources, while Robert's far inferior diptych cashed in on the Pagnol vogue in 1990, with *La Gloire de mon père* attracting 5.8 million spectators and *Le Château de ma mère* 3.4 million (Prédal 1991: 403).

Operatic tragedy in *Jean de Florette* and *Manon des sources*

Claude Berri's avowed ambition in filming his Pagnol adaptations, to make a French *Gone With the Wind* and launch a mythical 'cinéma populaire' (Ostria 1986: 62), coincided exactly with Jack Lang's vision of the medium. With financial aid from Lang, he shot both films simultaneously, on location, over a period of nine months and at an almost unprecedented cost of 110 million francs (Prédal 1991: 63). The *Cahiers* review of *Jean de Florette* noted that Berri's experience producing Roman Polanski's *Tess* (1979) had given him a taste for expensive and risky literary adaptation, far removed from his earlier films as director (Toubiana 1986: 49). It was a taste which Berri was subsequently to indulge as a producer and director of heritage films, in *La Reine Margot* (1994) and *Germinal* (1993) respectively (see below).

In 1952 Pagnol had shot the film *Manon des sources*, developing the narrative a decade later in written form, and adding to the saga a tragic dénouement and a prequel concerning Jean de Florette. The resultant two-part novel, *L'Eau des collines*, is the source for Berri's two films. Although these were shot simultaneously, *Jean de Florette* is generally the stronger, benefiting from a tight dramatic focus on its three protagonists. Berri's achievement in both films, particularly the first, is to eschew the public space of the heritage genre in favour of a private tragedy concerning disputed heritage (the farm left to Jean in part one and ultimately to his daughter Manon in part two). *Jean de Florette* follows the inevitable demise of the urban interloper of the title (Gérard Depardieu) after his peasant neighbours, César and Ugolin Soubeyran (Yves Montand and Daniel Auteuil), block his water supply in order to buy his land on the cheap. Although the Provençal landscape shown is spectacular, high camera angles are rare, while throughout the film Bressonian ground-level close-ups of Ugolin's carnations or Jean's withering crops convey the central importance to the narrative of earth, water, and cultivation. This elemental factor structures the rhythm of the narrative as well, with rainfall and drought prolonging and finally confirming Jean's fate. As *Cahiers* suggested, Jean can be identified with the director since both are outsiders entering Provence (Toubiana 1986: 49), but he also appears to embody the heritage genre which this film at least plays against. Hence Jean's conception of Provence as a pastoral idyll, and his intention to 'cultiver l'authentique', a parody of the heritage film's characteristic claims to authenticity; moreover his naive ambition is interpreted as literary (like so many heritage projects) when Ugolin assumes that 'l'authentique' is an exotic plant Jean has read about in a text on horticulture. The character of Jean departs from a naturalistic

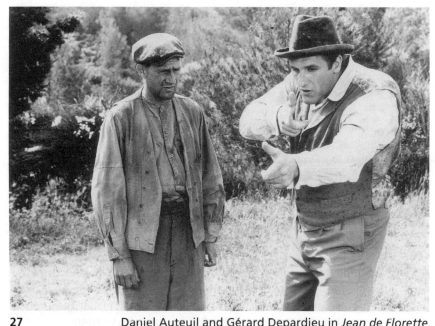

27　　　　　　　　Daniel Auteuil and Gérard Depardieu in *Jean de Florette*

portrayal of the Provençal peasant community in two other ways: first through Depardieu's appearance – he is a hunch back, recalling the archetype from popular literature, Victor Hugo's Quasimodo – and melodramatic acting style, and second through his association with music and above all with opera. His wife Aimée (Elisabeth Depardieu), an ex-opera singer, suggests that *Jean de Florette* is an ideal name for an opera, while an early scene shows him playing his harmonica as she sings the theme from Verdi's *The Force of Destiny*. The absurdity here stems from the gulf between an idealised, musical fantasy of rural living and the harsh reality to which the family are exposed through the Soubeyrans' plotting. Jean's illusions remain, however, encapsulated above all in the scenes in which he pauses to play the operatic theme on his harmonica. These musical interludes, as well as qualifying Berri's realism with a romanticised element, convey a touristic, facile picture of Provence which was uncritically reproduced not just in Yves Robert's Pagnol adaptations but, with the Verdi theme intact, in an advertising campaign for a beer (Stella Artois).

If *Jean de Florette* is a sombre and at times melodramatic tragedy, *Manon des sources* is a simple revenge narrative. After Jean's death, Manon (Emmanuelle Béart) is avenged upon the Soubeyrans, and in the final twist César is revealed as Jean's father and thus the destroyer of his own son. Again, the score is dominated by the harmonica theme from Verdi, here played by Manon at several points in the film. Like her father, and again in part through the operatic association of the music, Manon is a mythical rather than naturalistic character. An elusive goatherd, she is already a legendary figure at the start of the film, associated with the Provençal landscapes she inhabits, and reminiscent of the folk archetype of the water nymph (de la Bretèque 1992: 65). As in *Jean de Florette*, the characterisation is balanced between realism and fantasy: while César and Ugolin function at one end of the scale, Manon belongs to the other, and the villagers, sketchy stereotypes akin to those presented by Yves Robert, fit uneasily between them. It is above all the evocation of village life – largely absent from the narrower frame of *Jean de Florette* – which links *Manon des sources* to Pagnol's own films and also to a touristic image of Provence: the tableaux of villagers working recall the supposedly ethnographic set pieces 'beloved alike by opera (Gounoud's *Mireille*), advertising agencies and the cinema', while the increasing importance of the village square in the film is analogous not only to conceptions of a public heritage space but also to the traditional symbolism of the square 'as a metonymy for the "territory" of Provence' (de la Bretèque 1992: 63, 67). Although envisioned as a simplification of Pagnol, avoiding picturesque images of folk ritual, of villagers drinking pastis and playing *pétanque* (Ostria 1986: 62), *Manon des sources*, unlike the prequel, falls back with increasing regularity on such scenes. Manon's revenge – the drying up of the fountain – and her denunciation of César and Ugolin both take place in the village before an audience, as do the public rituals which follow: the religious procession, the wedding, the Christmas service. Only in the revelation of César's relation to Jean, and in his decline and self-willed death does Berri return to the spare, private spaces so frequent in *Jean de Florette*. César's death scene also sees the Verdi theme return with a fresh status, narrative rather than decorative: playing over an image of César's body, Jean's theme finally unites father and son.

Sentimental tourism in *La Gloire de mon père* and *Le Château de ma mère*

Yves Robert's apparently cynical attempt to emulate the format and thus the popularity of Berri's Pagnol adaptations proved hugely successful, despite the marked difference in styles. Robert's two films seem to owe as much to Disney as to Pagnol, despite being based on the latter's memoirs, *Souvenirs d'enfance*. The first part introduces the young Marcel (Julien Ciamaca) and his family, including his schoolteacher father Joseph (Philippe Caubère) and his mother Augustine (Nathalie Roussel). Beginning in 1900, the film evinces a nostalgia for childhood and for the early years of the century as well as a certain geographical exoticism. Like *Jean de Florette* and *Manon des sources*, *La Gloire de mon père* and *Le Château de ma mère* were shot largely on location in Provence, but tragic intrigue is replaced by domestic and sentimental comedy, while the peasant milieu of the Berri films here becomes a picturesque diversion for bourgeois tourists. As such, *La Gloire de mon père* and *Le Château de ma mère* reflect tellingly the spatial and temporal tourism fundamental to the heritage film, Berri included. The spectacular landscape, the rustic archetypes and the folk rituals of the genre are all here, while Robert's use of high camera angles to realise public places, whether the parks and avenues of Marseille or the Provençal mountains, epitomises the construction of 'heritage space' (Higson 1993). The model of the heritage spectator as a kind of temporal, as well as spatial, daytripper is evoked – without a hint of irony or awareness – by the narrative of both films. If in *La Gloire de mon père* the family stay in a country villa for the school holidays, in *Le Château de ma mère* they travel to Provence, and to the château of the title, every Sunday. Naturally, they meet none of the hostility with which Jean de Florette is greeted, but are in fact fêted by the locals. The tone is consistently one of light comedy until the conclusion of the second part, which relates the deaths of Marcel's mother, his brother Paul and his peasant friend Lili. The coda which follows legitimises the narrative, not merely via the male voice-over – implicitly the voice of Pagnol's text, which punctuates both films – but also by representing the now adult Pagnol as a film-maker in the thirties, and by including a brief sequence from one of his films. Thus in a gesture characteristic of the heritage genre, Robert ultimately 'authorises' his work by reference to an original source, indeed to two, Pagnol's text *Souvenirs d'enfance* (the voice-over) and Pagnol's cinema (the black-and-white sequence).

Literary legitimacy

As a novelist and film-maker, Pagnol has occupied both sides in the relationship between film and literature, adapting the work of Alphonse Daudet, but adapted in turn by Claude Berri and Yves Robert. The heritage film as a genre relies heavily on a cultural legitimacy derived from 'the adaptation of literary and theatrical properties already recognised as classics within the accepted canon', and in each adaptation, 'the "original" text is as much on display as the past it seeks to reproduce' (Higson 1993: 114–15). These films sell themselves by invoking not only 'the familiarity and prestige of the particular novel or play, but also [...] the pleasures of other such quality literary adaptations and the status of a national intellectual tradition' (Higson 1993: 115). Thus Yves Robert's Pagnol adaptations invoke both Marcel Pagnol and Claude Berri, while less cynically, Claude Chabrol's *Madame Bovary* (1991) refers directly to the original novel by Flaubert and implicitly to Jean Renoir's film version of 1933. As regards 'a national intellectual tradition', literary adaptations in France during the eighties and nineties have consistently celebrated the nineteenth-century novel, a high point of French cultural history. Since the heritage genre 'can also invent new texts for the canon by treating otherwise marginal texts or properties to the same modes of representation and marketing' as the recognised classics (Higson 1993: 115), Pagnol – Berri's *Jean de Florette* (1986) – appears beside Proust – Volker Schlöndorff's *Un Amour de Swann* (1983) – and Dumas – Patrice

Chéreau's *La Reine Margot*, Bertrand Tavernier's *La Fille de Dartagnan* (both 1994) – beside Flaubert, Zola and Balzac (see below).

Beyond the illustration of the text in *Madame Bovary*

The most common way for a literary adaptation to display the original text is to use part of it as a narrative voice-over, often read by an anonymous voice which one is free to identify as that of the author. In Tavernier's *Un Dimanche à la campagne* (1984) the director himself provides the voice-over, reading passages from Pierre Bost's novel. (Alternatively, adaptations of plays – such as Jean-Paul Rappeneau's highly popular version of Edmond Rostand's *Cyrano de Bergerac* (1990) – function simply as filmed theatre. The result is a collective spectacle which often presents a stage on which Cyrano performs to an audience who revel in his rhetoric and his swordplay, and which only opens up a wider perspective in the action-oriented battle sequences.) Giving the text a voice within the film is a crucial question when the literary source is idiosyncratic in its expression. This is perhaps a reason why realist novels are often adapted: the staple of literary realism, graphic description, is easily reproduced by a detailed *mise en scène*. But with a writer like Flaubert, renowned for his unusual style, the transposition of text to image may not seem sufficient. Hence Claude Chabrol's efforts, in *Madame Bovary* (1991), to find a suitable filmic vehicle for the original novel.

Chabrol's film follows the plot of Flaubert's novel scrupulously, although to simplify the narrative the opening chapter is cut and the epilogue narrated in a brief voice-over rather than shot in detail. Emma (Isabelle Huppert) marries a country doctor, Charles Bovary (Jean-François Balmer), but soon after the birth of their daughter, she tires of her dull husband and her constrained small-town life. She embarks on an affair with the local landowner, Rodolphe (Christophe Malavoy) and harbours illusions of an escape into a romantic idyll. When Rodolphe breaks with her and refuses to pay her secret debts, she commits suicide. In a gesture which epitomises the heritage genre's claims to authenticity, Chabrol declared that his aim was to make the film that Flaubert himself would have made of the story (de Biasi 1991: 106). In visual terms, this entails the detailed reconstruction of nineteenth-century Normandy, with three hundred extras in period dress. As for sound, Chabrol employs three or four passages of music, one of which is described in the novel, and of course the narrative voice-over. A male voice – which one might interpret as representing Flaubert or his narrator – reads five or six passages of text during the course of the film, passages chosen by Chabrol because he felt the sublimity of Flaubert's expression could not be transposed into cinema (de Biasi 1991: 50). Thus during Emma's drawn-out death (from swallowing arsenic), a pause in the dialogue between husband and wife allows the off-screen voice to read 'five of the most beautiful lines Flaubert ever wrote' (de Biasi 1991: 105). A concluding voice-over reaffirms the film's

Contemporary French cinema

dependence on the text, as part of the last page of the novel is read over the final image. A similar strategy is employed at the end of Claude Berri's 1993 adaptation of Zola's *Germinal* (see below). This use of voice-overs taken from the original text can jeopardise what Chabrol identifies as the need for film-making to remain autonomous, rather than merely the 'illustration' of a literary work (de Biasi 1991: 56). In the latter case, images merely duplicate the sound-track, as in Yves Robert's Pagnol adaptations: 'Le narrateur nous dit d'une voix profonde: "Le ciel était bleu", et vlan, on nous sert à l'écran un grand ciel bleu avec la musique appropriée, non, ça, je n'en veux pas' [The narrator tells us in a deep voice: 'The sky was blue', and bang, we're given a big blue sky on the screen with the appropriate music. No, I don't want that] (de Biasi 1991: 62). In order to avoid this redundancy of the narrated image, Chabrol attempted to be faithful to Flaubert not merely in *mise en scène*, but in montage too, and to match his editing to the 'interior rhythm' of Flaubert's narrative (de Biasi 1991: 79). In the agricultural show sequence, for example, the cross-cutting between Rodolphe's declaration of love for Emma and the speeches from the square below follows precisely the alternation of voices given in the text (de Biasi 1991: 84).

Certain scenes in Chabrol's *Madame Bovary* are none the less represented in a manner at variance with the novel: Emma's hallucination just before her suicide is rendered not by any fantasy sequence but by the glimpse of a bright red backdrop behind her as she pleads with Rodolphe for money. Chabrol claims that this sudden burst of colour evokes a kind of vertigo which matches Emma's desperate state of mind (de Biasi 1991: 93). But it is much less powerful than François Truffaut's blood-red close-up at a crucial moment in *Les Deux Anglaises* (1971). More evocative in *Madame Bovary* are the virtuoso camera movements, which do not simply realise the events of the novel, but actually equate the heritage format with Emma's desires, so that she almost personifies the genre. In contrast with the generally static shots of cramped interiors which characterise much of the photography, the moments when Emma glimpses a romantic escape from her lifestyle are conveyed in self-consciously sumptuous sweeps of the camera, conveying her state of mind but also foregrounding the favoured techniques of the heritage film. This first happens at the ball she and Charles attend early in the film, during which the camera rises elegantly to give an aerial view of the dancers, before descending again to floor level. Emma's rising hopes – and the construction of heritage space – are again conveyed by fluid camera work when she and Rodolphe have made love in the woods: the camera rises ecstatically into the trees, to the accompaniment of choral music. But again, as in the ball sequence, the camera motion also encapsulates the pattern of Emma's life, by returning to earth like her dreams which, we are told in a voice-over from the text, fall into the mud like wounded swallows.

Germinal 'is more than just a film'

Émile Zola's novel of 1885 explores the living and working conditions of miners in the north of France, and contrasts their suffering with the greed of the mine owners. Claude Berri's adaptation of 1993 tends to neglect the latter group, who are subject to sketchy characterisation in the film, and concentrates on the miners. Étienne Lantier (Renaud) comes to the Voreux coal mine looking for work. He is hired and works alongside the experienced Maheu (Gérard Depardieu). Étienne soon moves in with Maheu, his wife Maheude (Miou-Miou) and their family, falling for their daughter Catherine (Judith Henry). Prompted by his socialist convictions and the management's decision to reduce the miners' pay, Étienne organises a strike fund. When the strike begins, Catherine and her brutal lover Chaval (Jean-Roger Milo) work as 'scabs' at a nearby pit. Although the miners manage to close this pit, at Voreux they are fired on by the army, and Maheu is killed. The strike ends, and Étienne, Catherine and Chaval return to work, only to find themselves trapped underground when the mine is sabotaged. Étienne fights with Chaval and kills him; Catherine dies in Étienne's arms before he himself is rescued. On his return to the surface, he finds Maheude – the most committed striker – preparing to go down the mine to keep her family alive. It is at this closing moment that Berri – like Chabrol in *Madame Bovary* – falls back on the original text in the form of a voice-over. The last page of Zola's novel is read off-screen, heralding a future blossoming of the miners' struggle even as Étienne leaves the scene of the abortive strike. Ironically, Berri's *Germinal* was interpreted in *Cahiers du cinéma* in the opposite sense, as a closing down of the miners' struggle in much the same way as the French government had closed down the mines: 'La "gauche" qui a fermé les mines [...] a donc eu son film qui ferme la mémoire vive des mineurs et la voue, comme leurs mines, au musée' [The 'left wing' which has closed down the mines has thus got the film it wanted, which closes down the vivid memory of the miners and condemns it, like the mines, to the museum] (Scala 1993: 25).

At the time of release, *Germinal* was rated the most expensive French film ever made, with a budget of more than 160 million francs. It attracted 5.8 million spectators, coming third behind *Les Visiteurs* and *Jurassic Park* at the French box office in 1993 (Robinson 1995: 127). This fact led *Cahiers* to establish a distinction between the genuinely popular cinema of Jean-Marie Poiré's *Les Visiteurs* (see chapter 6) and the worthy, government-sponsored project that is *Germinal*. In an editorial entitled 'Vous avez dit populaire?', Thierry Jousse credited *Les Visiteurs* with a carnival-like power, while attacking *Germinal* for vulgarising and fossilising literature (Jousse 1993). This critique was elaborated by Andréa Scala, who remarked that the marketing of *Germinal* as an exemplar of national culture – a marketing carried out by the then Education Minister Jack Lang as well as by the film's producers and distributors – merely converted a cultural object into a commodity in a vain attempt to persuade the public to consume *Germinal* as avidly as they did *Les Visiteurs* (Scala 1993: 24). In short, the film was a theme-park version of the novel and of history, emptied of any attack on capitalism and populated by stereotypes (Scala 1993: 25). This criticism is at least partly justified. Berri's portrayal of the mine owners is perfunctory and close to caricature, while the marching strikers are rendered strangely theatrical and false by Jean-Louis Roques's jolly score. Both the music and the camera work are more effective in conveying the conviviality of public rituals – the tavern, the fair – than the tension of the strike or the claustrophobia of the flooded pit. The generally bleak colour scheme is none the less impressive, the persistent brown tones suggesting realist paintings of the period. The prime contribution that *Germinal* makes to the heritage genre does not lie, however, in painterly allusions or period reconstruction, but in an attempt to go beyond cinema and to achieve a socio-cultural function typical of Jack Lang's conception of film. The didactic imperative of the project – to celebrate the working class and remember the days of French heavy industry – was emphasised at the government-sponsored première of the film in Lille. In the months that followed Lang – as Spielberg was to do in the United States and Britain with *Schindler's List* – peddled the film as a form of national education by sending free videotapes to schools (Scala 1993: 24). This is the ultimate function of the heritage film in the Lang/Mitterand years: to provide a facile public education about the literary and historical past. As Depardieu claims at the start of the French video: '*Germinal* is more than just a film'.

Reflecting the war in Bosnia: *La Reine Margot*

If, as the director of *Germinal*, Berri attempted to relate the heritage form to the social circumstances of the 1990s – namely the recession – as the producer of Patrice Chéreau's *La Reine Margot* (1994) he oversaw another adaptation of a nineteenth-century novel with claims to reflect the political realities of the moment. In Chéreau's film, based on a popular historical potboiler by Alexandre Dumas, the allusions are to the religious divisions and civil war in Bosnia. A major concern of French foreign policy in the nineties, the former Yugoslavia was, naturally enough, subject to documentary representation, as in Marcel Ophüls's *Veillée d'armes* and Bernard-Henri Lévy and Alain Ferrari's *Bosna!* (both 1994). To reflect on Bosnia through a literary period drama is altogether more unexpected, but in fact provides a means of reaching a wide audience while exploiting the potential of the heritage film, 'in the displaced form of costume drama,' to create 'an important space for playing out contemporary anxieties and fantasies of national identity [...] and power' (Higson 1993: 118).

Patrice Chéreau, who made his first film in 1975, is noted for his subversions of realism and his attention to *mise en scène*. In fact, during the 1980s he worked more extensively in theatre – as director of the Théâtre des Amandiers in Paris – than in cinema, although in 1987 he did combine the two in simultaneous stage and screen versions of Chekov's *Platonov*. For *La Reine Margot* – previously filmed in 1954 – fidelity to the text was not stressed. Unlike Chabrol's *Madame Bovary*, Chéreau's project did not require the actors to read the original novel. Instead of an 'authentic' literary adaptation, 'Chéreau saw the film partly as a tale that would echo religious, political and social conflicts in the modern world: the highly effective score is by the Serbo-Croatian Goran Bregovic, while the carnage on view is unusually explicit for a historical drama' (Andrew 1995: 24). While Chéreau and the lead, Isabelle Adjani, stressed the Bosnian subtext in their interviews, critics also linked *La Reine Margot* to the 'new violence' epitomised by the work of Quentin Tarantino. An editorial on screen violence in *Sight and Sound* called the film 'an interesting if only fitfully successful hybrid of the costume drama and the contemporary violent thriller. [...] What *La Reine Margot* suggests is that it may be possible to fuse these two idioms, the costume drama and the revenge thriller, and use such a hybrid to address the whole European nightmare of ethnic cleansing' (Dodd 1995).

The focus of the plot and the central metaphor of religious intolerance and 'ethnic cleansing' is provided by the Saint Bartholomew's Day Massacre of August 1572, in which six thousand Protestants were slaughtered throughout Paris. In the opening sequence, Chéreau portrays the arranged wedding between the Catholic Marguerite de Valois, known as Margot (Adjani) and the Protestant Henri de Navarre (Daniel Auteuil), a political device intended to keep the peace in France. This sequence also introduces the court and Margot's Machiavellian family, including her brother, the unstable King Charles IX (Jean-Hugues Anglade), and her mother, the sinister Catherine de Medici (Virna Lisi). Following a frantic order from Charles, all Protestants gathered in Paris for the wedding are massacred. Navarre, rejected by Margot, is kept under house arrest but gradually befriends the king and saves his life after a hunting accident. When Catherine attempts to dispose of Navarre by giving him a poisoned book to read, it is the king who inadvertently succumbs to the trap, licking his fingers to turn the pages. Charles dies sweating blood, in one of the gruesome images which typify the graphic violence of the film. After Charles's death, and partly reconciled with Navarre, Margot leaves Paris in secret to join the Protestants. On a more private scale, the narrative includes two subplots concerning La Môle (Vincent Perez), a Protestant who engages in an illicit romance with Margot and a buddy relationship with his Catholic adversary, Conconnas (Claudio Amendola).

As the plot outline suggests, *La Reine Margot* is a visceral experience, the blood, sweat and dirt far removed from the niceties of heritage convention. Bregovic's menacing score creates a brooding atmosphere heightened by the constant rumbling of thunder and ringing of unseen bells. Filmed often in red and bloody tones, the action is frequently confined to claustrophobic interiors. The conventional reliance on wide-angle shots and luscious *mise en scène* is restricted to the opening wedding sequence, which functions to situate the film in the heritage genre and to present the public façade behind which brutal, private acts are hidden. Moreover both of the key exterior sequences, the massacre and the hunting scene, subvert generic expectations. In the former, the painterly tableaux beloved of the genre present a horrific spectacle, that of the dead and dying in the streets of Paris, reminiscent of images from the Holocaust or from Bosnia. As in Yves Angelo's Balzac adaptation *Le Colonel Chabert* (1994), where the French dead are piled high after the battle of Eylau, the static poise of the tableau has been transformed into a pile of still or frozen bodies. The shock of such images breaches the normally assured, touristic distance between spectator and spectacle which is the usual premise of the heritage film. In the hunting sequence from *La Reine Margot*, the gaze of the Duke of Anjou (Pascal Greggory), aimed directly at the camera, also erodes this distance. In contrasting such chilling self-consciousness with the heat of brutal passions, in balancing the 'illustrative tableaux' and the 'Olympian' perspectives of the heritage film against the claustrophobic 'two-shots, close-ups and [...] interior spaces of the Mafia film', and above all in reflecting on the urgent realities of the moment through a literary period drama, *La Reine Margot* clearly stands as the 'powerful apotheosis of the French heritage film' (Darke 1995). As *Cahiers du cinéma* declared in an editorial, the film brings to the genre an impressive energy and brutality never seen before (Jousse 1995).

References

Andrew, G. (1995), Isabelle époque, London, *Time Out*, 1273, 22–6.

Biasi, P.-M. de (1991), Un Scénario sous influence: Entretien avec Claude Chabrol, in Boddaert, F., *et al.*, *Autour d'Emma: Madame Bovary, un film de Claude Chabrol*, Paris, Hatier, 23–109.

Daney, S. (1982), Le Cinéma explore le temps, Paris, *Cahiers du cinéma*, 338, 65.

Darke, C. (1995), La Reine Margot, London, *Sight and Sound*, January 1995, 55.

Darnton, R. (1984), Danton and double-entendre, New York, *New York Review of Books*, 16 February 1984, 19–24.

De la Bretèque, F. (1992), Images of 'Provence': ethnotypes and stereotypes of the south in French cinema, in R. Dyer and G. Vincendeau (eds), *Popular European Cinema*, London and New York, Routledge, 58–71.

Dodd, P. (1995), History nasties, London, *Sight and Sound*, February 1995, 3.

Forbes, J. (1992), *The Cinema in France After the New Wave*, London, BFI/Macmillan.

Higson, A. (1993), Re-presenting the national past: nostalgia and pastiche in the heritage film, in L. Friedman (ed.), *British Cinema and Thatcherism: Fires were Started*, London, UCL Press.

Jousse, T. (1993), Vous avez dit populaire?, Paris, *Cahiers du cinéma*, 473, 5.

Jousse, T (1995), La Reine et le fou, Paris, *Cahiers du cinéma*, 479:80, 5.

Le Péron, S. (1982), L'Affiche douze ou le retour du grand public, Paris, *Cahiers du cinéma*, 336, 19–20.

The heritage film

Neale, S. (1986), Melodrama and tears, Glasgow, *Screen*, 27: 6, 6–22,

Ostria, V. (1986), Les Saisons et les jours, Paris, *Cahiers du cinéma*, 380, 60–66.

Pauly, R. M. (1993), *The Transparent Illusion: Image and Ideology in French Text and Film*, New York, Peter Lang.

Prédal, R. (1991), *Le Cinema français depuis 1945*, Paris, Nathan.

Reader, K., (1989) 'L'Air du temps' – three recent popular French films, paper given at Warwick University Conference.

Robinson, D. (1995), *The Chronicle of Cinema, 5: 1980-1994*, London, *Sight and Sound*.

Sainderchin, G.-P. (1982), La Rupture, Paris, *Cahiers du cinéma*, 336, 18,

Scala, A. (1993), Le 18 Brumaire de Claude Berri, Paris, *Cahiers du cinéma*, 374, 24–5.

Tavernier, B. (1993), I wake up, dreaming: a journal for 1992, London, *Projections*, 2, 251–378.

Toubiana, S. (1983), L'Histoire en dolby, Paris, *Cahiers du cinéma*, 343, 54–5.

Toubiana, S. (1986), L'Opéra Pagnol, Paris, *Cahiers du cinéma*, 387, 49–51.

Toubiana, S., *et al.* (1986), L'Image a bougé: Abécédaire du cinéma français, *Cahiers du cinéma*, 381, 18–34.

Truffaut, F. (1988), *Le Cinéma selon François Truffaut*, edited by A. Gillain, Paris, Flammarion.

Vincendeau, G. (1993), Catherine Deneuve and French womanhood, in P. Cook and P. Dodd (eds), *Women and Film: a Sight and Sound Reader*, London, Scarlet Press, 41-9.

Walker, J. A. (1993), *Art and Artists on Screen*, Manchester and New York, Manchester University Press.

Conclusion

Predictions of French cinema's demise as the millennium approaches, although commonplace, seem to have been overly pessimistic. This is largely because the dual threat of Hollywood and of television has proved less fatal than supposed. The hard-won exclusion of cinema from the GATT trade agreement – and the success of *Les Visiteurs* in head-to-head competition with *Jurassic Park* – signals that French screens are not yet condemned to showing one hundred per cent American product. Of course, to continue to compete with Hollywood, French cinema must also continued to reinvent itself as it has done over the last century. In the mid-nineties, the signs of this are promising: not only the healthy development of the heritage genre (*La Reine Margot*), the perennial appeal of the popular comedy (*Les Visiteurs*), and the resurgence of the fantasy film (*La Cité des enfants perdus*), but also the reinvention of the urban thriller (*J'ai pas sommeil*).

Perhaps most significantly, 1994 saw the launch of the newest wave of *auteurs* intent on revitalising traditional French realist cinema. In a move which demonstrated that television need not be a threat to cinema, but can actually support it, a series of nine films entitled *Tous les Garçons et les filles de leur âge* was commissioned by IMA Productions and the television station La Sept. Three of the films – André Téchiné's *Les Roseaux sauvages*, Olivier Assayas's *L'Eau froide* and Cedric Khan's *Trop de Bonheur* – were shown at the Cannes festival in May 1994, while all nine were screened on French television in autumn that year. Most recently, in the summer of 1995, twenty-seven year-old Mathieu Kassovitz won the best director award at Cannes for *La Haine*, a black-and-white portrayal of life in the deprived Parisian suburbs. It is a measure of the current health of French cinema that half-way through 1995, three of the five biggest-grossing films in France are domestic productions, *La Haine* among them. In 1895 the inventor of cinema, Louis Lumière, called the new medium 'an invention without a future'. A century later, he is still being proved wrong.

Filmography

Key d: director sc: screenplay c: cinematography l.p.: leading players p: production company

Annaud, Jean-Jacques

L'Amant

d: Jean-Jacques Annaud – sc: Gérard Brach, Jean-Jacques Annaud, from the novel by Marguerite Duras – c: Robert Fraisse – l.p.: – Jane March, Tony Leung, Frédérique Meininger, Arnaud Giovanetti – p: Renn Productions/Films A2/Burrill Productions/Giai Phong Film, colour, 1992.

Angelo, Yves

Le Colonel Chabert

d: Yves Angelo – sc: Jean Cosmos, Yves Angelo, from the novel by Honoré de Balzac – c: Bernard Lutic – l.p.: Gérard Depardieu, Fanny Ardant, Fabrice Luchini – p: Film par film, in association with D.D. Films/TF1 Films production/Orly Films, colour, 1994.

Becker, Jean

L'Été meurtrier

d: Jean Becker – sc: Sebastien Japrisot from his own novel– c: Étienne Becker – l.p.: Isabelle Adjani, Alain Souchon, Suzanne Flon, Jenny Clève, Michel Galabru – p: Premier/SNC/CAPAC /TF1, colour, 1983.

Beineix, Jean-Jacques

Diva

d: Jean-Jacques Beineix – sc: Jean-Jacques Beineix, Jean Van Hamme, from the novel by Delacorta – c: Phillipe Rousselot – l.p: Wilheminia Wiggins Fernandez, Frédéric Andréi, Richard Bohringer, Thuy Ann Luu – p: Irène Silberman/Films Galaxie/Greenwich Film Productions, with the participation of Antenne 2, colour, 1980.

La Lune dans le caniveau

d: Jean-Jacques Beineix – sc: Jean-Jacques Beineix, Olivier Mergault, from the novel by David Goodis – c: Philippe Rousselot – l.p.: Gérard Depardieu, Nastassia Kinski, Victoria Abril, Vittorio Mezzogiorno – p: Gaumont/TF1/SFPC/Opera Film Produzione, colour, 1983.

37,2 le Matin

d: Jean-Jacques Beineix – sc: Jean-Jacques Beineix, from the novel by Phillipe Djian – c: Jean-François Robin – l.p.: Béatrice Dalle, Jean-Hugues Anglade, Consuelo de Havilland, Gérard Darmon – p: Constellation/Cargo Films, colour, 1986.

Roselyne et les lions

d: Jean-Jacques Beineix – sc: Jean-Jacques Beineix – c: Jean-François Robin – l.p.:

Isabelle Pasco, Gérard Sandoz, Philippe Clévenot – p: Cargo Films/Gaumont, colour, 1989.

IP5
d: Jean-Jacques Beineix – sc: Jean-Jacques Beineix, Jacques Forgeas – c: Jean-François Robin – l.p.: Yves Montand, Olivier Martinez, Sekkou Sall – p: Cargo Films/Gaumont, colour, 1992.

Berri, Claude

Jean de Florette
d: Claude Berri – sc: Claude Berri, Gérard Brach, from Marcel Pagnol, L'Eau des collines – c: Bruno Nuytten – l.p.: Yves Montand, Gérard Depardieu, Daniel Auteuil, Elisabeth Depardieu – p: Renn Productions/Films A2/RAI2/DD, colour, 1986.

Manon des sources
d: Claude Berri – sc: Claude Berri, Gérard Brach, from the novel and film by Marcel Pagnol – c: Bruno Nuytten – l.p.: Yves Montand, Daniel Auteuil, Emmanuelle Béart – p: Renn Productions/A2/RAI2/DD, colour, 1986.

Germinal
d: Claude Berri – sc: Claude Berri, Arlette Langmann, from the novel by Emile Zola – c: Yves Angelo – l.p.: Renaud, Gérard Depardieu, Miou-Miou – p: Renn productions, in association with France 2 Cinéma/D.D. productions/Alternative Films/Nuova Artisti Associati, colour, 1993.

Besson, Luc

Le Dernier Combat
d: Luc Besson – sc: Luc Besson, Pierre Jolivet – c: Carlo Varini – l.p.: Pierre Jolivet, Fritz Wepper, Jean Bouise, Jean Reno – p: Les Films du Loup/Constantin Alexandrov, black and white, 1983.

Subway
d: Luc Besson – sc: Luc Besson, Pierre Jolivet, Alain Le Henry, Marc Perrier, Sophie Schmit – c: Carlo Varini – l.p.: Isabelle Adjani, Christophe Lambert, Richard Bohringer, Michel Galabru – p: Les Films du Loup/TSF Productions/Gaumont/TF1 Films Productions, colour, 1985.

Le Grand Bleu
d: Luc Besson – sc: Luc Besson, Robert Garland – c: Carlo Varini – l.p.: Jean-Marc Barr, Rosanna Arquette, Jean Reno – p: Les Films du Loup/Gaumont Productions, colour, 1988.

Nikita
d: Luc Besson – sc: Luc Besson– c: Thierry Arbogast– l.p.: Anne Parillaud, Jean-Hugues Anglade, Tcheky Karyo, Jeanne Moreau, Jean Reno – p: Palace/Gaumont/Cecci/Tiger, colour, 1990.

Atlantis
d: Luc Besson – sc: Luc Besson – c: Christian Petron – p: Les Films du Loup, colour, 1991.

Léon
d: Luc Besson – sc: Luc Besson– c: Thierry Arbogast – l.p.: Jean Reno, Gary Oldman, Natalie Portman, Danny Aiello – p: Gaumont/Les Films du Dauphin, colour, 1994.

Blier, Bertrand

Les Valseuses
d: Bertrand Blier – sc: Bertrand Blier, Philippe Dumarçay, from the novel by Bertrand Blier – c: Bruno Nuytten – l.p.: Gérard Depardieu, Patrick Dewaere, Miou-Miou, Jeanne Moreau – p: CAPAC/Uranus/UPF/Prodis, colour, 1974.

Préparez vos Mouchoirs
d: Bertrand Blier – sc: Bertrand Blier – c: Jean Penzer – l.p.: Carole Laure, Gérard Depardieu, Patrick Dewaere – p: Films Ariane/CAPAC/Belga Films/SODEP, colour, 1978.

Buffet froid
d: Bertrand Blier – sc: Bertrand Blier – c: Jean Penzer – l.p.: Gérard Depardieu, Bernard Blier, Jean Carmet, Geneviève Page – p: Sara Films/Antenne 2, colour, 1979.

Tenue de soirée

d: Bertrand Blier – *sc:* Bertrand Blier – *c:* Jean Penzer – *l.p.:* Gérard Depardieu, Michel Blanc, Miou-Miou – *p:* Hachette Première/DD Productions/Ciné-Valse/Philippe Dussart/SARL, colour, 1986.

Merci la Vie

d: Bertrand Blier – *sc:* Bertrand Blier – *c:* Philippe Rousselot – *l.p.:* Charlotte Gainsbourg, Anouk Grinberg, Gérard Depardieu, Michel Blanc, Jean Carmet – *p:* Ciné Valse/Film par Film/Orly/DD/ SEDIF/A2, colour/black and white, 1991.

Bresson, Robert

Lancelot du Lac

d: Robert Bresson – *sc:* Robert Bresson – *c:* Pasqualino de Santis – *l.p.:* Luc Simon, Laura Duke Condominas, Humbert Balsan, Vladimir Antokek-Oresek – *p:* Mara Film/Laser Productions/ ORTF/Gerico Sound, colour, 1974.

Buñuel, Luis

Cet Obscur Objet du désir

d: Luis Buñuel – *sc:* Luis Buñuel, Jean-Claude Carrière – *c:* Edmond Richard – *l.p.:* Fernando Rey, Carole Bouquet, Angela Molina, Julien Bertheau – *p:* Greenwich/Galaxie/In Cine, colour, 1977.

Carax, Léos

Boy Meets Girl

d: Léos Carax – *sc:* Léos Carax – *c:* Jean-Yves Escoffier – *l.p.:* Denis Lavant, Mireille Perrier, Carroll Brooks, Elie Poicard – *p:* Abilène, black and white, 1984.

Mauvais Sang

d: Léos Carax – *sc:* Léos Carax – *c:* Jean Yves Escoffier – *l.p.:* Michel Piccoli, Juliette Binoche, Denis Lavant, Julie Delpy – *p.:* Les Films Plain-Chant/Soprofilms/FR3 Films Production/Unite 3, colour, 1986.

Les Amants du Pont-Neuf

d: Léos Carax – *sc:* Léos Carax– *c:* Jean-Yves Escoffier– *l.p.:* Juliette Binoche, Denis Lavant, Klaus-Michael Gruber– *p:* Christian Fechner, colour, 1991.

Caro, Marco *see* Jeunet, Jean-Pierre

Chabrol, Claude

Le Boucher

d: Claude Chabrol – *sc:* Claude Chabrol – *c:* Jean Rabier – *l.p.:* Stéphane Audran, Jean Yanne, Antonio Passalia, Mario Beccaria – *p:* La Boétie/Euro International, colour, 1969.

Les Innocents aux mains sales

d: Claude Chabrol – *sc:* Claude Chabrol, from the novel by Richard Neely – *c:* Jean Rabier –*l.p.:* Romy Schneider, Rod Steiger, Paolo Giusti, Jean Rochefort – *p:* Films la Boétie/Terra/Juppiter, colour, 1975.

Le Cri du hibou

d: Claude Chabrol – *sc:* Odile Barski and Claude Chabrol, from the novel by Patricia Highsmith – *c:* Jean Rabier – *l.p.:* Christophe Malavoy, Mathilda May, Jacques Penot – *p:* Italfrance Films/ Civitesca Films, with the participation of TF1 Films Production, colour, 1987.

Une Affaire de femmes

d: Claude Chabrol – *sc:* Colo Tavernier O'Hagan, Claude Chabrol– *c:* Jean Rabier – *l.p.:* Isabelle Huppert, François Cluzet, Marie Trintignant – *p:* MK2 Productions/Films A2/Films du camélia/La Sept, in association with Sofinergie, colour, 1988.

Madame Bovary

d: Claude Chabrol – *sc:* Claude Chabrol, from the novel by Gustave Flaubert – *c:* Jean Rabier – *l.p.:* Isabelle Huppert, Jean-François Balmer, Christophe Malavoy, Jean Yanne – *p:* MK2/CED/ FR3, colour, 1991.

L'Oeil de Vichy

d: Claude Chabrol – *sc:* Jean-Pierre Azema, Robert Paxton – *c:* Jean-Claude Boukriss – *p:* Fit Production/INA/TF1 Films Production/Sylicone, black and white, 1993.

L'Enfer
d: Claude Chabrol – *sc:* Henri-Georges Clouzot, adapted by Claude Chabrol – *c:* Bernard Zitzermann – *l.p.:* Emmanuelle Béart, François Cluzet, Nathalie Cardone, André Wilms – *p:* MK2 Productions, colour, 1994.

Chalonge, Christian de

Docteur Petiot
d: Christian de Chalonge – *sc:* Dominique Garnier, Christian de Chalonge– *c:* Patrick Blossier – *l.p.:* Michel Serrault, Pierre Romans, Zbigniew Horoks – *p:* Electric/MS/Sara/ Ciné 5, colour/black and white, 1990.

Chibane, Malik

Hexagone
d: Malik Chibane – *sc:* Malik Chibane –*c:* Patrice Guillou – *l.p.:* Jalil Naciri, Farid Abdedou, Hakim Sarahoui, Karim Chakir, Faiza Kaddour – *p:* Alhambra Films, colour, 1994.

Collard, Cyril

Les Nuits fauves
d: Cyril Collard – *sc:* Cyril Collard, Jacques Fieschi, from the novel by Collard – *c:* Manuel Teran – *l.p.:* Cyril Collard, Romane Bohringer, Carlos Lopez – *p:* Banfilm Ter/La Sept Cinéma/Erre Produzioni/SNC with the participation of Sofinergie 2/CNC/Canal +/ Procirep, colour, 1992.

Corneau, Alain

Série noire
d: Alain Corneau – *sc:* Georges Perec, from the novel *A Hell of a Woman* by Jim Thompson – *c:* Pierre-William Glenn – *l.p.:* Patrick Dewaere, Myriam Boyer, Marie Trintignant, Bernard Blier – *p:* Prospectacle/Gaumont, colour, 1979.

Fort Saganne
d: Alain Corneau – *sc:* Henri de Turenne, Louis Garde, Alain Corneau– *c:* Bruno Nuytten – *l.p.:* Gérard Depardieu, Catherine Deneuve, Philippe Noiret, Sophie Marceau – *p:* Albina Productions/Films A2/SFPC, colour, 1984.

Tous les Matins du monde
d: Alain Corneau – *sc:* Pascal Quignard, Alain Corneau, from the novel by Quignard – *c:* Yves Angelo – *l.p:* Gérard Depardieu, Jean-Pierre Marielle, Guillaume Depardieu, Anne Brochet – *p:* Film par film/D.D./Divali/Sédif/FR3/Canal+/Paravision, colour, 1992.

Chéreau, Patrice

La Reine Margot
d: Patrice Chéreau – *sc:* Danièle Thompson, Patrice Chéreau, from the novel by Alexandre Dumas – *c:* Phillipe Rousselot – *l.p:* Isabelle Adjani, Daniel Auteuil, Jean-Hugues Anglade, Vincent Perez – *p:* Renn Productions/France 2 Cinéma/D.A. Films/NEF Filmproduktion/Degeto/R.C.S. Films, colour, 1994.

Denis, Claire

Chocolat
d: Claire Denis – *sc:* Claire Denis, Jean-Pol Fargeau – *c:* Robert Alazraki – *l.p:* Isaach de Bankole, Giula Boschi, François Cluzet, Jean-Claude Adelin – *p:* Electric/Cinemanuel/MK2/Cerio/Wim Wenders Produktion/TF1/SEPT/Caroline/FODIC, colour, 1988.

Deray, Jacques

Borsalino
d: Jacques Deray –*sc:* Jean-Claude Carrière, Claude Sautet, Jacques Deray, Jean Cau – *c:* Jean-Jacques Tarbès – *l.p.:* Jean-Paul Belmondo, Alain Delon, Michel Bouquet – *p:* Adel-Marianne-Mars, colour, 1970.

Devers, Claire

Noir et blanc
d: Claire Devers – *sc:* Claire Devers, from *Desire and the Black Masseur* by Tennessee Williams –*c:* Daniel Desbois, Christopher Doyle, Alain Lasfargues, Jean-Paul de Costa – *l.p.:* Francis Frappat, Jacques Martial, Joséphine Fresson – *p:*

Electric/Les Films du Volcan, black and white, 1986.

Deville, Michel

Péril en la demeure
d: Michel Deville – *sc:* Michel Deville, Rosalinde Damamme, from the novel *Sur la terre comme au ciel* by René Belletto – *c:* Martial Thury – *l.p.:* Michel Piccoli, Nicole Garcia, Anemone, Christophe Malavoy, Richard Bohringer – *p:* Gaumont, colour, 1985.

La Lectrice
d: Michel Deville – *sc:* Michel Deville, Rosalinde Deville, from the novel (and other texts) by Raymond Jean – *c:* Dominique Le Rigoleur – *l.p.:* Miou-Miou, Régis Royer, Christian Ruché, Maria Cesars – *p:* Curzon Films/Elefilm/AAA/TSF/Ciné 5/Sofimage, colour, 1988.

Dugowson, Martine

Mina Tannenbaum
d: Martine Dugowson – *sc:* Martine Dugowson – *c:* Dominique Chapuis – *l.p:* Romane Bohringer, Elsa Zylberstein, Florence Thomassion – *p:* IMA Films in association with UGC Images/Christian Bourgois Productions/La Sept Cinéma/FCC/SFPC/Les Films de L'Etang/Belbo Film Productions, colour, 1993.

Duras, Marguerite

India Song
d: Marguerite Duras – *sc:* Marguerite Duras – *c:* Bruno Nuytten – *l.p.:* Delphine Seyrig, Michel Lonsdale, Mathieu Carrière – *p:* Sunchild/Armorial, colour, 1975.

Ferreri, Marco

La Grande Bouffe
d: Marco Ferreri – *sc:* Marco Ferreri, Rafaeil Azcona, Francis Blanche – *c:* Mario Vulpiani – *l.p.:* Marcello Mastroianni, Ugo Tognazzi, Philippe Noiret, Michel Piccoli, Andréa Ferréol – *p:* Mara/ Les Films 66/Capitolina, colour, 1973.

Girod, Francis

René la canne
d: Francis Girod – *sc:* Jacques Rouffio, Francis Girod, from the novel by Roger Borniche – *c:* Aldo Tonti – *l.p.:* Gérard Depardieu, Sylvia Kristel, Michel Piccoli, Jean Carmet – *p:* Président/Rizzoli, colour, 1977.

Godard, Jean-Luc

Tout va bien
d: Jean-Luc Godard, Jean-Pierre Gorin– *sc:* Jean-Luc Godard, Jean-Pierre Gorin– *c:* Armand Marco – *l.p.:* Yves Montand, Jane Fonda, Vittorio Caprioli, Jean Pignol – *p:* Anouchka Films/Vicco Films/Empire Film, colour, 1972.

Sauve qui peut (la vie)
d: Jean-Luc Godard – *sc:* Anne-Marie Miéville, Jean-Claude Carrière – *c:* William Lubtchansky – *l.p.:* Jacques Dutronc, Nathalie Baye, Isabelle Huppert, Roland Amstutz– *p:* Sara Films/MK2/Saga Productions/Sonimage/CNC/ZDF/SSR/ORF, colour, 1979.

Passion
d: Jean-Luc Godard – *sc:* Jean-Luc Godard – *c:* Raoul Coutard– *l.p.:* Isabelle Huppert, Hannah Schygulla, Michel Piccoli, Jerzy Radziwilowicz– *p:* Sara Films/Sonimage/Films A2/Vidé Production SA, colour, 1982.

Prénom Carmen
d: Jean-Luc Godard – *sc:* Anne-Marie Miéville – *c:* Raoul Coutard– *l.p.:* Maruschka Detmers, Jacques Bonnaffé, Myriam Roussel, Hippolyte Girardot– *p:* Sara Films/Jean-Luc Godard Films, colour, 1983.

Je vous salue Marie
d: Jean-Luc Godard – *sc:* Jean-Luc Godard – *c:* Jean-Bernard Menou, Jacques Firmann– *l.p.:* Myriam Roussel, Thierry Rode, Philippe Lacoste– *p:* Pégase Films/SSR/JLG Films/Sara Films/Channel 4, colour, 1985.

Jeunet, Jean-Pierre, and Caro, Marco

Delicatessen
d: Jean-Pierre Jeunet, Marc Caro– *sc:* Jean-Pierre Jeunet, Marc Caro– *c:* Darius Khondji– *l.p:* Dominique Pinon, Marie-Laure Dougnac, Jean-Claude Dreyfus – *p:* Electric/Constellation/ UGC/Hachette Première, colour, 1990.

Kurys, Diane

Coup de foudre
d: Diane Kurys – *sc:* Olivier Cohen, Diane Kurys – *c:* Bernard Lutic – *l.p.:* Miou-Miou, Isabelle Huppert, Guy Marchand, Jean-Pierre Bacri – *p:* Alexandre Films/ Hachette Première/A2/SFPC, colour, 1983.

Un Homme amoureux
d: Diane Kurys – *sc:* Diane Kurys, Olivier Schatzky – *c:* Bernard Zitzermann – *l.p:* Peter Coyote, Greta Scacchi, Claudia Cardinale, Jamie Lee Curtis – *p:* Alexandre Films/JMS, colour, 1987.

Après l'Amour
d: Diane Kurys – *sc:* Diane Kurys, Antoine Lacomblez – *c:* Fabio Conversi – *l.p.:* Isabelle Huppert, Bernard Giraudeau, Hippolyte Girardot – *p:* Alexandre Films/TF1 Films Production/Prodeve, with the participation of Sofiarp/Investimages/Canal+, colour, 1992.

Lanzmann, Claude

Shoah
d: Claude Lanzmann –*p:* Aleph/Historia, colour, 1985.

Leconte, Patrice

Monsieur Hire
d: Patrice Leconte – *sc:* Patrice Leconte, Patrick Dewolf, from the novel *Les Fiançailles de M. Hire* by Georges Simenon – *c:* Denis Lenoir – *l.p.:* Michel Blanc, Sandrine Bonnaire, André Wilms – *p:* Cinéa/Hachette Première/FR3, colour, 1989.

Le Mari de la coiffeuse
d: Patrice Leconte – *sc:* Patrice Leconte – *c:* Edouardo Serra – *l.p.:* Jean Rochefort, Anna Galiena, Roland Bertin, Maurice Chevit – *p:* Lambart Productions/TF1 Films in association with Soficas Investimage 2 and 3 and Créations, colour, 1990.

Tango
d: Patrice Leconte – *sc:* Patrice Leconte – *c:* Edouardo Serra – *l.p.:* Philippe Noiret, Thierry Lhermitte, Richard Bohringer, Carole Bouquet, Miou-Miou – *p:* Cinéa/Hachette Première in association with TF1 Films/Zoulou Films with the participation of Soficas/Sofinergie/ Canal+, colour, 1993.

Le Parfum d'Yvonne
d: Patrice Leconte – *sc:* Patrice Leconte, from the novel *Villa Triste* by Patrick Modiano – *c:* Edouardo Serra – *l.p.:* Jean-Pierre Marielle, Hippolyte Girardot, Sandra Majani, Richard Bohringer – *p:* Lambart Productions/Zoulou Films/Éuropéen Cinématographique Rhône-Alpes/M6 Films in association with Cofimage 5/Investimage 4/Sofiarp 2, colour, 1994.

Margolin, François

Mensonge
d: François Margolin – *sc:* Denis Saada, François Margolin – c: Caroline Champetier – *l.p.:* Nathalie Baye, Didier Sandre – *p:* Cuel Lavalette/FR3/Alain Sarde, colour, 1991.

Malle, Louis

Le Souffle au cœur
d: Louis Malle – *sc:* Louis Malle – *c:* Ricardo Aronovich – *l.p.:* Léa Massari, Benoit Ferreux, Daniel Gelin – *p:* NEF/Marianne Films/Video Films/Seitz, colour, 1971.

Lacombe, Lucien
d: Louis Malle – *sc:* Louis Malle, Patrick Modiano– *c:* Tonino Delli Colli– *l.p.:* Pierre Blaise, Aurore Clément, Holger Lowenadler, Thérèse Gieshe– *p:* NEF/UPF/Vides/Hallelujah Films, colour, 1974.

Au Revoir les Enfants
d: Louis Malle– *sc:* Louis Malle – *c:* Renato Berta– *l.p.:* Gaspard Manesse, Raphaël Fejto, Francine Racette– *p:* MK2/Stella Films, colour, 1987.

Molinaro, Edouard

La Cage aux folles
d: Edouard Molinaro –*sc:* Francis Veber, Edouard Molinaro, Marcello Danon, Jean Poiret, from the play by Jean Poiret – *c:* Armando Nannuzzi – *l.p.:* Ugo Tognazzi, Michel Serrault, Michel Galabru – *p:* PAA/DAMA, colour, 1978.

La Cage aux folles II
d: Edouard Molinaro –*sc:* Jean Poiret, Francis Veber, Marcello Danon – *c:* Armando Nannuzzi – *l.p.:* Ugo Tognazzi, Michel Serrault, Marcel Bozzuffi – *p:* PAA/DAMA, colour, 1980.

Niermans, Edouard

Poussière d'ange
d: Edouard Niermans – *sc:* Edouard Niermans, Jacques Audiard, Alain le Henry – *c:* Bernard Lutic – *l.p.:* Bernard Giraudeau, Fanny Bastien, Fanny Cottençon, Michel Aumont – *p:* UGC/President Films/Top No 1/FR3/Films de La Saga/SOFICA, colour, 1987.

Nuytten, Bruno

Camille Claudel
d: Bruno Nuytten – *sc:* Bruno Nuytten, Marilyn Goldin, from the book by Rheine-Maris Paris – *c:* Pierre Lhomme – *l.p.:* Isabelle Adjani, Gérard Depardieu, Laurent Grevill – *p:* Films Christian Fechner/Lilith Films/Gaumont/Films A2/DD Productions, colour, 1988.

Ophüls, Marcel

Le Chagrin et la pitié
d: Marcel Ophüls– *sc:* Marcel Ophüls, André Harris– *c:* André Gazut, Jurden Thieme– *p:* Télévision Rencontre/Société suisse de radiodiffusion/Norddeutscher Rundfunk, black and white, 1971.

Palcy, Euzhan

Rue Cases Nègres
d: Euzhan Palcy – *sc:* Euzhan Palcy – *c:* Dominique Chapuis – *l.p:* Garry Cadenat, Darling Legitimus, Douta Seck – *p:* Su Ma Fa/Orca/NEF Diffusion, colour, 1983.

Pialat, Maurice

Police
d: Maurice Pialat – *sc:* Catherine Breillat, Maurice Pialat – *c:* Lucian Tovoli – *l.p.:* Gérard Depardieu, Sophie Marceau, Richard Anconina – *p:* Gaumont/TF1 Films Production, colour, 1985.

Sous le Soleil de Satan
d: Maurice Pialat – *sc:* Maurice Pialat, from the novel by Georges Bernanos – *c:* Willy Kurant – *l.p.:* Gérard Depardieu, Sandrine Bonnaire, Maurice Pialat – *p:* Erato Films/Films A2/Flack Fims/CNC/SOFICA, colour, 1987.

Van Gogh
d: Maurice Pialat – *sc:* Maurice Pialat – *c:* Gilles Henry– *l.p.:* Jacques Dutronc, Alexandra London, Bernard Le Coq – *p:* Erato/Canal+/A2/Livradois, colour, 1991.

Poiré, Jean-Marie

Papy fait de la Résistance
d: Jean-Marie Poiré – *sc:* Christian Clavier, Martin Lamotte, Jean-Marie Poiré – *c:* Robert Alazraki – *l.p.:* Christian Clavier, Michel Galabru, Gérard Jugnot, Martin Lamotte – *p:* Films Christian Fechner, colour, 1983.

Les Visiteurs
d: Jean-Marie Poiré – *sc:* Christian Clavier, Jean-Marie Poiré – *c:* Jean-Yves Le Mener – *l.p.:* Christian Clavier, Jean Reno, Valérie Lemercier, Marie-Anne Chazel – *p:* Alain Terzian, colour, 1993.

Rappeneau, Jean-Paul

Cyrano de Bergerac
d: Jean-Paul Rappeneau – sc: Jean-Paul Rappeneau, Jean-Claude Carrière, from the play by Edmond Rostand – c: Pierre Lhomme – l.p.: Gérard Depardieu, Anne Brochet, Vincent Pérez – p: Hachette Première/Camera One/Films A2/D.D. Productions/UGC, colour, 1990.

Resnais, Alain

Nuit et brouillard
d: Alain Resnais – sc: Jean Cayrol – c: Ghislain Cloquet, Sacha Vierny – p: Argos/Como, colour/black and white, 1955.

Muriel
d: Alain Resnais – sc: Jean Cayrol – c: Sacha Vierny – l.p.: Delphine Seyrig, Jean-Pierre Kérien, Nita Klein – p: Alpha/Eclair/Films de la Pléaide/Dear Films, colour, 1963.

Rivette, Jacques

Céline et Julie vont en bateau
d: Jacques Rivette – sc: Edouardo de Gregorio, Juliet Berto, Dominique Labourier, Bulle Ogier, Marie-France Pisier, Jacques Rivette, plus material from two stories by Henry James – c: Jacques Renard – l.p.: Juliet Berto, Dominique Labourier, Bulle Ogier, Marie-France Pisier, Barbet Schroeder – p: Les Films du Losange, colour, 1974.

Robert, Yves

La Gloire de men père
d: Yves Robert – sc: Jérôme Tonnerre, Louis Nucera, Yves Robert, from the auto-biography of Marcel Pagnol – c: Robert Alazraki – l.p: Philippe Caubère, Nathalie Roussel, Didier Pain – p: Gaumont/La Guéville/TF1, colour, 1990.

Le Château de ma mère
d: Yves Robert – sc: Jérôme Tonnerre, Yves Robert, from the autobiography of Marcel Pagnol – c: Robert Alazraki – l.p.: Philippe Caubère, Nathalie Roussel, Didier Pain – p: Gaumont/La Guéville/ TF1, colour, 1990.

Rohmer, Eric

Le Genou de Claire
d: Eric Rohmer – sc: Eric Rohmer – c: Nestor Almendros – l.p.: Jean-Claude Brialy, Aurora Cornu, Béatrice Romand – p: Les Films du Losange, colour, 1970.

La Marquise d'O
d: Eric Rohmer – sc: Eric Rohmer, from the novel by Heinrich von Kleist – c: Nestor Almendros – l.p.: Edith Clever, Bruno Ganz, Peter Luhr – p: Les Films du Losange/Gaumont/Janus-Film/Artémis, colour, 1976.

Perceval le Gallois
d: Eric Rohmer – sc: Eric Rohmer, from Chrétien de Troyes – c: Nestor Almendros – l.p.: Fabrice Luchini, André Dussolier, Gérard Falconetti – p: Les Films du Losange/Barbet Schoeder/FR3, colour, 1978.

Le Rayon vert
d: Eric Rohmer – sc: Eric Rohmer, Marie Rivière – c: Sophie Maintigneux – l.p.: Marie Rivière, Lisa Heredia, Vincent Gauthier, Béatrice Romand – p: Les Films du Losange, colour, 1986.

4 Aventures de Reinette et Mirabelle
d: Eric Rohmer – sc: Eric Rohmer – c: Sophie Maintigneux – l.p.: Jessica Forde, Joëlle Miquel, Philippe Laudenbach, Marie Rivière, Fabrice Luchini – p: Les Films du Losange, colour, 1986.

Schoendoerffer, Pierre

Le Crabe-Tambour
d: Pierre Schoendoerffer – sc: Jean-François Chauvel, Pierre Schoendoerffer, from the novel by the director– c: Raoul Coutard – l.p.: Jean Rochefort, Claude Rich, Jacques Perrin – p: Alain Sarde, colour, 1977.

Dien Bien Phu

d: Pierre Schoendoerffer – *sc:* Pierre Schoendoerffer – *c:* Bernard Lutic– *l.p.:* Donald Pleasance, Ludmila Mikael, Patrick Catalifo, Jean-François Balmer – *p:* Mod Films/Antenne 2/Films A2/Flach Film/Production Marcel Dassault/GM Aviation Services/Seco Film, colour, 1992.

Serreau, Coline

Trois Hommes et un couffin

d: Coline Serreau – *sc:* Coline Serreau – *c:* Jean-Yves Escoffier, Jean-Jacques Bouhon – *l.p.:* Roland Giraud, Michel Boujenah, André Dussolier – *p:* Flach Films/Soprofilm/TF1 Films Production, colour, 1985.

Romuald et Juliette

d: Coline Serreau – *sc:* Coline Serreau – *c:* Jean-Noel Ferragut – *l.p.:* Daniel Auteuil, Firmine Richard, Pierre Vernier, Maxime Leroux – *p:* Cinéa/FR3 Films, colour, 1989.

La Crise

d: Coline Serreau – *sc:* Coline Serreau – *c:* Robert Alazraki – *l.p.:* Vincent Lindon, Patrick Tinsit, Zabou – *p:* Les Films Alain Sarde/TF1 Films Production/Leader Cinematografica/Raidue, with the participation of Canal+, colour, 1992.

Swaim, Bob

La Balance

d: Bob Swaim – *sc:* M. Fabiani, Bob Swaim – *c:* Bernard Zitzermann – *l.p.:* Nathalie Baye, Phillipe Léotard, Richard Berry, Maurice Ronet – *p:* Les Films Ariane/Films A2, colour, 1982.

Tanner, Alain

Une Flamme dans mon cœur

d: Alain Tanner – *sc:* Myriam Mézières – *c:* Acacio de Almeida – *l.p.:* Myriam Mézières, Benoit Regent, Aziz Kabouche – *p:* Garance/La Sept/Filmograph, black and white, 1987.

Tavernier, Bertrand

L'Horloger de Saint-Paul

d: Bertrand Tavernier – *sc:* Jean Aurenche, Pierre Bost, from the novel *L'Horloger d'Everton* by Georges Simenon – *c:* Pierre-William Glenn – *l.p.:* Philippe Noiret, Jean Rochefort, Sylvain Rougerie – *p:* Lira Films, colour, 1974.

Coup de torchon

d: Bertrand Tavernier – *sc:* Jean Aurenche, from the novel *Pop.1280* by Jim Thompson – *c:* Pierre-William Glenn – *l.p.:* Philippe Noiret, Isabelle Huppert, Jean-Pierre Marielle – *p:* Les Films de la Tour/A2/Little Bear, colour, 1981.

Un Dimanche à la campagne

d: Bertrand Tavernier – *sc:* Bertrand Tavernier, Colo Tavernier, from the novel by Pierre Bost – *c:* Bruno de Keyser – *l.p.:* Louis Ducreux, Sabine Azéma, Michel Aumont – *p:* Sara Films/Films A2, colour, 1984.

La Vie et rien d'autre

d: Bertrand Tavernier – *sc:* Jean Cosmos, Bertrand Tavernier –*c:* Bruno de Keyser – *l.p.:* Philippe Noiret, Sabine Azéma, Pascale Vignal – *p:* Hachette Première/GPE Europe/AB Films/Little Bear/ Films A2, colour, 1989.

La Guerre sans nom

d: Bertrand Tavernier – *sc:* Bertrand Tavernier, Patrick Rotman – *c:* Alain Choquart – *p:* Le Studio Canal+/GMT Productions/Little Bear, colour, 1992.

L.627

d: Bertrand Tavernier – *sc:* Bertrand Tavernier, Michel Alexandre – *c:* Alain Choquart – *l.p.:* Didier Bézace, Charlotte Kady, Jean-Paul Comart, Nils Tavernier – *p:* Little Bear/Les Films Alain Sarde, colour, 1992.

Truffaut, François

Domicile conjugal

d: François Truffaut – *sc:* François Truffaut, Claude de Givray – *c:* Nestor Almendros – *l.p.:* Jean-Pierre Léaud, Claude Jade – *p:* Les Films du Carrosse, colour, 1970.

Les Deux Anglaises et le continent
d: François Truffaut – *sc:* François Truffaut, Jean Grualt, from the novel by Henri-Pierre Roché – *c:* Nestor Almendros – *l.p.:* Jean-Pierre Léaud, Kika Markham, Stacy Tendeter, Philippe Léotard – *p:* Les Films du Carrosse, colour, 1971.

Une Belle Fille comme moi
d: François Truffaut – *sc:* Jean-Loup Dabadie, François Truffaut, from the novel by Henri Farrell – *c:* Pierre-William Glenn – *l.p.:* Bernadette Lafont, Claude Brasseur, Charles Denner – *p:* Les Films du Carrosse/Columbia, colour, 1972.

La Nuit américaine
d: François Truffaut – *sc:* François Truffaut, Jean-Louis Richard, Suzanne Schiffman – *c:* Pierre-William Glenn – *l.p.:* Jacqueline Bisset, Valentina Cortese, Alexandra Stewart, Jean-Pierre Aumont, Jean-Pierre Léaud, François Truffaut – *p:* Les Films du Carrosse/PCCF/PIC, colour, 1973.

L'Histoire d'Adèle H.
d: François Truffaut – *sc:* Jean Gruault, Suzanne Schiffman, from the novel by Frances Vernor Guillie – *c:* Nestor Almendros – *l.p.:* Isabelle Adjani, Bruce Robinson, Sylvia Marriott – *p:* Les Films du Carrosse/Artistes Associés, colour, 1975.

L'Amour en fuite
d: François Truffaut – *sc:* François Truffaut – *c:* Nestor Almendros – *l.p.:* Jean-Pierre Léaud, Marie-France Pisier, Claude Jade – *p:* Les Films du Carrosse, colour, 1979.

Le Dernier Métro
d: François Truffaut – *sc:* François Truffaut, Suzanne Schiffman – *c:* Nestor Almendros – *l.p.:* Catherine Deneuve, Gérard Depardieu, Jean Poiret – *p:* Les Films du Carrosse, colour, 1980.

Varda, Agnès

Sans Toit ni loi
d: Agnès Varda – *sc:* Agnès Varda – *c:* Patrick Blossier – *l.p.:* Sandrine Bonnaire, Macha Méril, Stéphane Freiss – *p:* Ciné-Tamaris/Films A2, colour, 1985.

Jane B. par Agnès V.
d: Agnès Varda – *sc:* Agnès Varda – *c:* Nurith Aviv – *l.p:* Jane Birkin, Philippe Léotard, Jean-Pierre Léaud, Farid Chopel – *p:* Ciné-Tamaris/La Sept, colour, 1987.

Jacquot de Nantes
d: Agnès Varda – *sc:* Agnès Varda – *c:* Patrick Blosier, Agnès Godard, Georges Strouve – *l.p.:* Phillipe Maron, Edouard Joubeaud, Laurent Monnier – *p:* Ciné-Tamaris/Canal +/La Sept/La Sofiarp, black and white/colour, 1991.

Vigne, Daniel

Le Retour de Martin Guerre
d: Daniel Vigne – *sc:* Jean-Claude Carrière, Daniel Vigne – *c:* André Néau – *l.p.:* Gérard Depardieu, Nathalie Baye, Sylvie Meda – *p:* SFPC/Marcel Dassault/FR3, colour, 1982.

Wajda, Andrzej

Danton
d: Andrzej Wajda – *sc:* Jean-Claude Carrière, from the play *L'Affaire Danton* by Stanislawa Przybyszweska – *c:* Igor Luther – *l.p.:* Gérard Depardieu, Wojciech Pszoniak, Anna Alvaro – *p:* Les Films du Losange/Group X (for Gaumont/TF1), colour, 1982.

Warnier, Régis

Indochine
d: Régis Warnier – *sc:* Erik Orsenna, Louis Gardeal, Catherine Cohen, Régis Warnier – *c:* François Catonne – *l.p.:* Catherine Deneuve, Vincent Perez, Linh Dan Pham – *p:* Paradis/La Générale d'Images/BAC/Orly/Ciné Cinq, colour, 1992.

Index

A bout de souffle, 14, 106, 110,
  128, 132, 133, 134
Adjani, Isabelle, 60–1, 64, 155–6,
  168
Affaire Dreyfus, L', 2
Affaire de femmes, Une, 22, 31,
  33–4
Age d'or, L', 7
Akerman, Chantal, 82, 88, 90
Allegret, Yves, 12
Allen, Woody, 96
Alphaville, 15
Amant, L', 49, 50–1, 151
Amant magnifique, L', 91
Amants du Pont-Neuf, Les, 119,
  121, 126, 128, 132, 133–5
Ami de mon amie, L', 67
Amour l'après-midi, L', 67
Amour fou, L', 66
Amour en fuite, L', 51–2
Amour de Swann, Un, 144, 163
Amour violé, L', 82
Angelo, Yves, 157, 169
Annaud, Jean-Jacques, 50–1, 60,
  128, 129, 139, 151
Anthracite, 109
Antoine et Colette, 51
Apocalypse Now, 41
Après l'Amour, 89
Argent, L', 5, 7
Armée des ombres, L', 38
Arrieta, Adolfo, 76
*Arrivée d'un train en gare de La
  Ciotat, L'*, 2
Arroseur arrosé, L', 2

Artaud, Antonin, 6
Ascenseur pour l'échafaud, 29
As des as, L', 100
Assassin, The, 130
Assassinat du duc de Guise, L', 4
Assassinat du Père Noël, L', 10
Assayas, Olivier, 171
Astruc, Alexandre, 13
Atalante, L', 8, 124, 134
Atlantis, 129
Audry, Jacqueline, 81, 88
Aurenche, Jean, 13, 114, 149
Au revoir les enfants, 32–3
Autant-Lara, Claude, 12
auteurs, la politique des, 9, 13–14,
  135
Autour de Minuit, 27
Aveu, L', 99
Avoir 20 ans dans les Aurès, 40

Badham, John, 130
Badlands, 86
Bahloul, Abdelkrim, 42
Baisers volés, 51–2
Balance, La, 108–9, 116
Bal du gouverneur, Le, 94
Barbarella, 136
Barbe-Bleue, 2
Bardot, Brigitte, 15
Bataille du rail, La, 12
Batman, 128
Bâton Rouge, 42
Battle of Algiers, The, 39
Bazin, André, 13
Beau Serge, Le, 15

Becker, Jacques, 11, 12
Becker, Jean, 54, 60–2, 63
Beineix, Jean-Jacques, 42, 55,
    63–4, 99, 111, 119, 120–6,
    132, 134, 135, 144
Belle et la bête, La, 131
Belle Fille comme moi, Une, 101
Belle de jour, 57, 60, 106
Belle Noiseuse, La, 156
Bellon, Yannick, 81, 82, 109
Belmondo, Jean-Paul, 100, 106–7
Belmont, Charles, 81
Berri, Claude, 120, 140, 142, 144,
    149, 158–62, 163, 165, 166–7
Bertolucci, Bernardo, 151
Besson, Luc, 109, 111, 119, 121,
    126–32, 135, 144
Betty Blue, see 37,2 le Matin
Beur cinema, 42–4
Bilal, Enki, 136
Black Moon, 82
Blier, Bertrand, 32, 34, 37–8, 46,
    52–3, 56, 68–73, 77, 82, 86,
    137
Boisset, Yves, 40, 112
Bonnes Femmes, Les, 101
Bonnie and Clyde, 86
Borowczyk, Walerian, 136
Borsalino, 75, 100, 107–8
Borsalino et compagnie, 108
Bosna!, 167
Bost, Pierre, 13, 149, 153
Bouchareb, Rachid, 42
Boucher, Le, 39–40, 101
Boudu sauvé des eaux, 9
Boy Meets Girl, 132, 133
Breillat, Catherine, 91
Bresson, Robert, 12, 13, 134, 143,
    144, 154
Breton, André, 6
Brisseau, Jean-Claude, 94
Broken Blossoms, 5
Bronzés, Les, 55
Buffet froid, 52
Bunker Palace Hôtel, 136
Buñuel, Luis, 6, 7, 54, 57–60, 106

câfé-théâtre, 38, 55, 138
Cage aux folles, La, 73–5
Cage aux folles II, La, 75
Cahiers du cinéma, 13–14, 15, 64,
    67, 100, 119, 132
Calcutta, 29

Calmos, 56, 82
Camille Claudel, 60, 155–7
Camion, Le, 83
Camomille, 42
Camps de la mort, Les, 20
Carabiniers, Les, 37
Carax, Léos, 42, 76, 119, 121,
    126, 128, 132–5, 137
Carné, Marcel, 9, 11, 12, 122,
    126, 137
Caro, Marc, 34, 136–7, 138
Casque d'or, 12
Cavanni, Lilianna, 29, 30
Céline et Julie vont en bateau, 64–6,
    68
Cendrillon, 2
Cercle rouge, Le, 107
Cet Obscur Objet du désir, 54,
    57–60
Chabrol, Claude, 13, 14–16, 22,
    31, 33–4, 39–40, 85, 100,
    101–3, 104–6, 112, 163,
    164–5, 166, 168
Chagrin et la pitié, Le, 20, 22–4,
    25, 27, 28, 29, 30
Chalonge, Christian de, 34–7, 136,
    137
Chapeau de paille d'Italie, Un, 6
Chaplin, Charlie, 4, 133
Charef, Mehdi, 42
Chariots of Fire, 142
Charme discret de la bourgeoisie, Le,
    57
Chartreuse de Parme, La, 12
Château de ma mère, Le, 160,
    162–3
Cheb, 42
Chéreau, Patrice, 164, 167–9
Chibane, Malik, 42, 43–4
Chien andalou,Un, 6, 60
Chimère, 91
Chinoise, La, 19
Chocolat, 94–5
Christian-Jacques, 10, 12
Chronique d'un été, 18
Ciel est à vous, Le, 11
cinéma du look, 12, 91, 111,
    119–35, 136, 137
Cité des enfants perdus, La, 136,
    171
Clair, René, 6, 8, 10
Clément, René, 12, 120
Clémentine Tango, 91, 135

Cléo de 5 à 7, 85
Clouzot, Henri-Georges, 11, 12,
    101, 104, 112
Club de femmes, 88
Cocteau, Jean, 12, 13, 75, 131,
    133, 136
Cœur fidèle, 5, 6
Cœur en hiver, Un, 79
Collard, Cyril, 76, 78–9
Colonel Chabert, Le, 157, 169
Condamné à mort s'est échappé, Un,
    12
Conte d'hiver, 67
Coppola, Francis Ford, 41, 123
Coquille et le clergyman, La, 6
Corbeau, Le, 11, 101, 104
Corbiau, Gérard, 142
Corneau, Alain, 99, 112–14, 115,
    116, 142, 147–9, 151, 157–8
Costa-Gavras, 99, 112, 125
Coup de foudre, 33, 82, 88–9, 96
Coup de torchon, 99, 112, 114–16
Cousins, Les, 14
Crabe-Tambour, Le, 40–1, 42
Créatures, Les, 85
Cri du hibou, Le, 100, 101–3, 104
Crise, La, 91
Cyrano de Bergerac, 157, 164

Dadaism, 6
Dali, Salvador, 6
Dante, Joe, 38
Danton, 143, 144, 145, 146–7
Davy, Jean-François, 46
Déjeuner sur l'herbe, Le, 152
Delannoy, Jean, 11
Delicatessen, 34, 136–7, 138
Delluc, Louis, 4–5
Delon, Alain, 99, 100, 107–8
Demoiselles de Rochefort, Les, 15
Demy, Jacques, 15, 87
Deneuve, Catherine, 32, 148, 151
Denis, Claire, 94–5
Depardieu, Gérard, 32, 38, 70–3,
    116, 146–7, 148, 155–6,
    157–8, 160–1
Deray, Jacques, 75, 100, 106,
    107–8
Dernier Combat, Le, 126
Dernier Métro, Le, 32, 38, 51
Dernier Milliardaire, Le, 8
Desperately Seeking Susan, 64, 65
Destin de Juliette, Le, 91

Deux Anglaises, Les, 50, 142, 165
Deux ou Trois Choses que je sais
    d'elle, 47
Deval, Jacques, 88
Devers, Claire, 92–4
Deville, Michel, 52, 102
Diaboliques, Les, 12, 104
Diabolo Menthe, 96
Diehl, Gaston, 154
Dien Bien Phu, 41–2, 145, 150
Dimanche à la campagne, Un, 149,
    152, 153–4, 164
Diva, 111, 119, 120–2, 123, 125,
    134
Djamai, Cheikh, 42
Docteur Petiot, 34–7, 136, 137
Domicile conjugal, 51–2
Donaldson, Roger, 112
Double Indemnity, 51
Doulos, Le, 106
Drach, Michel, 37
Dugowson, Martine, 95–7
Dulac, Germaine, 5, 6, 7, 81, 88
Duras, Marguerite, 49, 50, 52,
    82–5, 87, 94, 144

Eau froide, L', 171
El Dorado, 5
Emmanuelle, 32, 46, 50, 64
Enfants du paradis, Les, 11, 122
Enfer, L', 104–6
Entr'acte, 6
Epstein, Jean, 5, 6
Eraserhead, 92, 93
E.T., 129
État de siège, 99
Et Dieu créa la femme, 15
Été meurtrier, L', 54, 60–2, 63, 64
Éternel Retour, L', 11
Eustache, Jean, 81
Exhibition, 46

Fahrenheit 451, 15
Fantômas series, 3, 99, 108
Fantôme de la liberté, Le, 57
Farinelli, 142
Fassbinder, Rainer Werner, 76,
    122
Femme de l'aviateur, La, 101
Femme d'à côté, La, 51
Femme est une femme, Une, 15
Femme du Gange, La, 83
Femme de nulle part, La, 5

Ferran, Pascale, 95
Ferrari, Alain, 167
Ferreri, Marco, 53–4
Fête espagnole, La, 5
Feu follet, Le, 29
Feuillade, Louis, 3, 99
Feyder, Jacques, 8, 139
Fille de Dartagnan, La, 164
Fille du puisatier, La, 10
film noir, 9, 51, 96, 99, 106, 108,
    109–11
Flamme dans mon coeur, Une, 48
Flic, Un, 107
Fort Saganne, 147–9, 150, 151
Français, si vous saviez, 23
Franju, Georges, 136
Frears, Stephen, 112
French Cancan, 112, 152, 155
French Connection, The, 127
Friedkin, William, 127
Fuller, Sam, 14

Gabin, Jean, 9
Gance, Abel, 5, 8, 147
Garce, La, 109
Gaumont, Léon, 3
Genou de Claire, Le, 67, 68
Germinal, 140, 149, 160, 165,
    166–7
Gervaise, 12
Getaway, The, 112
Girod, Francis, 32, 38, 107
Gloire de mon père, La, 160, 162–3
Godard, Jean-Luc, 13, 14, 15, 16,
    19–20, 23, 29, 34, 35, 37,
    47–9, 64, 85, 110, 112, 119,
    122, 125, 128, 132, 133, 134,
    152, 157
Golden Eighties, 88
Gone With the Wind, 160
Gorin, Jean-Pierre, 19, 23, 29
Gothic, 152
Goupi Mains-Rouges, 11
Grand Bleu, Le, 121, 126, 128–9,
    131
Grande Bouffe, La, 53–4
Grande Illusion, La, 9, 14
Grande Vadrouille, La, 16, 89
Greenwald, Maggie, 112
Grémillon, Jean, 11, 133
Griffith, D. W., 5
Grifters, The, 112
Guerre des boutons, La, 16

Guerre du feu, La, 50
Guerre sans nom, La, 27–8, 150
Guy, Alice, 3, 81

Haine, La, 171
Harris, André, 22, 23, 28
Hawks, Howard, 14
Hexagone, 42, 43–4
High Sierra, 107
Histoire d'Adèle H., L', 143, 156
Histoire d'un crime, L', 3
Histoires d'A, 81
Hitchcock, Alfred, 14, 40, 51, 57,
    69, 76, 100–2, 104
Homme amoureux, Un, 89
Homo-actualités, 76
Horloger de Saint-Paul, L', 114, 116
Hôtel Terminus, 23, 27

impressionism, 4–5, 6
India Song, 82–5, 94
Indochine, 145, 148, 150–2
Innocents aux mains sales, Les, 104
Inspecteur Lavardin, 101
Intrigues de Sylvia Couski, Les, 76
IP5, 124–6, 129
Issartel, Marielle, 81
Issermann, Aline, 82, 91

Jacquot de Nantes, 87
Jaeckin, Just, 46
J'ai pas sommeil, 95, 171
Jane B. par Agnès V., 49, 87, 125,
    152
Jasset, Victorien, 3
Jazz Singer, The, 7
Jean de Florette, 142, 144, 158–62,
    163
*Jeanne Dielman, 23 Quai du
    Commerce, 1080, Bruxelles*, 90
Jetée, La, 15
Jeunet, Jean-Pierre, 34, 136–7,
    138
Je vous salue Marie, 47, 48–9
Jewel in the Crown, The, 148
Joli mai, Le, 18
Journal d'un curé de campagne, Le,
    12, 154
Jour se lève, Le, 9
Judex series, 99, 108
Juge et l'assassin, Le, 149, 150
Jules et Jim, 96
Juliette ou la clé des songes, 12

Jurassic Park, 128, 138, 166, 171

Kassovitz, Mathieu, 171
Kermesse héroique, La, 8, 139
Khan, Cedric, 171
Killing, The, 112
Kill-Off, The, 112
King Kong, 36
Kubrick, Stanley, 112
Kurys, Diane, 33, 82, 87, 88–9, 91, 96

L.627, 116, 117–18
Lacombe, Lucien, 23, 29–32, 33, 38, 39
Lancelot du Lac, 143
Lang, Jack, 144, 145, 147, 160, 167
Langlois, Henri, 18
Lanzmann, Claude, 20, 22, 24–7, 28, 37
Last Emperor, The, 151
Lautner, Georges, 100
Lawrence of Arabia, 148
Lean, David, 148
Le Bargy, Charles, 4
Leconte, Patrice, 54, 55–7, 64, 100, 102–4
Lectrice, La, 52
Léon, 109, 129, 131–2
Le Roy, Mervyn, 130
Letter From An Unknown Woman, 96
Lévy, Bernard-Henri, 167
L'Herbier, Marcel, 5, 7
Limelight, 133
Linder, Max, 4
Little Caeser, 130
Loin du Vietnam, 16, 19
Lola Montès, 22
Loulou, 116, 154
Lucas, George, 127
Lumière, Auguste, 1, 2, 52
Lumière, Louis, 1, 2, 52, 171
Lune dans le caniveau, La, 99, 122–4, 126
Lynch, David, 92

Madame Bovary (Chabrol), 163, 164–5, 166, 168
Madame Bovary (Renoir), 163
Made in U.S.A., 112
Mais qu'est-ce qu'elles veulent?, 81

Malick, Terence, 86
Malle, Louis, 23, 29–31, 32–3, 38, 39, 82
Maman et la putain, La, 81
Manon des sources (Berri), 144, 158–62
Manon des sources (Pagnol), 160
Man Ray, 6
Ma Nuit chez Maud, 67, 101
Marboeuf, Jean, 36
Marche gay, La, 76
Marginal, Le, 100
Margolin, François, 77, 78
Mari de la coiffeuse, Le, 54, 55–6
Marker, Chris., 15, 16, 18
Marquis, 136
Marquise d'O, La, 152
Marseillaise, La, 145, 147
Marshall, Tonie, 95
Masculin-Féminin, 16
Mauvais Sang, 76–7, 121, 124, 132–3, 134
Mean Streets, 117
Meerson, Lazare, 8
Méliès, Georges, 2, 3, 4, 135
Melville, Jean-Pierre, 38, 99, 106–7
Memory of Justice, The, 23, 27
Menace, La, 112
Mensonge, 77, 78
Mépris, Le, 16, 122, 124, 130, 133, 157
Merci la Vie, 32, 34, 37–8, 68–70, 77, 137
Mina Tannenbaum, 95–7
Miss Mona, 42
Mistons, Les, 14, 52
mode rétro, la, 23, 28–9, 32, 94, 107
Molinaro, Edouard, 73–5
Monde sans pitié, Un, 134
Monsieur Hire, 55, 100, 102–4
Montand, Yves, 19, 99, 112, 125
Mort du soleil, La, 5
Munich, 22
Muriel, 21, 39
Murnau, F. W., 35

Nana, 9
Napoléon vu par Abel Gance, 5, 147
Nathalie Granger, 83
Nedjar, Michel, 76
Nick Carter series, 3

Niermans, Edouard, 109–11
Night Porter, The, 29–30
Nikita, 109, 111, 129–31, 132
Nimoy, Leonard, 89
Noir et blanc, 92–4
Nom de la rose, Le, 50, 139
North by North-West, 57
Nosferatu, 35
nouvelle vague, la, 13, 14–16, 47, 67, 85, 99, 112, 121, 132
Nuit américaine, La, 52
Nuit et brouillard, 20, 21, 22, 25, 37
Nuit du doute, La, 42
Nuit fantastique, La, 11
Nuit porte jarretelles, La, 135
Nuits fauves, Les, 78–9
Nuit de Varennes, La, 143, 145–6, 147
Numéro deux, 47
Nuytten, Bruno, 155–7

Œil du malin, L', 104
Œil de Vichy, L', 33, 101
Olivia, 88
Ombre du doute, L', 91
One from the Heart, 123
On s'est trompé d'amour, 90
Ophüls, Marcel, 20, 22–4, 27, 28, 167
Ophüls, Max, 10, 22
Orphée, 12, 75, 133
Ours, L', 50, 128, 129, 139
Oury, Gérard, 16, 89, 100
Outremer, 94

Pagnol, Marcel, 10, 158–63, 165
Palcy, Euzhan, 94
Papy fait de la Résistance, 38, 138
Parapluies de Cherbourg, Les, 15
Parfum d'Yvonne, Le, 57
Paris nous appartient, 65
Partie de campagne, Une, 14, 143, 152, 153, 155
Pascal, Christine, 109
Passage to India, A, 148
Passe ton Bac d'abord, 116
Passion, 48, 125, 152
Passion Béatrice, La, 149
Pas très catholique, 95
Pathé, Charles, 2, 3, 4
Paths of Glory, 112
Peckinpah, Sam, 108, 112, 130

Penn, Arthur, 16, 86
Perceval le Gallois, 143
Péril en la demeure, 102
Personne ne m'aime, 95
Pétain, 36
Petite Lise, La, 133
Petits Arrangements avec les morts, 95
Petit Soldat, Le, 39
Pialat, Maurice, 78, 91, 99, 116–17, 143, 152, 153–5, 156
Picabia, Francis, 6
Pickpocket, 12, 134
Pierrot le fou, 16, 130, 132
Pisier, Marie-France, 66, 94
Place de la République, 29
poetic realism, 8–9, 12, 108, 122, 126, 135, 137, 143
Pointe courte, La, 15, 81, 85
Point of No Return, 130
Poiré, Jean-Marie, 38, 138–40, 166
Polanski, Roman, 123, 160
polar, the, 99–118
Police, 91, 99, 116–17, 154
Police python 357, 112
Pompiers de Lyon, Les, 2
Pontecorvo, Gillo, 39
Portes de la nuit, Les, 9, 12, 126
Poulet au vinaigre, 101
Pourquoi Israël, 24
Pourquoi pas!, 82
Poussière d'ange, 109–11
Prénom Carmen, 48
Préparez vos Mouchoirs, 71
Prévert, Jacques, 9, 12
Professionnel, Le, 100
Psycho, 69
Pulp Fiction, 131

Quai des brumes, 9, 137
4 Aventures de Reinette et Mirabelle, 67–8, 69
400 Coups, Les, 14, 51, 86, 126, 134
Que la Fête commence, 149
Quelque part, quelqu'un, 81
Querelle, 76, 122, 123

Race d'ep!, 76
Raiders of the Lost Ark, 139
Rappeneau, Jean-Paul, 157, 164
R.A.S., 40

Rayon vert, Le, 67, 68
Rear Window, 57, 100, 101, 102
Règle du jeu, La, 9
Reine Margot, La, 160, 164, 167–9, 171
René la canne, 32, 38, 107
Renoir, Jean, 9, 10, 12, 13, 14, 38, 143, 145, 147, 149, 150, 152, 153, 154, 155, 158, 163
Resnais, Alain, 16, 20, 21, 22, 37, 39, 144, 154
Retour de Martin Guerre, Le, 143
Retour à la raison, Le, 6
Ripoux, Les, 100
Ripoux contre ripoux, 100
Rivette, Jacques, 15, 16, 64–6, 68, 156
Robert, Yves, 16, 160, 162–3, 165
Roboh, Caroline, 110, 158
Rochant, Eric, 134
Rohmer, Eric, 13, 15, 16, 67–8, 69, 85, 100–1, 132, 143, 152
Rollin, Jean, 46, 82, 88, 136
Romuald et Juliette, 91
Roseaux sauvages, Les, 171
Roselyne et les lions, 124, 126
Rotman, Patrick, 27
Rouan, Brigitte, 94
Rouch, Jean, 18, 19
Roue, La, 5
Rouge et le Noir, Le, 12
Rue Cases Nègres, 94
Russell, Ken, 152

Samourai, Le, 107
Sans Toit ni loi, 85–7
Sauve qui peut (la vie), 47–8, 49
Schindler's List, 34, 167
Schlöndorff, Volker, 144, 163
Schoendoerffer, Pierre, 40–2, 94, 150
Scola, Ettore, 145–6
Scorsese, Martin, 16, 117
Sedouy, Alain, 22, 23
Seidelman, Susan, 64
S'en fout la mort, 95
Sennet, Mack, 4
Sense of Loss, A, 23
Série noire, 99, 112–14, 115, 116
Serreau, Coline, 81, 82, 87, 89–91
Shoah, 20, 21, 22, 24–7, 28, 37
Si Jolie Petite Plage, Une, 12
Silence de la mer, Le, 38

Sœurs Brontë, Les, 143
Son Nom de Venise dans Calcutta désert, 83, 84
Souffle au coeur, Le, 31, 33, 39
Soukaz, Lionel, 76
Souriante Madame Beudet, La, 88
Sous le Soleil de Satan, 116, 154
Sous les Toits de Paris, 8
Spielberg, Steven, 34, 129, 138, 139, 167
Stargate, 136
Star Is Born, A, 96, 115
Starsky and Hutch, 108, 109
Star Wars, 127
Sting, The, 107
Strangers on a Train, 101
Strangulation Blues, 132
Subway, 121, 126–8
surrealism, 6–7, 135
Suzanne Simonin, la réligieuse de Diderot, 65
Swaim, Bob, 108–9, 116

Taggers, 79
Tango, 54, 56–7, 68
Tanner, Alain, 48
Tapage nocturne, 91
Tarantino, Quentin, 131, 168
Tasse, La, 76
Tati, Jacques, 13
Tavernier, Bertrand, 27–8, 99, 112, 114–15, 116, 117–18, 143, 149–50, 152, 153–4, 164
Téchiné, André, 143, 171
Tenue de soirée, 71–3, 77
Terry, Norbert, 76
Tess, 123, 160
Thé au harem d'Archimède, Le, 42
Thé à la menthe, Le, 42
Thèvenet, Virginie, 135
Three Men and a Baby, 89
Tirez sur le Pianiste, 15, 99, 121, 125
Toni, 158
Tous les Garçons et les filles de leur âge, 171
Tous les Matins du monde, 79, 142, 157–8
Tout va bien, 19–20
tradition de qualité, la, 11–12, 13, 14, 142, 149
Trauner, Alexandre, 8, 9, 10, 126
37,2 le Matin, 55, 62–4, 124

36 Fillette, 91
Tristana, 57
317e Section, La, 40
Trois Hommes et un couffin, 89–91
Trop Belle pour toi, 69
Trop de Bonheur, 171
Truffaut, François, 13, 14, 15, 16,
    32, 38, 50, 51–2, 64, 86–7, 96,
    99, 101, 121, 126, 132, 134,
    142–3, 149, 156, 165

Une chante, l'autre pas, L', 81, 85

Vadim, Roger, 15
Valseuses, Les, 37, 38, 46, 52–3,
    56, 64, 69, 70–1, 72, 86
Van Gogh (Pialat), 116, 152, 153,
    154–5, 156
Van Gogh (Resnais), 154
Varda, Agnès, 15, 16, 19, 49, 81,
    82, 85–7, 125, 144, 152
Vautier, René, 40
Veillées d'armes, 27, 167
Verneuil, Henri, 100
Vernoux, Marion, 95
Vertigo, 100, 101, 102, 104
Victimes de l'alcoolisme, Les, 3

Vie du Christ, La, 3
Vie est à nous, La, 9, 145
Vie et rien d'autre, La, 27, 149–50
Vigne, Daniel, 143
Vigo, Jean, 6, 8, 32, 124, 134,
    137
20 000 lieues sous les mers, 2
Violons du bal, Les, 37
Visiteurs, Les, 38, 138–40, 166,
    167, 171
Visiteurs du soir, Les, 11, 122
Vivement Dimanche!, 14

Wajda, Andrzej, 144, 145, 146–7
Walsh, Raoul, 107
Warnier, Régis, 94, 150–2
Week-End, 16, 19

Xhonneux, Henri, 136

Yeux sans visage, Les, 136

Z, 99
Zecca, Ferdinand, 3
Zéro de conduite, 8, 32
Zidi, Claude, 100, 120